WRITING
FOR THE
MEDIA

WRITING FOR THE MEDIA

William L. Rivers
Alison R. Work

Stanford University

Mayfield Publishing Company
Mountain View, CA 94041

Library of Congress Cataloging-in-Publication Data

Rivers, William L.
    Writing for the media.

    Bibliography: p.
    Includes index.
    1. Journalism—Authorship. 2. Reporters
and reporting. 3. Advertising copy.
4. Publicity. I. Work, Alison R. II. Title.
PN4775.R472 1988   808'.06607   87-24789
ISBN 0-87484-829-6

Manufactured in the United States of America

10 9 8 7 6 5 4 3 2 1

Mayfield Publishing Company
1240 Villa St.
Mountain View, California 94041

Sponsoring editor, C. Lansing Hays; manuscript editor, Joan Pendleton; text designer, Cynthia Bassett; cover designer, David Toy. The text was set in 10/12 ITC New Baskerville by Carlisle Graphics and printed on 50# Finch Opaque by George Banta Company.

CONTENTS

PREFACE

We wrote this book, *Writing For The Media*, with special joy. Why? Because its scope enabled us to show not only what good writing is, but also the many careers open to those who work at being good writers.

As the first course in journalism has moved from teaching straight newswriting to showing the range of techniques used in media writing, students have been able to learn about various writing careers. Journalism, public relations, and advertising are all richer because of practitioners who began their careers in introductory journalism classes.

In this book two themes should stand out: We think all writing follows a fundamental pattern, and we think it should be a pleasure to study and acquire that pattern. Anywhere you turn in the book we hope you will find evident our appreciation for writers and writing—an appreciation on which we hope to hook students.

The many colleagues who have given us criticism and advice on our manuscript are too numerous to name. The manuscript reviewers, Maurine H. Beasley, University of Maryland; Herb Strentz, Drake University; Nancy L. Roberts, University of Minnesota; Douglas Birkhead, University of Utah, and Charles Arrendell, University of Texas, Arlington, provided perceptive, detailed comments and suggestions. We thank them.

William L. Rivers
Alison R. Work

Nothing you write will ever come out as you first hoped.
Lillian Hellman

The point of good writing is knowing when to stop.
Lucy M. Montgomery

As to the adjective: When in doubt, strike it out.
Mark Twain

Care should be taken, not that the reader may understand, but that he must understand.
Quintilian

A people without reliable news is, sooner or later, a people without the basis of freedom.
Harold J. Laski

If all printers were determined not to print anything till they were sure it would offend nobody, there would be little printed.
Benjamin Franklin

Do you realize if it weren't for Edison we'd be watching TV by candlelight?
Al Boliska

C H A P 1 T E R

Writing Principles

Patience, diligence, painstaking
attention to detail—these are the
requirements.   *Mark Twain*

Ernest Hemingway started his career as a journalist and later won a Nobel Prize for literature. He observed, "A writer's problem does not change. He himself changes and the world he lives in changes, but his problem remains the same. It is always how to write truly and, having found out what is true, to project it in such a way that it becomes the experience of the person who reads it."

When Hemingway decided to become an outstanding journalist, then a novelist, television was a dream and radio was just beginning. Writing was the only way anyone had to communicate over a distance or to keep records. Consequently, people recognized that to succeed in the world, they had to be able to write with reasonable clarity and grace.

GOOD WRITING

Today, we tend to think of writing as a time-consuming, and perhaps unnecessary, chore. By picking up the telephone or photocopying somebody else's writing effort and then circling a pertinent message, we can accomplish what people once could do only by writing themselves, and we also save ourselves time and energy. Computers, satellites, and all the other communication devices at our disposal make our lives simpler, more leisurely, and more effective. Yet for the foreseeable future, none of these technologies can fully replace writing as a tool of thinking, learning, record-keeping, and communication. Writing is an extension of the human ability

1

to reason, and until we have devised a computer as complex and flexible and independent and creative as the human brain, we will continue to need to write effectively.

Many college students find writing difficult because they have never been taught the basic principles of the craft. Or if they were taught these principles in school, they may not have really *learned* them, because they weren't asked often enough to apply and practice them. You will find that most college and university instructors are more demanding; you will be expected to write often and well for most of your classes. And as information becomes more and more important in all professions, writing ability is also becoming more essential after college. The labor department estimates that 80 percent of the jobs into which Americans are now promoted require writing ability and expects that by the year 2000, about 90 percent of promotions will demand that those who advance be able to write well.

This book is designed to help you acquire the techniques you need for writing effectively. It can also help you overcome any mental blocks you may have about writing. As you study the guidelines in this chapter, you will discover that writing is not a mysterious talent given to a few lucky people at birth but rather a craft you can learn and use effectively in school and in your life's work. The tools you need to become a capable writer are here. Choosing to use them is up to you.

Understand that for even the most effective writers, writing is difficult.

When I stepped from hard manual work to writing, I just stepped from one kind of hard work to another.   *Sean O'Casey*

When you see a writer's work in print, be it in an ad or a news story, it may look as if it had been effortlessly composed. You see no scribbled revisions, no crossed-out words and passages, no crumpled and discarded pages. Nevertheless, not even the most seasoned writer can smoothly and easily write the words that end up under his or her byline.

Roald Dahl, the author of many novels and stories, wrote, "By the time I am nearing the end of a story, the first part will have been reread and altered and corrected at least one hundred and fifty times. I am suspicious of both facility and speed." An effective craftsman like Dahl knows writing is difficult and time-consuming. You can't expect that a story good enough for publication will be written quickly and flawlessly. What you can expect for your hard work is that your writing will be worth printing and reading.

During the last two decades, researchers have begun studying and recording what good writers do before their words become public. Until recently, though, most of the hard work that went into good writing was known only to writers themselves. Let's see how the author of some of the most stirring words in history may have composed them.

In June 1940, many American college students gathered around dormitory·radios early one evening to listen to a speech given to the British Parliament by Winston Churchill. At that time, several months after the outbreak of World War II, Churchill had just been appointed prime minister and faced the responsibility of reassuring a frightened and demoralized British people. France was about to fall to the Nazis, and the Germans seemed sure to invade England soon. Here is a passage from Churchill's speech:

> Even though large tracts of Europe and many old and famous states have fallen or may fall into the grip of the Gestapo and all the odious apparatus of Nazi rule, we shall not flag or fail. We shall go on to the end. We shall fight in France, we shall fight on the seas and oceans, we shall fight with growing confidence and growing strength in the air, we shall defend our island, whatever the cost may be. We shall fight on the beaches, we shall fight on the landing grounds, we shall fight in the fields and in the streets, we shall fight in the hills. We shall never surrender!

This passage has many features that make it effective. One is Churchill's use of the phrase "we shall fight . . . , we shall fight . . . , we shall fight . . . ," demonstrating his mastery of a tricky writing technique: repetition. In the hands of an inept or careless writer, repetition can produce monotony or even unintentional humor. But Churchill, a superb craftsman, used this technique to produce the effect of hammer blows.

Churchill's brilliant combination of the repeated "we shall fight" with a carefully thought-out progression of battlefields contributes even more to the passage's impact. He begins with France, where the British troops were then fighting the Germans; then moves to "the seas and oceans" (still at a distance from English soil); then to the air, the beaches, the fields, the streets. And finally he ends the series with a retreat into the hills—implying that, rather than surrender, the British would carry on a guerrilla war against Germany's armies.

Most important, Churchill's goal in writing this speech was to rally the British to fight, and no one then or now could deny that his writing perfectly matched his purpose. When he ended the speech with the simple, climactic declaration "We shall never surrender!" American students, the British citizens, the whole nonfascist world was thrilled and inspired.

How did Churchill write this paragraph? Almost certainly, he thought about his purpose and his audience before he wrote, searching for a *theme*— an idea or point for the paragraph—that would inspire his country to resist the Nazis. His thoughts may have followed these lines:

> I must convince my people to resist, to remain determined and courageous, even though Hitler now seems invincible. We must fight; we must never surrender to this evil force. If the Nazis invade, we must

continue to fight in every city and town and, finally, in the fields and hills of Scotland and Wales.

Expert writer that he was, Churchill probably reflected on this theme and then condensed it to a sentence that served the paragraph's purpose and could provide a starting point for writing. He might have begun, for instance, by writing:

> Even though Hitler seems invincible, and even if the evil Nazi forces invade our island, we shall fight—we shall never surrender.

Using this topic sentence to start a draft of his paragraph, Churchill could then have added more sentences to expand on and explain his theme. He might, for instance, have added this after his topic sentence:

> We shall go on to the end. We shall fight in France. We shall fight on the beaches and in the streets and fields. We shall fight in the hills.

These sentences could have given him the idea to list the battlefields in a geographic progression to dramatize both the danger faced by his country and the courage and determination he would demand of his people.

Using this geographic progression as the framework for organizing his paragraph, Churchill probably went back over what he had written, revising the topic sentence to make it more subtle and interesting, adding several new potential battlegrounds, and rearranging the sentences to fit his progression from a foreign state—France—to his own country's hills.

Knowing Churchill's mastery of the English language, we can be sure he revised the paragraph several more times, refining words and phrases to incite and inspire the British people. For example, he chose to use many alliterative words—words that repeat a similar consonant sound—because he knew that this writing device, used carefully and sparingly, has a pleasing and exciting effect on the ear. Note all the alliteration in the first sentence:

*fa*mous states have *fa*llen
*g*rip of the *G*estapo
odio*us* apparat*us*
*f*lag or *f*ail

This was probably also the stage when Churchill chose to use the technique of repetition—the "we shall fight" sentences—because he meant this speech to be a call to arms and because repetition is at the core of every battle cry, from a high school cheerleader's yell ("Touchdown! Touchdown! We want a touchdown!") to the anguished outcry of Shakespeare's Richard III ("A horse! A horse! My kingdom for a horse!"). But Churchill was aware that repetition can become monotonous and, therefore, counterproductive. To relieve monotony, then, he interrupted the long series of "we shall fight" sentences with a summary statement: "We shall defend our island." He also varied the rhythm of the words following "we shall fight" to build the drama of his paragraph and focus his audience's attention.

Lastly, Churchill chose words and phrases carefully calculated to steel his people for the possibility of an invasion. He offered them some hope by reminding them of the remarkable successes of the outnumbered Royal Air Force ("with growing confidence and growing strength in the air"). But he also emphasized the danger posed by the Nazis, using fear to convince his listeners that they must resist. Churchill didn't say that "large tracts of Europe" had fallen to the "German armies" or to the "German government." He chose instead to name only the Gestapo, the cruel and fanatical secret police of the Nazi party, in connection with "all the odious apparatus of Nazi rule."

By using only the most frightening words and images related to Germany's government, Churchill made clear to his people that this war was not the traditional sort, which ends with one government winning and one losing and then the two simply negotiating a settlement of lands. He was warning, indirectly but not subtly, that if Great Britain surrendered to Hitler, the British people could expect to be subjected to all the cruelties of Nazi rule: suspension of all civil rights; destruction of Parliament, political parties, labor unions, and churches; corruption of the law and the courts; persecution of Jews and other minorities; concentration camps, torture, and mass executions. In short, Churchill was telling his people that they faced a fight, but that the alternative could be far worse than warfare.

As you can see from the lengthiness of this analysis of one fine paragraph, the right words rarely flow effortlessly from brain to fingertips and then onto paper. Writing is a mixture of art and craft, and even masterful writers like Churchill have had to struggle with that portion of writing—usually the greater portion—that is *craft:* the application of rules and training to a creative effort.

Although Churchill the man won a Nobel Prize for literature, Churchill the young student failed so often at his studies that he was tutored over and over again in the fundamentals of writing. He recalled those difficult years with gratitude: "I gained an immense advantage over the cleverer boys. I got into my bones the essential structure of the ordinary British sentence."

If you are aware of the hard work involved in good writing, you will be ready to succeed at the actual task of writing: the process of thinking and organizing, drafting, and revising until your words have accomplished your goal, which is to elicit the response you want from your readers. The rest of this chapter will show you exactly how effective writers compose. When you learn and consistently use the techniques familiar to able writers and explained in this chapter, you will enjoy the pleasure and power that come from writing well.

Make reading a habit.

I never desire to converse with a man who has written more than he
has read. *Samuel Johnson*

During the first few years of your life, you gained command of spoken
English. Without formal teaching, you learned how to use the various parts
of speech and how to form sentences. You learned to listen and speak
because both were essential for doing what you saw older children and
adults doing around you; you wanted to wield the same power you saw
them using. And to gain that power, you paid attention to the language
around you and tried—over and over again—to use it as you heard others
using it. Gradually you became familiar with and capable of using the
language that surrounded you.

Just as you once needed to master spoken English, you now need to
master written English. As we've already emphasized, nearly all adults need
to be able to write well in order to succeed professionally. For many people
in the media, writing is the focus of their careers. Now that you've decided
to gain command of written English, you need just what you needed when
you learned to speak: to be surrounded by the language you are learning
to use.

A generation ago, books like the Hardy Boys and Nancy Drew mysteries,
westerns, and romances were as common a part of growing up as sitcoms,
evening soap operas, and TV adventure shows are now. The language in
these books was the written English people had the most contact with as
they were learning to write. To sell, these books had not only to tell an
entertaining story but also to tell it in clear, readable sentences. And for
the most part, the people who grew up reading for fun wrote with the same
directness that flavored the books they read.

Now that many students and adults read not for recreation but only as
required for school or job, the language many people read most often is
what they find in textbooks and in forms and letters from government and
business. This writing tends to be full of long words, passive verbs, and
strings of prepositional phrases, all of which make understanding difficult.
Imagine how your spoken English would sound if you had patterned it
after language like this sentence from a health-insurance policy, printed by
U.S. News and World Report on September 15, 1980:

> Whenever Plan payment does not constitute payment in full, the
> amount, if any, thereof, (toward, but not in excess of, the physician's
> charges for such services) shall be up to but not in excess of that which
> then would have been payable by the Plan for Eligible Services, in
> accordance with the Plan's Schedule of Maximum Plan Payments for
> Eligible Services, (Series 750) applicable to this Certificate, and the Plan
> shall not be liable for any balance.

Fortunately, if someone had said aloud what they meant by this written sentence, it would probably have sounded something like this:

> If your doctor charges more for a covered service than the maximum we list, you'll have to pay the difference. Even if the doctor's fee is less than the maximum we allow, we won't pay more than he charges.

Because the language you've heard spoken tends to use active verbs and everyday words, you've learned to speak using active verbs and everyday words. If you are to write in a clear, direct style, you must regularly read clear written English.

For now, at least, many of the forms, letters, and books you have to read for school and business will continue to be so ponderous that reading them will hurt your writing as much as it will help it. You certainly can't stop reading the contracts you sign and texts that, although they may be poorly written, present valuable information. What you can do is make reading for pleasure a regular habit. A book doesn't have to be centuries old or concern a subject you don't care about to be good for your writing. Find books and magazines you enjoy and read them regularly—for at least twenty minutes a day. Make reading the parts of a newspaper that appeal to you a daily habit. The more you expose yourself to readable prose, the better your own writing will become.

Over the years, many researchers have found again and again that good writers do more reading for pleasure than less-skilled writers do. Just as continual exposure to spoken language helped you learn almost effortlessly to speak well, continual exposure to written language—articles and books written well enough to interest you—will help you learn to write effectively. Habitual reading will do more for your writing than any writing manual, including this one, can. By choosing books and magazines you enjoy and reading them regularly, you will expand your vocabulary, become familiar with devices for organizing your writing, learn a variety of sentence structures, learn how to punctuate and use words correctly, and learn to recognize the sound of good English, all the while enjoying yourself. Television and the overblown language you find in some of what you're required to read won't keep you from learning to write well; isolating yourself from good written English will.

BEGINNING TO WRITE

When you have become familiar with good writing (by reading it regularly) and have recognized the hard work involved in writing well (perhaps through trying to do so over and over again), you're ready to successfully learn the writing craft.

Carry out three processes as you write: invent, draft, and revise.

The act of composing is best described not as a sequence of stages, but as a set of distinguishable processes, which the writer must orchestrate in the act of writing.   *John Hayes and Linda Flower*

Good writers work back and forth, focusing on one of three processes, as they compose. The first of these processes is *invention:* discovering what to say and how to present it. The second is *drafting:* quickly recording what you have to say on paper. And the third process is *revision:* criticizing and then changing what you have written in drafts. Successful writers spend 25–50 percent of their writing time inventing, only about 25 percent of it drafting, and 25–50 percent of it revising.

These three processes fit together in a roughly linear sequence—focus on invention first, drafting second, and revision third—but as you carry them out, you will also find yourself moving back and forth to the other two stages. As you are writing your first draft, for example, you may find that you need to go back and search out new material. And almost as soon as you begin to draft, you may find yourself revising: You may write a few sentences, read them, and cross them out, realizing you have strayed from the point you want to make; or you may write a word, hear how it sounds, and choose a substitute.

Being open to change as you invent, draft, and revise is essential to writing well. Be willing to abandon what you have to say, change your subject, and start again; respond to the facts you gather when they lead you to refine, alter, or even abandon your purpose for writing; find a new audience when you realize the people whose needs you can serve best aren't those you're writing to; expand or limit your subject as you plan your first draft. Good writing is a messy, complicated process, not an orderly, rigid sequence of steps.

If you have no set method of revising your writing, perhaps you can model your revision on the work of Tim Quirk, who has used this method since he was a freshman:

> Many times I rewrite word by word, sentence by sentence. That is, I rewrite my first sentence two or three times before starting my second, and, once the second is finished, the first ends up needing further revision. So I rarely start my second paragraph before I'm satisfied with my first. Of course, once I have finished the second paragraph, the first needs more work. The same holds for pages and sections. I don't enjoy this method, and I try not to use it, but I can't help myself.
>
> I write everything by hand first, and, as the above method suggests, my paper is basically one big inkspill by the time I reach the end. If I have time, I do another hand-written rewrite before typing, making my

paper legible, but also making substantial revision. When I have a neat hand-written copy, I start typing. Each page of the typewriter usually gets crumpled and redone. Eventually, I have a complete typewritten paper. If I'm out of time, I call it the final draft. Otherwise, I set it aside for anywhere from two hours to two weeks. When I look at the paper again, I take my pen to it, deleting, adding, transposing. Then everything gets typed once more.

Observe constantly and search for connections.

An artist observes, selects, and combines.   *Anton Chekhov*

Although editors work with writers to plan stories, *all* good reporters—staff and freelance—combine curiosity and initiative to find good story topics on their own. One newspaper publisher says, "If you have a reporter who only does what the editor tells him to, you don't have much of a reporter."

How, then, do you go about finding good topics? The strength of your writing will rely directly on the strength of the topic you begin with. One professional writer, Kurt Vonnegut, has suggested, "Find a subject you care about and which you in your heart feel others should care about. It is this genuine caring, and not your games with language, that will be the most compelling and seductive element in your style."

To find a subject worth caring about, you must be receptive to the world around you. The germ from which a piece of good writing grows is usually commonplace: a chance remark, an experience had by someone the writer knows, a picture in the newspaper, an article read, or an incident that was part of the writer's everyday life. A huge ocean of stimuli for good writing surrounds you; talk to the people around you, read widely, and use your senses. Constant curiosity is the most valuable habit a writer can have, and there is *no* good writer who isn't curious.

As you seek to understand the environment you and your readers live in—whether you're exploring your school or global politics—you should look for relationships. When the answer to a question you asked or an article you read leads you to seek more information, you will discover patterns. Those patterns, supported by the details that made you recognize them, provide the best topics for writing.

How can it be, then, that so many people find themselves protesting "I don't have anything to write about!" when everyone is surrounded by rich resources for articles? First of all, many beginning writers fail to value their own experiences. Years of writing school compositions that simply reword material from the library or comment only on the work of other writers can lead students to believe that what they know from experience is not worth putting into writing. Actually, though, the strongest beginning for writing is what you have discovered in your own surroundings; when you write about what you have figured out yourself, you bring to your readers events and ideas they don't already know and can't understand without your help.

A second obstacle to recognizing the worthwhile subjects for writing that surround you is failing to observe fully. Unless you wonder at and about the world around you, you can't focus on the parts of your experience that will enrich other people's lives when you put them into words. If you ride a bus to school or work, you can either screen out the conversations around you and glance at other passengers' faces without really concentrating or you can give your surroundings your full attention: See the frayed, gray lace on the edge of her slip when the woman beside you sits down and crosses her legs, wait a few minutes and see the makeup that has collected in a crease on her cheek, and make a connection; listen to what the three boys behind you are saying—the words they choose, the sound of their voices, the interplay among them as camaraderie deepens or a fight brews; smell and feel the warm, stale air that surrounds you and the stickiness of the floor against the soles of your shoes; ask, tactfully, that woman beside you the questions that will satisfy your curiosity about her; read the graffiti. The most important experiences you have are often the easiest to miss. Test yourself often: Did I really listen to what that person just said to me? Did I ask questions to find out what I'd like to know? Did I really see the people around me today—my family, my friends, the strangers at the market or at the corner waiting for the light to change? By consciously observing—talking with people, using your senses fully, and reading widely—you will discover the unique experiences readers respond to.

You also need the initiative to seek out experiences that are accessible to you but not part of your routine. No matter how small the community you live in is, there are facets of it you have never explored. When you take the time to find out what is happening beyond your home, work, and social life—when you have the initiative, for instance, to visit the trade fair at your community center or talk with the people who congregate at a local diner every morning—you will enrich your idea bank and come across many good topics for stories. Good writers know experience is essential to lively writing. William Faulkner, winner of the Nobel Prize for literature, acknowledged the value of observation in his writing when he said, "I always write out of my personal experience, out of events I've been present at, out of stories I've heard from people. . . . All [any author] is trying to do is to tell what he knows about his environment and the people around him in the most moving way possible. He writes like a carpenter uses his tools."

Once you learn to observe skillfully, to search for connections, and to value your insights, only one obstacle to finding worthwhile subjects remains. How can you *remember* all the details you notice so that you can use them later to show your readers what you have perceived yourself?

Most writers keep written records of their experiences in files, on cards, or in a journal. Many famous writers, including Nathaniel Hawthorne and

Franz Kafka, have used journals to collect material for writing. Excerpts from their journals show how keeping written records of experiences will help you write.

Collect many observations and ideas in notes to yourself, and you will find that some of them are dead ends. Others, though, will turn out to be the ideas you need to make your writing work. The next section, on exploratory thinking, complements this discussion of observation. It will explain how to supplement the habits of careful observation, searching for connections, and recording ideas with specific techniques for beginning individual stories.

When your instructor assigns you to, say, a color story on a football game, think of the people and things that appeal to you. An author of this book has remembered for thirty years a woman student who returned from a football game and wrote a captivating story about how the salespeople sell soft drinks. In fact, she did more: She asked the sales manager how many bottles of soft drinks his employees had sold. When your class has the same assignment, think about what most interests you.

Begin writing by thinking exploratively.

How do I know what I think until I see what I say?   *E. M. Forster*

A blank piece of paper—or an empty display screen on a computer—can thoroughly intimidate the writer who doesn't know how to prepare to write. Experienced writers, though, expect to spend much of the time they put into writing just discovering what they want to say. Ernest Hemingway, for example, said, "My working habits are simple: long periods of thinking, short periods of writing." Conscious exploration is what helps good writers get started and keep going, figuring out the plans that help them write their first drafts and then doing their actual writing.

People may have told you in the past that writing an outline is a good way to start writing. Outlines can be tremendously helpful, but formal outlines don't work well as tools for starting to write. Before you can decide on an order for your ideas, you have to come up with good ideas in the first place.

To start writing, you should deliberately *explore,* seeking out a wide variety of possibilities. By discovering many options before you commit yourself to a particular, limited plan, you can later settle on the *strongest* of the choices available to you. The thinking you should rely on as you start to compose, then, should not be critical. Instead of criticizing your ideas too early, concentrate on collecting as many ideas as you can.

Simply talking about your topic is one technique that will help you prepare to write. As you talk with another person, in a group of people, or even into a tape recorder, ask yourself what you already know about the topic you plan to pursue and then what additional information you'll need to collect.

These nine questions are worth asking your listener(s) or yourself:

What subject will I write about?

Which aspects of the subject will I include and which will I ignore?

What incidents do I know about that illustrate my particular topic?

Where can I find out about aspects of my topic I'm not already familiar with myself?

What questions can I ask about my topic?

What are the answers to these questions?

Do I have any problems with this topic?

What are the problems?

Who is my audience?

If you take notes while or just after you talk about your topic, you will have a collection of ideas that is much less cumbersome to sift through than a tape recording and one that you don't have to worry about forgetting. By "notes," we mean not neat, complete sentences, but whatever *you* need to have on paper in order to remember an idea later. Note-taking is also at the heart of two other dependable techniques for exploring a topic: free-writing and brainstorming.

Free-writing is uncensored, nonstop writing. With your subject in mind, begin writing and do not allow yourself to stop, even for a second. Don't let yourself go back to something you have already written to revise it; just keep writing—new ideas or versions of ideas you've already used that you like better than what you came up with earlier. If you get stuck, write the last word you used over and over until a new idea occurs to you. And when you free-write, don't let trying to write in complete, correct sentences distract you. You may be halfway through a sentence, think of a better idea, and start a new sentence. Or you may find yourself writing phrases and leaving out unimportant words. Free-writing is for your eyes only and should be a messy collection of ideas: brilliant ones, useless ones, and mediocre ones, all mixed together. By putting off criticism until later, you will compile the richest group of ideas possible from which to choose the material you'll actually use.

For the same reason, brainstorming also demands that you compile ideas and put off criticizing them until later. Brainstorming consists of generating all the ideas you can, jotting them down as you go. One way to brainstorm is to write the general idea for your story in the center of a piece of blank, unlined paper. Then, suspending the impulse to question, jot down randomly—all over the paper—all the ideas you can think of that are related to your general idea. As a third step, use arrows or lines to join related ideas.

Some writers use index cards or separate pieces of paper for brainstorming. If you jot down ideas and details one to an index card, later you will easily be able to set aside material you don't plan to use and also experiment with different plans for organizing your writing. You will be able to group related cards in piles and choose an overall order for the piles that works like an outline to guide your writing. One of the authors of this book uses a less expensive variation of the index-card system, jotting down all the ideas she can think of on the front side of sheets of notebook paper. She then cuts the paper into pieces, one idea to a piece, and puts related ideas in piles, adding the ideas that she came up with away from her desk and jotted down on paper napkins, MasterCard receipts, or whatever else was handy. After identifying her audience and purpose, she forms a plan for her first draft, by setting aside individual ideas or piles of related ideas she doesn't plan to use, putting the slips of paper for related ideas together, and then choosing an order for the piles of related ideas. After adding whatever details she needs for achieving her purpose—also on slips of paper for individual ideas, placed wherever in the ordered piles of ideas they fit—and making whatever changes in the order and content of the piles the new details call for, she writes her first draft. The piles of scribbled ideas remind her of the material that belongs in each paragraph, section, and chapter and give her each idea that belongs in the first draft right when she needs to remember it.

As you can see, exploratory techniques like brainstorming ease the difficulty of the rest of writing. They give you good answers to the questions "What am I going to write about?" and "What do I have to say about this topic?" They also give you the resources you need to come up with a strong plan for your writing, saving you anguish and wasted effort. (Some writers even find that preliminary ideas on how to organize their articles emerge as they explore their topic.)

Combine and vary these techniques for exploratory thinking in whatever way fits your personality. No one of them is magical or indispensable. What *is* essential, though, is that you harness your experience—gathering the ideas you already know and searching out whatever additional material you need—before you write. As Kurt Vonnegut advised student writers, "your own winning style must begin with ideas in your head."

BECOMING AN EFFECTIVE WRITER

Now that you have used curiosity, a sense of relationships, and exploratory thinking to compile a rich stockpile of ideas and observations, you are almost ready to assemble the material for a specific article. Choosing the content of a written composition is like deciding how to compose a photograph within its frame. You must decide what to include within the frame and what to leave outside it before you can convey your vision to others.

Consider your audience and define your purpose before you write.

Everything that is written merely to please the author is worthless.
Blaise Pascal

The photographer and the writer both have to know their audience to decide what to capture on film or in words. The success of any composition depends on how well the composer has identified his or her audience and responded to its needs. You may discover you have already started thinking about your readers as you collected ideas for writing. Or you may find that, for you, exploring and observing first and then figuring out who your readers will be works better. Either approach—subconscious or conscious—is fine. Be sure, though, that you wait to plan and draft until after you know exactly who your readers will be and have thought about what they will need and want.

Every piece of writing you have ever produced had a specific audience: the students, faculty, and staff who read your campus newspaper; a professor, teacher, or teaching assistant; classmates; a friend or relative; or even just you, the writer, yourself. Professional writers also write for a specific audience whenever they submit an article for publication.

Many beginning writers are at a disadvantage because they have written almost exclusively for the teachers who have taught them what they are writing about and then assigned their grades. This kind of writing is poor training for professional writing for several reasons. First, professional writers usually write for people who know less than they do about the subject of an article. Second, professionals write for people whose goal as they read is understanding or entertainment rather than evaluation. And third, professional writers usually aim toward groups of people rather than a single individual. Studies have also shown that high school teachers' preferences can diverge from those of newspaper and magazine readers. Anyone who picks up a periodical wants to be able to grasp the meaning of articles without unnecessary strain in order to understand and enjoy them. In contrast, it has been shown that some high school English teachers tended to rate poorly reasoned compositions written in exotic vocabulary as better than simply written, logically organized papers.

The audience you have written for in school, then, may have been an artificial one. Unless your teachers have valued clarity in your writing and provided you with assignments written for a variety of audiences—classmates, students in other classes and grades, parents, other adults in your

community, and teachers not primarily concerned with grading your work—
you will need to learn how to write as professionals do: to inform and
entertain.

Writing for an English instructor is not very different from writing for a media instructor.

The difference between literature and journalism is that journalism is
unreadable, and literature is not read.   *Oscar Wilde*

A journalism professor who had also taught English composition asked his
journalism class to read *The Elements of Style* by William Strunk and E. B.
White, then compare its instructions with those of the journalism textbook
the students were reading. When the students had completed this task, the
professor asked, "What is the difference in what *The Elements of Style* and
the journalism text teach you?"

Nearly all students responded that there is only one difference: Journalism teaches us not to use a comma before "and," while *The Elements of
Style* teaches us to use a comma before "and."

One student, who majored in English, disagreed, saying, "The difference isn't great, but I've noticed especially in writing news stories our text
stresses simplicity. Compare this simplicity to Thomas Wolfe's writing." He
then produced a paperback book, *Look Homeward, Angel:*

> He knew the inchoate sharp excitement of hot dandelions in young
> spring grass at noon; the smell of cellars, cobwebs, and built-on secret
> earth; in July, of watermelons bedded in sweet hay, inside a farmer's
> covered wagon; of cantaloupe and crated peaches; and the scent of
> orange rind, bittersweet, before a fire of coals.

To a limited extent, the student was correct. Had he gone further in
analyzing journalism—such as some newspaper and magazine features,
reviews, editorials, and columns—he might have changed his mind. Nonetheless, he and his instructor are right in emphasizing simplicity.

Every beginning writer, trying to become a novelist or an advertising
copywriter, should master simple expression. If you are meant to be creatively different, your nature will force you to it, perhaps even force you
to become a writer like the intricate, misunderstood James Joyce. But you
will be a better one if you master simplicity first. We are not saying that
simplicity is a primitive form. It should certainly be the beginning, but most
of the great writers have made it the end as well. Leo Tolstoy is a prime
example. His *War and Peace* is a complex structure because of the many
plots, subplots, and characters, but its prose is simple.

E. B. White

E. B. White may have been first among the great modern American essayists. A longtime worker for the *New Yorker*, White received the National Medal for Literature, the Presidential Medal for Freedom, and many other awards. He was honest, almost beyond belief. He wrote a letter to Dale Kramer, the author of a book about the *New Yorker:*

> I can't very well say whether I brought anything to the early *New Yorker*, except a certain eagerness (which was characteristic of many of the early employees in that shop) and a certain naivete, which was particularly characteristic of me as I was late in developing, was ill at ease, and fairly perceptive about the city. I was unhappy and unproductive in the jobs I held after getting out of college—I didn't like advertising, or publicity, and although I liked newspapers and reporting I couldn't qualify on newspapers or press associations (although I tried hard) as I wasn't quick enough or wise enough, and was scared of them.

Moreover, White may also be the most brutal critic of his own writing. When he had written "The Morning of the Day They Did It," he submitted it to Harold Ross, the editor of the *New Yorker*. Ross was delighted with it, set it in type, then sent proofs to White, who had settled in Maine. White then wrote to Ross: "I've read my piece over in proof, don't like it, and don't want it published. . . . A writer should have the privilege of submitting one, and I just don't happen to like this piece." After nearly a year of arguing with White, who finally relented, Ross published it.

The experience of Tolstoy suggests yet another reason to work for simplicity. Toward the end of his life, Tolstoy became obsessed with the need to write for the peasants of Russia in the simple language they understood. You do not need to think of yourself writing for peasants to learn the lesson this teaches: Remember the audience. To communicate complex ideas and paradoxical facts simply enough that any literate person can understand you is to address the largest possible audience.

Let us suppose that you are going to write for the media. What will you write?

Defining "news."   A political scientist who became convinced that he had to learn about political journalism to understand fully how the federal government works interviewed fifty Washington correspondents. He was baffled to discover that few of them were able to define "news" precisely, even though their work included gathering information and opinions from

Later, when Ross tried to pay White richly for his work, White objected, saying, "Since I agree to perform this service for the *New Yorker*—and am very glad to get the work—there is no reason to pay me a large sum of money. I would regard such a payment as a gift, or a stunt, or a device."

How could a man be so apologetic in his comments about himself? As you're no doubt beginning to suspect, E. B. White was a complex man.

Then the Book-of-the-Month Club directors heard that White's book, *The Second Tree From the Corner,* would be published in January. They asked the publisher to delay publication until August so that the book could be made a club selection. That would result in at least $20,000 more in royalties. White wrote to the publisher, saying, "After mulling over the Book-of-the-Distant-Month proposal, I have decided not to accept it." One of the editors told White that that had been the breeziest thing that had ever happened at Harper & Row. He explained with, "I don't want to wait around to suit a book club's fancy."

Although White didn't care about money, here is a typical critic's measurement of White, made by Irwin Edman: "E. B. White is the finest essayist in the United States. He says wise things gracefully; he is the master of an idiom at once exact and suggestive, distinguished yet familiar. His style is crisp and tender, and incomparably his own."

As for White's love of writing, here are his acceptance remarks for the National Medal for Literature: "I fell in love with the sound of an early typewriter and have been stuck with it ever since. I believed then, as I do now, in the goodness of the published word: it seemed to contain an essential goodness, like the smell of leaf mold."

officials who make news and selecting, reporting, and interpreting events. Moreover, the few who constructed succinct definitions disagreed with each other. The simplest definition offered was "News is what happens," to which the political scientist replied that one of the things that happened twenty minutes earlier was that he had walked in the door of the correspondent's office. Surely, he protested, *that* was not news anyone was likely to consider interesting.

The first lesson this episode teaches us is that there is nearly always confusion about basic terms among knowledgeable practitioners. The poet A. E. Housman said he could not define poetry any more than a terrier could define a rat, but the terrier certainly knew a rat when he saw one. Just as poets know a poem when they see one, reporters can recognize news when it happens. Here is the most useful definition: News is the *timely* report of events, facts, and opinions that *interest a significant number of people.* It is not enough that a report be timely; if it does not interest at least a large minority of its potential audience, it is not news. Similarly, information that is only interesting cannot be considered news; it must have some element of timeliness.

Types of news writing.   The most common type of news story is the *straight-* or *hard-news* report—also known as the *objective report*—which is a timely account of an event. A newspaper report of a speech is usually straight news. Because it covers only what happened during a brief period, straight news provides a valuable focus. It is valuable also because it makes such limited demands on reporters that they can come close to presenting an objective report of verifiable fact.

The *depth report* is a step beyond straight news. Instead of merely trying to mirror the highlights of an event, the reporter gathers additional information that is independent of the event but related to it. A reporter who covers a speech on medical practices in China may consult experts and reference sources, then present the speaker's words in a larger framework. In some cases, additional information is placed in the report on the speech; in others, it is reported separately. In either case, depth reporting calls for transmitting information, not the reporter's opinion. Verifiable fact is as pivotal in depth reporting as it is in straight-news reporting.

Interpretive reports—also known as *news analyses*—are another step beyond straight news. These usually focus on an issue, problem, or controversy. Here, too, the substance is verifiable fact, not opinion. But instead of presenting facts as straight news or a depth report and hoping the facts speak for themselves, the interpretive reporter clarifies, explains, analyzes. The interpretive report usually focuses on why: Why did the president take that trip, appoint that man, make that statement? What is the real meaning of the event?

Investigative reporting, sometimes called *muckraking,* is the practice of opening closed doors and closed mouths. As in interpretive reporting, the focus is on problems, issues, and controversies. In fact, interpretive and investigative reports are the same in cases where the reporter must unearth hidden information in order to clarify, explain, and analyze. Normally, though, interpretive reporters have relatively little trouble finding facts because they are endeavoring to explain public events, and they can usually find many sources who are happy to help them. (In fact, the danger in all reporting is that sources may want to provide information serving their own private interests.) In contrast, the investigative reporter must try to discover facts that have been hidden for a purpose—often an illegal or unethical purpose.

Features differ from the news reports already itemized primarily in their intent. A news report ordinarily presents information that is likely to concern readers, but a feature is usually designed to capture their interest. The feature reporter casts a wide net in search of facts, sometimes pulling in and using things a news reporter would consider frivolous. The feature writer's report provides a reading experience that depends more on style, grace, and humor than on the importance of the information.

Opinion writing—which encompasses editorials—also includes the work of columnists and those who review books, films, and music. Opinion writing is a presentation of facts and opinion to entertain and influence the public.

Any editorial writer must contend with the thoughts of his or her superiors: a publisher, an editor-in-chief, an editor of the editorial page, a newspaper board, and the like. In our definition, the *editorial* is the public thought of an institution; the editorial is also the presentation of fact and opinion that interprets significant news and influences public thoughts.

A few magazines—for example, *Editor & Publisher*—reflect all newspaper terms. Other magazines reflect most newspaper terms, such as interpretive reports, investigation reporting, features (known as magazine articles), editorials, columns, and reviews.

The electronic news media embrace all newspaper terms, usually under other names. *This* radio or television station may not include all, but *that* station may include most of them while another station will include the rest.

Writing for public relations and advertising.   As for public-relations practitioners, to borrow two sentences from Robert Beyers, a PR man who directs news and publications at Stanford University: "Think like a journalist, and you'll serve your institution well. Write like a journalist, and you'll do even better." Most public-relations practitioners must use *all* forms of journalism, print and broadcast.

Advertising is a different discipline, but many ad people and journalists can learn from one simple anecdote: A novice in advertising, assigned to produce copy on the outstanding quality of a bar of soap, wrote:

> The alkaline element and the fats in this product are blended in such a way as to secure the highest quality of saponification, along with specific gravity that keeps it on top of the water, relieving the bather of the trouble and annoyance of fishing around for it at the bottom of the tub during his ablutions.

Later, the story goes, a veteran copywriter looked appalled at the long, long sentence, and reduced it to these words:

It floats.

This story has a lesson for all advertising people—and for those who work in journalism: Keep everything simple. Nearly all those who attempt to reach the great mass of people—even the small masses—must remember what Winston Churchill said: "The old words are the best."

Understand the different purposes served by the broadcast media, magazines, newspapers, public relations, and advertising.

He said that there was only one good, knowledge; and only one evil, ignorance. *Diogenes Laërtius*

At the risk of oversimplifying, let us say that as *information media*, radio, television, and cable television are useful primarily in reporting spot events— alerting the public to breaking news. Periodic newscasts, most of which are repetitive in varying degrees throughout the day, cannot flesh out news and place it into a context that gives it meaning. The nature of most newscasts requires that announcers skim along the top of the news, presenting just headlines, leads, and brief news bulletins. Some radio, television, and cable reporters, of course, do work occasionally on news analysis and documentary programming. Although these programs provide a deeper focus than regular broadcast news does, they usually concentrate on a single event or, at most, a cluster of related events. For the most part, broadcast news provides little depth.

Magazines, on the other hand, come in a vast variety, which allows them to specialize in an entirely different way. Magazine articles almost always run at length, in depth, or both. Even the newsmagazines, which attempt to cover a wide range of subjects in some depth, publish less information in a weekly issue than appears in a single day's issue of a large metropolitan newspaper. Because they cannot match the timeliness of radio, television, and cable television, magazines often seek out unreported news. Magazine writers also have time to explore issues and polish their presentation, lending grace and color to events and personalities that most newspaper and broadcast journalists can show only in silhouette.

The American newspaper shares some of the benefits and some of the handicaps of magazine and broadcast journalism. Newspapers cannot compete with radio, television, and cable for rapid transmission, and few newspapers can give more than a handful of reporters the leisure for lengthy investigation and graceful writing that magazine writers enjoy. But once off the press, the newspaper is available at any time of day, unlike a broadcast, and it provides a considerable volume of information on many subjects, unlike a magazine. A man interviewed during a newspaper strike gave a good summary of what people miss without a daily paper: "I don't have the details now; I just have the result. It's almost like reading the headlines of the newspaper without following up the story. I miss the detail of and explanation of events leading up to the news."

Advertising and public relations (PR) are usually ignored, but they also have vital roles in giving news and features to the general public. Of course, advertising is concerned primarily with selling a product. PR is concerned about many things, of which selling a product can be one. For example, someone invents a new chewing gum that helps people stop smoking. To inform people about it and buy it, you go on the road doing talk shows throughout the country. Your intent is to advertise, but, strictly speaking, you're involved in PR. You're certainly attempting to sell the product, but you're also dealing with news people, to inform the public about the product, your company, and yourself.

PR is also concerned about things other than selling. Foremost among the concerns of PR people is to present a favorable picture of their organizations. Thus, public relations sometimes means "community relations," as when a company is involved in a community project such as helping build a swimming pool.

Pacific Gas & Electric (PG&E) in 1986 solicited and received news stories and editorials in major newspapers throughout the United States, including the *Wall Street Journal* and the *New York Times* about an important issue involving hydropower. Congress was considering legislation that would have been detrimental to PG&E's interest, and the company convinced the editors that the legislation was unfair. Congress eventually agreed.

Institutional advertising also plays this role. Ten years ago, Mobil Oil Company started running a series of ads that address issues of importance to oil companies. The intent is not to sell gasoline, but to encourage people to see oil companies in a more sympathetic light.

Truthful reporting is accurate, objective, and balanced.

. . . we should tell it like it is, and it is often better than we say it is.
Howard K. Smith, ABC News commentator

Accuracy. Giving in to the urge to stretch the truth can undermine trust that has taken years to develop. One of the authors of this book, for example, had read and trusted her community's leading morning newspaper for five years and had chosen it as a model for the school newspaper staff she advised. Reading the newspaper's editorials one morning, she came across this sentence: "About 39 schools are circulating petitions against Star Wars research on their campuses. They include prestigious institutions like the California Institute of Technology, Harvard University, and the Massachusetts Institute of Technology."

Surely, the reader thought, this sentence was wrong and the writer meant some of the faculty members at these institutions opposed research on space weapons. When the reader called the newspaper, an editorial-page staff member confirmed that individuals affiliated with the universities, and not the universities as institutions, had sponsored the petitions.

Then the reader asked whether the paper would correct the sentence, and the staff member immediately said that because the writer had *meant* individuals affiliated with the universities and not the universities themselves, no correction would be issued. The newspaper, she continued, printed corrections only for "major errors." The conversation ended after the caller asked whether her inquiry about a correction would be forwarded to the writer's supervising editor. The staff member's answer was, "We *are* the editors."

This five-minute incident left the reader's trust in her newspaper badly shaken. In a series of actions reflecting a lack of respect for truth, the staff member who wrote the editorial and the editor who answered the phone demonstrated how quickly journalists' loss of regard for accuracy can undermine public confidence. Some inaccuracies are inevitable even in the most careful reporting, and some reader complaints are unjustified. Nothing, however, is more important than truthfulness in reporting: especially not a reporter's ego.

Accuracy, then, has two components. The first is getting facts straight in print, and the second is exhibiting more concern for truthfulness than defensiveness when you have made a mistake.

The most obvious and elementary inaccuracy is a misspelled name. Make sure every name is spelled correctly and avoid assumptions; you may know fifteen women who spell their first name "Mary," but the speaker at the convention whose comments you report may be "Meri Jones." When a reader notices a misspelled name, he or she is apt to wonder whether, if you can't even get the spelling of someone's name right, you can be trusted to be accurate in any of the other facts you provide.

Other facts you should check to ensure accuracy are numbers, dates, addresses, photo identifications, technical information, and direct quotations. If you use addition, percentages, or some other mathematical explanation in a story, do the math yourself to make sure it works; you can be sure some of your audience will. Choose your authorities carefully; if the "police chief" calls, get his or her telephone number and call back to check part of the story. Check any story that sounds implausible with an experienced reporter, and label all opinion and rumor as such, identifying its source.

As *Washington Post* reporter Janet Cooke learned after receiving a Pulitzer Prize and then losing her job because her award-winning story had been about a character who did not exist except as a composite of many different individuals, reporting on imaginary people or events as if they were real—even when a story illustrates a truth—is fiction writing, not journalism. Never allow yourself to alter the facts.

Finally, be careful not to distort the meaning of a comment by twisting or eliminating its context. One reporter asked a famous British diplomat this question when the diplomat arrived in New York: "Do you plan to visit any night clubs while you are in New York, Lord Selwyn?" The diplomat parried, "*Are* there any night clubs in New York?" The next day the reporter's newspaper carried a story beginning: " 'Are there any night clubs in New York?' That was the first question British diplomat Lord Selwyn asked yesterday as he arrived. . . ." The inaccuracy created by this kind of distortion of context shows contempt for those who read or listen to a reporter's work.

When you have made a mistake—in a news story, a PR release, or even an ad—and an inaccuracy is called to your attention, remember that whoever notifies you that your facts may need correcting is doing you a service. When you have been working against a deadline and putting time and care into your work, you may have to fight the impulse to defend it. If a reader, listener, or viewer calls and suggests you have made a mistake, make no immediate promise or rejection of a printed correction; just thank them and tell them you'll notify your supervisor immediately.

Objectivity.   Complete objectivity, like flawless accuracy, is an impossible ideal that journalists must pursue tirelessly. Try to report your observations in a way that several unbiased observers would agree is accurate, and realize that your background and beliefs affect your judgment.

Everyone, including the professional journalist, tends to protect his or her beliefs through selective exposure, selective perception, and selective retention. We tend to read and listen to information that supports our beliefs and ignore what opposes our assumptions. We tend to register information that bolsters our views more than information that contradicts them. And we tend to forget facts that fail to support our conclusions and remember facts that mesh with what we believe. We can balance some of our biases by working at self-examination. Reporters must recognize their prejudices, fight the impulse to make assumptions, and seek information that challenges their views in order to serve their audiences responsibly. Analyze your own weaknesses and try to compensate for them through careful observation and questioning. One technique that will help is being wary of concluding that anything you report is good or bad. Let the reader, listener, or viewer decide.

If you work as a specialist, you need to guard your ability to report objectively with special care. When you have to depend on the same sources over and over again for information, when you understand the problems of those whose actions you report, and when you chat, dine, and live with your subjects day after day, it is easy to fall into the habit of favoring those whose activities you are bound to report as objectively as you can. If a coach wants you to play down a player's injuries, you may have trouble not co-operating if you have accepted free game tickets for your family or friends. If the restaurant you are reviewing advertises in the paper you work for, you may be tempted to focus on the tasty apple pie and ignore the lumps in the mashed potatoes. Or if you know that the director of the community theater's dreary Christmas play has an alcoholic wife, you may want to help him by giving the play a favorable review. Remember whom you work for: your audience.

Balance.   Conflict is more interesting than harmony, but journalists need to produce a picture of reality that informs readers and viewers of successes as well as failures. Readers and viewers object, for example, to what they perceive as discrepancies in how different classes are covered. One black newspaper reader complains, "If you read the paper, you'd think everyone on my side of town is a robber or a mugger. That's the only coverage we get."

When a story contains a negative comment about some person or activity, that person or someone connected with the activity should have an opportunity to respond. Talk with a spokesperson for an activity that has been criticized and include that version of the event before you report it. Realize also that controversial issues may have more than two sides. Interview all sides: managers as well as subordinates, owners and neighbors as well as tenants.

EXERCISES

1. Read one long feature story in a newspaper and another in a magazine. Decide for yourself which is better. Then write a report of no more than 200 words on both stories in which you explain why the story you preferred was better than the other feature.

2. In class, explain why the story you have chosen is better. For example, did it have anecdotes? Did it describe people more precisely than the other story did? Did it have an identifiable beginning and end (or did it just conclude as though the writer had nothing more to write)?

3. Free-write a story at least a page and a half long. Then, taking your time, painstakingly rewrite your story. Bring both drafts to class and read them aloud.

There is no worse lie than a truth misunderstood by those who hear it.
William James

In any really good subject, one has only to probe deep enough to come to tears.
Edith Wharton

In your work and in your research there must always be passion.
Ivan Pavlov

Research is to see what everybody else has seen, and to think what nobody else has thought.
Albert Szent-Györgyi

There are no embarrassing questions—just embarrassing answers.
Carl Rowan

Discussion is an exchange of knowledge; argument, an exchange of ignorance.
Robert Quillen

The first rule is the first rule in life: see everything yourself.
Richard Melba

Perfection is achieved by a series of disgusts.
Walter Pater

2

Research: Gathering Facts

> ... the first essence of journalism is to know what you want to know; the second, to find out who will tell you.
> *John Gunther*

When you question a speaker, you should remember an anecdote about the late J. Edgar Hoover, former director of the FBI. Hoover had become irritated as he read a long report because the writer had not observed the FBI's margin requirements. At the top of the first page, Hoover wrote, "Watch the borders." Because no one asked Hoover exactly what he meant, orders to "watch the borders" went out to FBI field offices, and for weeks agents guarded our borders with Canada and Mexico. Your questions about what a speaker has said should clear up this sort of ambiguity.

Learning about mistakes by the FBI, which is not a journalistic institution, should tell you that this chapter is for public relations practitioners and advertising writers as well as journalists. In fact, all students should learn how the various methods of research can be used. In fact, many basic principles of research should be employed in everyday living.

GATHERING FACTS THROUGH OBSERVATION

Although interviews and "library research" are basic ways of getting information, we begin with methods that you might consider less traditional—although good writers have probably always relied on them.

Make a sustained effort to improve your listening habits.

The difficulty in life is the choice.   *George Moore*

The key to improving your listening ability is objectivity. No one has such good listening ability that he or she doesn't need to eliminate some bad habits. Be honest with yourself about which listening skills you're good at and which you need to enhance. For instance, some people need practice at blocking out extraneous noises and visual distractions. Others need to stop assuming they know what will be said before it is said.

To become an effective listener, strive to bring your habitual listening up to the quality of your capacity to listen. Deal with your weaknesses in listening habits as if they must be corrected immediately to prevent serious problems, and continually practice the habits you want to be able to rely on as a reporter. Daily practice—not just for a week or two, but over months and years—will help you replace sloppy habits with the rare talents of a good listener.

Pay attention to nonverbal communication.

No mortal can keep a secret! If his lips are silent, he chatters with his fingertips; betrayal oozes out of every pore!   *Sigmund Freud*

Part of listening is noting a speaker's tone of voice. Is his or her voice overbearingly loud, so soft it's difficult to hear, rushed, or breathy? Does the speaker's voice reflect his or her vitality? Is it flat and colorless? Do you hear any tension in the speaker's voice?

Expressions that a speaker uses over and over can also help you understand his or her attitude. A speaker who says, "I don't mean to change the subject," for example, probably intends to do just that. Ending sentence after sentence with "You know what I mean?" or "OK?" may mean the speaker doubts your ability to listen and understand.

Gestures and facial expressions make up an important part of what a speaker says. A single gesture may not mean anything; a speaker who rubs the back of her neck, for example, may simply be massaging a sore muscle pulled during a touch football game the day before. If she rubs the back of her neck repeatedly, however, combs her fingers through her hair, and uses fistlike or karate-chop motions, she is probably feeling frustrated. Note speakers' facial expressions and clusters of two or three of the following gestures:

Defensiveness: arms crossed over chest, crossed legs, hands on the hips, fistlike gestures, karate chops, and pointing an index finger at others while talking

Suspicion: crossing the arms, glancing sideways, drawing away, touching or rubbing the nose, rubbing the eyes, and buttoning a jacket

Cooperativeness: sitting on the edge of a chair, hand-to-face gestures, tilting the head, and open hands

Frustration: rubbing the back of the neck, combing fingers through hair, using fistlike gestures, karate chops, pointing an index finger while speaking, wringing the hands, and breathing or speaking in short breaths

Insecurity: rubbing one thumb over another, keeping hands in pockets, biting fingernails, chewing a pen or pencil, and pinching own flesh

Nervousness: covering mouth with hand while speaking, tugging at pants while seated, tugging at ear, fidgeting in chair or with some object, picking or pinching own flesh, not looking at listener, wringing hands, whistling, smoking, and clearing throat

Confidence: steepling hands, placing hands behind back, sitting up straight, hands in pockets with thumbs out

Evaluation: stroking chin, tilting head, hand-to-face gestures, putting hand to bridge of nose, peering over glasses, taking glasses off or cleaning them, pipe-smoking gestures, biting on earpiece of glasses

Rather than assuming in print or on the air that a subject's gestures reveal a particular state of mind, show the gestures themselves. When you show how a subject behaves, your audience can understand what a subject's gestures reveal as well as you do. Assuming in print or on the air that a subject feels a certain way is risky: You may be wrong. Reporting a subject's facial expressions and gestures, on the other hand, can only contribute to understanding. Nora Ephron used description of nonverbal communication to describe the first woman umpire in a professional baseball game:

> . . . but if you ask Bernice Gera a question about that suit—where she bought it, for example, or whether she ever takes it out and looks it over—her eyes widen and then blink, hard, and she explains, very slowly so that you will not fail to understand, that she prefers not to think about the suit, or the shoes, or the shirt and tie she wore with it one summer night last year, when she umpired what was her first and last professional baseball game.

Ephron allows her readers to see for themselves how Gera feels.

As you can see from Ephron's description, observation enlivens reports based on interviews. In addition to observing and reporting tone of voice, facial expression, and gesture, you can also observe:

Body characteristics: physique or body shape, features, skin color and tone, fragrance or odor, clothes, makeup, hairstyle

Proxemics: how a subject uses and perceives personal and social space—how one acts at a family gathering; in a small group of friends, colleagues, customers, or constituents; in a crowd; on stage

Personal surroundings: the environment a subject creates at home or in the office—furniture, objects on walls and on tables or desks, lighting, temperature, smells, colors, noises, and music

Albert Mehrabian of the University of California at Los Angeles has reported research indicating that only 7 percent of what a speaker communicates is conveyed through words. Mehrabian concluded that 38 percent is conveyed by the manner of speaking and 55 percent is conveyed by facial expression, eye behavior, posture, and gestures. In another study, Ray Birdwhistell of the University of Pennsylvania found that in an average two-person conversation, words carry less than 35 percent of the interaction's social meaning; more than 65 percent is nonverbal. The differences in the two studies' percentages arose because the researchers investigated different speech situations. The conclusion of both studies is the same: Most communication is nonverbal.

If research findings have failed to convince you, consider the true story of von Osten's horse, bought in Berlin in 1900. Von Osten's horse Hans became famous for counting, doing arithmetic (adding, subtracting, multiplying, and dividing), telling time, using a calendar, and performing other feats—all by tapping his hoof. At public demonstrations, Hans counted the number of people in the crowd and the number wearing glasses.

A committee of psychology and physiology professors, cavalry officers, veterinarians, a circus director, and the director of the Berlin Zoological Garden examined Hans when von Osten was not present. The horse still counted correctly, and the committee concluded that Hans actually was able to perform as advertised.

When a second committee was formed, however, one of the examiners told von Osten to whisper a number in one of Hans's ears and another examiner to whisper a second number in Hans's other ear. Hans could not add the numbers. Similar tests revealed why Hans had failed: He couldn't see anyone who knew the answer. When Hans had been asked questions, anyone who knew the answer had unwittingly become expectant and assumed a tense posture. When Hans's hoof-taps had reached the correct total, onlookers would relax and, unwittingly, make a slight head movement. Hans had learned to respond to this nonverbal signal by stopping the hoof-tapping.

Hans's ability hints at how much people say nonverbally. Careful observation is vital to truthful reporting.

To observe well, focus on significant details.

You see, but you do not observe.   *Sir Arthur Conan Doyle*

To become a skilled observer, you must correct vagueness of vision as well as bad listening habits. There is so much around us to see that to focus on anything, we have to ignore most of our surroundings. Unlike verbal information, which comes in neat linear succession, one word after another, visual information comes in a simultaneous flood of details. To cope with competing details, we tend to ignore the customary to focus on the unusual. A series of studies at a Geneva university found, for example, that most students tested could not describe the university's main entrance.

The reporter who fails to focus his or her vision cannot succeed. Fremont Older, a demanding San Francisco newspaper editor, decided that one beginning reporter would be able to write a lively report only by immersing himself in his subject. Older assigned the reporter a story about the Salvation Army and said the reporter could take all the time he needed to thoroughly research his subject. After three weeks, the reporter turned in a flavorless story. "Didn't you observe *anything?*" Older bellowed. "At night, for instance, *where did they hang the bass drum?*" The reporter didn't know and was fired.

Older repeated this story to young reporters for decades. One of those reporters, Bruce Bliven, said he was still pushing himself to observe well fifty years after his own experiences with Older. "After I meet someone," Bliven said, "I ask myself questions about his personal appearance, to make sure I really *saw* him."

Reporters for the electronic media must also be able to observe significant details. To write well for radio, you must help your audience see the scenes you've witnessed. To write well for television, you must know what visual elements of a story are important and how to use words to show the elements that will be missing or difficult to make out on the TV screen.

Everyone with vision can learn to focus it. Like all observers, reporters must simplify their surroundings by selecting only some details to report and observe. Before you cover an event or conduct an interview, think about what details you'll focus on. Then, as you observe, be guided rather than bound by your plans. If you train yourself to be a good observer, you'll find that before you sit down to compose a story, you've already finished some of the toughest work of writing.

Understand how your beliefs and feelings and even your physical position can distort your perceptions.

Our most important sights are those which contradict our emotions.
Paul Valéry

As you prepare to report, first ask yourself what you expect to see. Then ask yourself what you want to see. Even the best reporters cannot completely avoid distorting as they observe. By assuming that some distortion is inevitable, though, you'll be better able to keep it to a minimum.

Emotional distortion.   When an event makes you react emotionally, you're particularly vulnerable to the impulse to distort. Reporters have to deal with all facets of life, and some of what is newsworthy is bound to make you angry or make you want to cry. Many reporters make a practice of joking about what other people would find disturbing. Without this defense mechanism, some stories would be too grim to contemplate. Despite the joking, though, reporters feel the same emotions all humans do. Professionalism demands that those emotions be kept in check.

Print reporters can often resolve the problem caused when emotions distort their observations by first recording their impressions immediately after an event that stirs their emotions, while their memories are still vivid, and then later, at a more tranquil time, examining their initial account to find and correct distortions. Sometimes a reporter can even harness emotional reactions by reporting them. When Mary Kay Blakely started to collect information on the gang rape that occurred in a New Bedford, Massachusetts, bar in March 1983, she felt sure she would be able to contain her emotions. The hard reality that other men in the bar not only failed to report the rape but also cheered it on was more than she could overcome, though. Blakely drew on her emotions to write an effective article aimed at male readers:

> Since I can think of nothing more to ask of women—except that we keep doing what we're doing—I am asking you to hand this section of the magazine to the man you love, perhaps the man sitting in the easy chair in the living room, reading the newspaper. If he is a man who shares your vision of equality, if he shares your horror over the tragedy in New Bedford, I need to talk to him.
>
> I will not try to lean over my typewriter and grab him by the lapels and pull him into my panic. But the probability that another generation of children will be sacrificed to the brutal violence of rape makes me wild with pain. I believe with every inch of my being that rape is preventable . . . but it can't be stopped without the help and commitment of good men.

Usually you should sidestep your emotional reactions and report dispassionately. And even if you do choose to report your own emotional reactions, you must check to make sure they haven't led you to distort the truth.

For broadcast reporters, the pressure to keep emotions under control is even more intense than for those who write for print. Even if broadcast material is not live, it must often be broadcast soon after it is recorded. Broadcasting allows little time for stepping back to cool off or for rewriting. You must distance yourself emotionally from the events you cover: You cannot be carried away by a crowd's enthusiasm; you cannot be outraged by someone's behavior or statements; and you cannot be too full of pity or fear to be able to do your job.

Remind yourself that your responsibility is to get the story on the air. After that if you want to yell, cry, or shake—fine. The story and your responsibility as a reporter have to come first.

Perspective.   Any single perspective is limited and should be supplemented with others. When you report on an event, ask yourself how someone viewing the event from a different location would see it and move around as much as you can to observe from different physical perspectives. Imagine, for example, viewing an antinuclear rally from within feet of the speakers' platform; you are close enough to read the speakers' expressions and see their intensity, surrounded by applause and chanting, and you are aware of organizers carrying clipboards and bustling through the packed crowd. Now imagine yourself at the same rally but far from the stage. You can hear every word of the speeches, but the speakers' voices are amplified by microphones, their facial expressions are blurred by distance, and the crowd, except for the knot of onlookers chanting and clapping near the stage, is lounging on the grass. A handful of utility workers, attracted by the noise and signs, mutters "Bunch of dummies" and "What about the Russians . . . my job . . . the Arabs?" on your right. In addition to moving from place to place as you observe an event, you should also arrange whenever you can to have another reporter accompany you as a second observer.

Observing from more than one location can be difficult for broadcast reporters. They have equipment to move and need good placement for microphones and cameras. The best place for the equipment may not be the best observation point; microphones must be close to subjects and long cables can create an obstacle. Cameras can be bulky and usually work best from a tripod, and cameras on tripods are usually assigned positions in back of other reporters to keep the cameras from blocking the reporters' view. Video recorders can also be large and hard to move. Positioning equipment so that a cable or microwave signal can get to a receiver also can limit your choice of locations. When time permits, even if you cannot move cameras and microphones, observe with your own eyes and ears from a variety of locations.

You may think television reporters can count on cameras to do their observing for them. Cameras can distort the truth, though. Thirty-five years ago, a study by Kurt and Gladys Lang illustrated this problem. The Langs studied television coverage of a Chicago parade welcoming home General Douglas MacArthur. President Harry S. Truman had relieved MacArthur of his command of the Korean War, and most Republican members of Congress and some conservative Democrats supported MacArthur. MacArthur's return was one of the first events to be covered thoroughly by television.

The Langs placed thirty-one observers along the parade route, and other observers kept track of television reports on the parade. Here is a typical report made by an observer on the parade route:

... I had expected roaring, excited mobs; instead, there were quiet, well-ordered, dignified people. .... The air of curiosity and the casualness surprised me. Most people seemed to look on the event as simply something that might be interesting to watch.

Another observer along the parade route said:

Everybody strained but few could get a really good glimpse of him. A few seconds after he had passed most people merely turned around to shrug and to address their neighbors with such phrases: "That's all," "That was it," "Gee, he looks just like he does in the movies," "What'll we do now?"

Those who watched the television coverage of the parade found that because the camera followed the general, cheering seemed constant and seemed even to reach a crest as the telecast ended. One television viewer said:

... the last buildup on TV concerning the "crowd" gave me the impression that the crowd was pressing and straining so hard that it was going to be hard to control. My first thought, "I'm glad I'm not in that" and "I hope nobody gets crushed."

Lenses, and especially telephoto lenses, foreshorten perspective, making people who are standing quite far apart from each other appear as a closely packed mass on film. A typical 50-millimeter camera lens also takes in an angle of only 25 degrees, and a telephoto lens takes in only 5 degrees; the human eye can accommodate a 120-degree angle. When a camera is held low and pointed up, a subject appears important; holding a camera high makes a subject look insignificant. And moving a camera's focus over a subject's body to look him or her over head-to-toe can be derogatory. In short, cameras can lie or at least can distort the truth. Unless you describe events you cover from the perspective of an observer, you are failing to tell the truth.

Recognize the benefits and pitfalls of observation under cover and as a participant.

When the book of life is opening, our readings are secret.   *E. M. Forster*

The act of observation alters what is being observed. A reporter who observes a family's sixteen adopted children helping prepare a typical evening's dinner, for example, makes the evening atypical simply by being in the house. The degree to which an observer's presence alters behavior varies, though. If the observer is relatively unimportant to those being observed, as a reporter on a battlefield would be, his or her presence is unlikely to have much effect.

Subjects who are unaware they are being watched behave normally. Undetected observation raises an ethical question, though: Should a subject's privacy be invaded? Many argue that concealment is only justified when the behavior being observed is open to public inspection. Circulating in a public singles bar to observe the patrons' interactions, then, would be permissible, whereas doing the same at a private cocktail party wouldn't be.

Some also argue that unobtrusively observing behavior at private gatherings is ethical as long as a reporter does not identify people. Reporters commonly record conversations heard on the street, in theater lobbies, and at concerts; this standard carried to an extreme, however, would also permit eavesdropping from behind someone's curtains.

One way of minimizing changes in the behavior of those being observed is by observing as a participant not identified as a reporter. One of the most widely known reports based on observation as a participant is Gloria Steinem's 1963 article, "I Was a Playboy Bunny." Steinem wrote:

> Serving lunch for four hours wasn't quite enough to open up all my old foot wounds, but the piled-up plates of roast beef . . . make a tray even heavier than a full load of drinks. The customers are all men: the heavy sprinkling of dates and wives in the evening crowd disappears. One told me over and over again that he was vice president of an insurance company and that he would pay me to serve at a private party in his hotel. Another got up from his fourth martini to breathe heavily down my neck. When I pulled away, he was sincerely angry. "What do you think I come here for," he said, "roast beef?"

Even though Steinem was observing public behavior, the consequences of her choosing to conceal herself as a participant were substantial: an unsuccessful but harassing libel suit, several weeks of threatening phone calls, temporary loss of serious journalistic assignments, repeated publication of her employee photograph in *Playboy,* and twenty years of occasional phone calls from working and retired Bunnies who wanted to talk about working conditions and sexual demands at Playboy Clubs.

If you choose to observe as a participant, be especially careful if you already share the goals of the group you join. The benefits of participating may be more than outweighed by your lack of detachment. Before you report from the perspective of a participant, ask yourself "Why am I going to participate: to be a part of this group or to observe and report?"

Even observers who do not begin by sharing the values of a group they participate in may find themselves unable to remain objective. Two scientific observers of audience behavior at a Billy Graham crusade in New York left their posts at the end of Graham's sermon to walk to the altar and make their "Decision for Christ." When you are observing as a participant, leave the group as regularly as you can to discuss your observations with outsiders.

Gloria Steinem

When Gloria Steinem published her book *Marilyn* in late 1986, readers were surprised that this book carried so many new observations of Marilyn Monroe that it became a best-seller. Here is an example of Steinem's reporting on Monroe:

> As an actress, she often objected to playing a "dumb blonde," which she feared would also be her fate in real life, but she might have attempted the "serious actress" appeal of playing Cecily, a patient of Sigmund Freud. After all, the director of this movie was John Huston and the screenwriter was Jean-Paul Sartre, who considered Marilyn "one of the greatest actresses alive." Ironically, Dr. Ralph Greenson, a well-known Freudian who was Marilyn's analyst in the last months of her life, advised against it, because, he said, Freud's daughter did not approve of the film. Otherwise, Marilyn would have been called upon to enact the psychotic fate she feared most in real life, and to play the patient of a man whose belief in female passivity may have been part of the reason she was helped so little by psychiatry.

Steinem had written of Monroe for *Ms.* magazine in 1972, suggesting that problems the actress had, such as guilt over not having children, also were felt by many women. Steinem's article led Henry Holt & Company to ask her to write a text on Monroe, which would accompany pictures of Monroe taken by a photojournalist before her death.

Steinem said, "One aspect of writing about a woman like Marilyn is that you feel you're exploiting her all over again." But because Steinem spends much time raising funds for women's causes, she decided to donate her money from this book to a Marilyn Monroe Children's Fund.

Observing over time is usually preferable to undercover or participant observation. Subjects who erect facades to conceal their attitudes and regular behavior rarely succeed at maintaining their poses. Nearly every study of the degree to which an observer's presence changes behavior emphasizes that the effect shrinks over time and that, in many cases, the observer is eventually forgotten.

GATHERING FACTS FROM INTERVIEWS

Interviewing is the nucleus of most reporting. The process of interviewing is highly personal, and some people's warmth, intelligence, and curiosity make them talented interviewers.

"Not to be presumptive, I thought Marilyn would like to see the money go to children's projects."

What of Steinem's own money? Happily, Letty Cottin Pogrebin, Steinem's agent, sold at auction in March 1987 proposals for two books at a total of $1,200,000. The first proposal at the auction was for Steinem's *Bedside Book of Self-Esteem*. Little, Brown outbid sixteen other publishers with an offer of $700,000. On the second proposal for a book about women from rich and powerful American families, Simon & Schuster outbid seven other publishers with a $500,000 offer. Pogrebin said, "Now maybe Gloria can grow old without worrying about having to go to the Feminist Old Folks Home."

Perhaps no one would have predicted this success for a teenager in blue-collar Toledo, Ohio, who was taking dance lessons as a means "of dancing my way out of the neighborhood." Steinem is a product of a working-class background. When she was nine, her parents separated. Steinem took care of her mother, who became an invalid; "her spirit was broken." Everything she has done as an adult—especially writing—has carried her forward and up.

Now at fifty-three (in 1987), Steinem must be satisfied with her life so far. She may think of a *New Statesman* review of one of her books, *Outrageous Acts and Everyday Rebellions:*

> The most engaging feature of this collection, apart from its maturity and humour, is Steinem's habit of turning the world outside-in at the stroke of a pen, in her own observations and in snappy anecdote. . . . In a collection that ranges widely and with brilliant clarity from articles on Linda Lovelace (a shocker) to Alice Walker (the best review of *The Color Purple* I've ever read), to pieces on the sexual politics of conversation, little facts are constantly popping up to surprise, horrify or amuse.

Prepare for interviews.

It's always easy to do the next step, and it's always impossible to do two steps at a time.   *Seymour Cray*

Even a gifted interviewer must prepare; and by preparing carefully and devoting time and effort to following basic guidelines, anyone can become at least a competent interviewer.

Learning the basic facts about those you interview compliments your subjects and encourages them to respect and respond to you. Writer John Gunther has warned, "One thing is never, never, never to ask a person about his or her own first name, job, or title. These the interviewer should know beforehand." These details, of course, are just the minimum you should gather.

Even broadcast reporters, who have less time than newspaper and magazine reporters do to prepare for interviews, must determine (1) how the interviewee's first and last name are spelled and pronounced, (2) what the person does, (3) the person's official title, and (4) the purpose of the interview. Because broadcast reporters must prepare for interviews quickly, they must stay up-to-date on a broad spectrum of events. Staying informed will keep you at least somewhat knowledgeable about the people you interview even before you receive your assignments.

Extensive preparation will help you develop a line of questioning that is both relaxed and perceptive. By easily recognizing your subject's references and knowing what he or she has thought and said in the past, you can often give an interview added energy and substance. Consider how Catharine Stimpson, a professor of English, demonstrated her familiarity with and interest in her subject's work in this interview with Gerda Lerner, a founder of the study of women's history:

STIMPSON No one has ever said that you are not strong and no one has ever said that you are not individualistic. But you write eloquently about the need for collective work. How did you reconcile an individualistic core and collective action?

LERNER In 1963, my position was necessarily individualistic. But I had been involved in organizing and working with women for 25 years before that—at the workplace, in the community. As a historian, I brought the questions I had experienced into my scholarship. The Women's Movement, in the late 1960s, made the scholarship collective.

STIMPSON You often speak of the need to connect the female experience and academic theory.

LERNER That's right. A feminist style of learning implies the fusion of theory and practice. . . .

This example comes from a friendly, noncombative interview. In interviews with evasive or hostile subjects, being familiar with relevant facts is even more important; knowing the facts enables a reporter to elicit information a source wants to withhold.

Your publication or station may have biographical data on your interview subjects in its library or morgue; and assorted *Who's Who* publications, a *World Almanac and Book of Facts,* or a one-volume desk encyclopedia may also help you learn about particular interviewees. Most public libraries contain reference books describing major personalities in practically every field. If no reference book or news clippings include information on someone you are planning to interview, telephone calls to those who know about your source may be your only option.

An essential part of doing your homework before interviews is formulating the questions you plan to ask. Some experienced journalists can jot down just a few key words before interviews, but beginners should write down a number of questions and leave space between them for recording answers. Until you gain experience as an interviewer, having written questions will keep you from collapsing into silence or forgetting important questions. The process of writing questions will also help you determine an interview's focus.

Ask questions that will keep your interviews focused.

INTERVIEWER **Willie Sutton, why do you rob banks?**

SUTTON **Because that's where the money is.**

Although even veteran interviewers prepare questions before they interview, they don't limit themselves to asking only the questions they have thought of ahead of time. Keep your prepared questions in mind and use them whenever your subject drifts away from the interview's focus or comes to a dead end. But don't stick to your prepared questions so slavishly that you drag the conversation away from a new and fruitful direction.

Don't be afraid to ask questions not on your prepared list. Useful questions often grow out of what a subject says, and questions should stem naturally from your conversation, following up on a subject's comments. What the subject says may even be so significant that it changes an interview's focus as the interview develops. With practice, focused flexibility will become natural.

When you ask questions that you haven't composed beforehand, however, be careful not to pursue a line of questioning irrelevant to your interview's focus. Keep your conversation's direction in mind, and if a source rambles, politely bring him or her back to the focus of the interview.

When you ask questions based on your subject's responses, you must also be careful not to imply through a question's phrasing that any particular answer is right or wrong. This interviewer failed to keep questions open-ended:

Q: What kind of writers are left in television then?

A: Those who are still around are trained in the taboos of the business. . . .

Q: Again, this stems from the commercial exigencies of television, doesn't it?

A: It comes from the commercial nature. I don't want to be unfair to the businessman, but . . .

Q: But all these purposes—artistic, commercial, etc.—are at war with each other.

A: Continually at war. The thing I object to is that the world of commerce is using the resources of the theater, of all our culture, for sales purposes.

Broadcast interviewers must also make sure their questions are short and free of jargon. If your question is included in the forty seconds or so of material likely to be used in a radio interview or the minute or more in an interview for television, it must be very brief to keep the focus of the report on the interviewee. Because many television stations like to develop an image for their reporters, your questions are especially likely to be included in televised reports.

Be as personable as possible, and save tough questions until an interview's end.

Manners must adorn knowledge, and smooth its way through the world.   *Philip Dormer Stanhope, Earl of Chesterfield*

The stereotype of the reporter as an abrasive crusader is generally false. For every reporter who acts out this role, you'll find a hundred others who are personable and, usually, more effective. Sometimes, of course, all reporters must stand firm and ask tough questions. A reporter's main source of information, though, is people, and treating people courteously is usually the best way to get information from them.

Appearance and manner.   Before interviews, consider what manner and even what physical appearance will aid conversational rapport. You must recognize the "social distance" between you and whomever you will interview, a division widened by factors like class differences, age, race, sex, and fashion. Reporters usually try to reduce the social distance between themselves and their interview subjects. Only a few journalists, like the extremely flamboyant Tom Wolfe, have found emphasizing social distance useful.

Part of preparing for an interview is finding out enough about the person you'll be interviewing to know how to modify your manner and appearance; you may choose to be more or less formal than you are by nature, deferential or familiar, grammatically correct or streetwise in your speech. Sometimes the person you interview will set the tone of the conversation for you. Saul Pett, a veteran writer for the Associated Press, described two interviews for which his subjects set dramatically different tones. When Pett met Dr. Albert Kinsey, the sex researcher, Kinsey took a travel clock from his pocket, wound it, set the alarm, placed the clock on a table, checked the clock's time against his watch, and—looking up for the first time—said, "Yes." Dorothy Parker, the writer, on the other hand, greeted Pett at the door by asking, "Are you married, my dear?" When Pett said he was, Parker turned her back to him: "Well, in that case, you won't mind zipping me up."

The most basic interviewing courtesy of all is telling your source your name and whom you work for at the beginning of an interview. If you haven't done so in advance, you should also be sure all your sources know their comments may be broadcast or published.

Assertiveness and persistence.   Assertiveness and persistence are as important as courtesy. Too often, inexperienced interviewers allow a source to say whatever he or she wants to and then end the interview. As a reporter, you give everyone you interview a conduit to the public. In return for that privilege, your sources give you the chance to ask the questions that will yield accurate and reasonably detailed information for your audience.

Assertiveness is not the same as aggressiveness, though. The aggressive reporter who hits sources right away with rifle-shot questions can make interviewees wary of divulging information they might have been willing to discuss under more congenial circumstances. Instead of resorting to aggressiveness, strive to be assertive. After a source has dodged a question, politely point out that the question has not been answered and repeat it, even if you must repeat this process several times. Or when a source drifts away from the focus of your questions, politely bring him or her back to the point. If you report for the broadcast media, courteously remind sources who ramble that answers must be kept short.

You should usually save your toughest questions until the end of an interview. That way, if the source becomes guarded or hostile, the entire interview won't be jeopardized. When a source does become hostile, remaining cordial can deflect the hostility. One veteran reporter commented:

> If I have any curves to throw . . . I save them until the end of the interview, when we're on pretty good terms; and then I don't throw spitballs, just curves.
> Once, a union boss hit me with a spitball before I could begin questioning him. He asked, "How much did Joe Sevier (an opponent of the boss) pay you for writing that story about him in *Nation's Business?*" I thought about it a minute, to keep from replying angrily, then told him, "Well, he paid me exactly what you're going to pay me for doing this story about you." He grinned, and then we had a long and congenial interview that ended with an invitation for me to attend a meeting of his union that night—an unheard-of invitation because reporters were usually excluded.

Although exceptions to the rule of saving tough questions for last do exist, they are rare. One exception is the interview designed from the outset to be adversarial; once in a long while, a reporter has no worthwhile questions to ask that a source will answer willingly. For most interviews, though, the basic rule of delaying hard questions to the end stands.

Finally, although you can't become so sympathetic you're unable to be objective, *empathy* can help you treat sources with respect. If you consider what emotions your sources are likely to be feeling, you're unlikely to make mistakes like asking a bereaved mother, "How did you feel when you saw your little boy fall out of the car?"

Maintain neutrality.

Surely human affairs would be far happier if the power in men to be silent were the same as that to speak. But experience more than sufficiently teaches that men govern nothing with more difficulty than their tongues.   *Benedict Spinoza*

Reporters are paid to report, not to comment—in print, on the air, on the phone, or in person. Gratuitous comments damage your credibility as a reporter.

If your opinions were what an audience wanted to know, you'd be writing a column or a reporter would be interviewing you. Whether you agree or disagree with a subject's opinions should not affect an interview, and you should usually keep your opinions to yourself.

The most common problem among beginning reporters is not showing hostility, but leading sources inadvertently by smiling, nodding, or leaning forward. These responses are particularly dangerous on camera, where they make reporters look as if they're agreeing enthusiastically with what an interviewee is saying. Always remember to use methods for encouraging response without sacrificing your neutrality as an observer.

When a source hides behind bland statements, however, you may need to inject your own opinion into the conversation to provoke a genuine response. Gloria Steinem used this technique to probe Patricia Nixon in 1968. Steinem recalls:

> Explaining my doubts about writing from clips, I asked if there were any persistent mistakes in the press that I should take care not to repeat. "No, no," she said, smoothing her skirt. "You ladies of the press do a fine job. I think the stories have been very fine." Did that mean she liked everything that had been written? "Well, actually, I haven't had time to read a lot of them lately." . . . We went round with that a few more times. Then she was, I told her, the only person I'd ever met, including myself, who liked everything written about them. There was a flicker of annoyance behind the hazel eyes—the first sign of life.

Much later in the interview, Steinem expressed her opinion again, finally triggering a flood of controlled resentment that showed Mrs. Nixon's real ideas and feelings.

Encourage response, and aim for a balance between monologue and dialogue.

It takes two to speak the truth—one to speak, and another to hear.
Henry David Thoreau

Most interviews should begin with small talk to put the interviewee at ease and set a relaxed, conversational tone. Direct the small talk at the topic that will be the focus of your interview so you won't have to make a strained leap, for example, from the weather to your source's candidacy for mayor. Only with sources who are under time pressure or who are obviously barely tolerating being interviewed should you start questioning right away.

The microphones, lights, and cameras of broadcast interviewing can make interviewees not accustomed to them especially uncomfortable. You may need to gently remind interviewees to speak into the microphone, to stay within view of the camera and in the lights, and to avoid making distracting noises by shuffling papers or drumming their fingers on a table. Sometimes you can alleviate the anxiety that equipment causes by explaining that the microphones and cameras are helping get the source's message across to a large audience and also prevent misquotation. Be careful if you use this approach not to raise new issues that may worry a particular source further, though. Radio and print reporters can help interviewees become comfortable with having their words written down as they speak.

The ideal interview falls about halfway between monologue and dialogue. If you let the person you're interviewing monopolize the conversation, he or she probably won't provide the information you need. The source's comments are more important than yours, though, so you must control the conversation without dominating it.

If you do even half of the talking, your source is likely to pull back and may even become annoyed. You must provide brief comments aimed at gaining your source's confidence. When you refer to what your sources have said and done both before and during interviews, you can draw out full responses. Your brief comments should help interviewees realize you're capable of understanding and reporting their ideas.

Sometimes you will also have to comment in order to repeat a question a source has dodged, to ask a source to repeat or clarify a complex answer, or to keep an interview on track.

When an interviewee answers only in monosyllables—"Yes," "No," "Who knows?"—you can often elicit a more detailed response by asking "Why?" or "How?" People confronted with these simple questions can always shrug and remain silent, but most will feel obligated to defend the "yes" or "no" stance they've already taken with an explanation. When someone you want to interview answers with "no comment," respond by pointing out how commenting will benefit the source.

At the end of an interview, leave the door open for further questioning. If you explain to an interviewee that when you go over your notes you'll undoubtedly find questions you'll wish you had asked and then request permission to return with another question or two, you'll be free to deepen your understanding of what the source has said.

You may also get worthwhile results by ending an interview by turning control over to your subject. Peter Sandman explains how he customarily ends his interviews:

> I make it a habit to ask the source a broad leading question toward the end of the interview—something like, "Is there anything I haven't asked you that you think I ought to ask or that you are eager to answer?" It sometimes opens up whole new fields of exploration that I didn't even know existed.

Take notes.

But men are men; the best sometimes forget.   *William Shakespeare,* Othello

You read earlier about how jotting down a speaker's main points aids listening and enhances even tape-recorded interviews. More and more reporters are recording interviews on tape, and tape-recording often reassures interviewees afraid of being misquoted. A taped interview without accompanying notes must be listened to over and over again, though, before a reporter can turn it into a story. In general, you should tape interviews when you may need an exact record later to resolve disputes, and tape all interviews while you are learning how to record sources' words on paper. Rely on written notes to jot down the most salient direct quotations as you tape and, subsequently, to plan and write your articles.

As you decide which quotations to write down, be alert to the danger of quoting out of context. This kind of distortion is at its most blatant in advertising for movies and other performances, in which, for example, a critic's "The performance was remarkable only for its lifelessness" may be quoted as "Remarkable!" The problem is much more subtle among well-intentioned reporters. Reporters may become so intent upon the point expected to be the focus of an interview that they write down sentences that support that point and ignore others that contradict it. Or the reporter may quote part of an interview that fails to reflect the meaning of the interview as a whole. The best way to avoid misrepresenting sources and misleading your audience by quoting out of context is simply to remind yourself over and over that this kind of distortion is a persistent danger.

Avoid relying exclusively on an interview for numerical information.

He was a poet and hated the approximate.   *Rainier Maria Rilke*

Do you remember the last time you cleaned your room? When was it? You may answer this way: "It was last April, because I cleaned it after the weather got warm but school was still in session. No, it was May because I had to clean it right before I drove home for Mother's Day. I don't know exactly what day it was, but I'm sure it was on a Saturday early in May . . . I think."

The same kind of answer, disguised by the source by leaving out "I think," is what you're likely to get if you ask an interviewee for a specific date. Very few people can remember exact dates for most of their actions, although they may remember the actions themselves quite clearly. And often people remember actions as being more recent than they are.

Even sources who are trying to be honest are liable to give incorrect answers to questions asking for specific numbers: dates, amounts of money, and the like. If you have any way of checking figures supplied by interviewees, do the research. If no publications exist that can verify the numbers you've been given, search for another person who can answer the same questions. If both of these methods fail, be careful to attribute whatever numbers you quote to the interviewee and not to yourself.

Interview thoroughly and, when possible, repeatedly; base stories on interviews with more than one source.

The reporter has to talk to enough people so that he can reduce the degree to which he is misled.   *Joseph and Stewart Alsop*

You already know that multiple interviews of the same source are often a good idea. As sources become used to being observed and questioned by you, their facades are likely to crumble; repeat interviews give you time to review your notes, reflect, and then ask further questions.

Interviewing the same subject again and again is helpful for the same reason that a lengthy interview is usually better than a short one. Ricardo Diaz, a documentary filmmaker, interviewed a young American race-car driver seeking the world's land-speed record, then held by a foreigner. When Diaz asked the young man, early in the interview, why he was in such a dangerous occupation, the driver spoke eloquently of the challenge of speed and his desire to bring the world record home to the United States. Much later, when the interview had covered many other subjects and Diaz and the driver had become much more comfortable with each other, Diaz rephrased the question: Why was the driver seeking the world record? The driver then admitted that because he had little education and expensive tastes, he saw no other path for himself. Perhaps the truthful answer incorporated elements of the first and the second, but the incident points out the unreliability of single, brief interviews.

Even multiple interviews of the same subject, though, are not enough to ensure accuracy. Interviews with additional sources and careful library research allow reporters to triangulate: Here is what my primary source says, here is what others say, here is what the records show. Beat reporters, for example, should talk to the heads of the groups they cover, not just to whoever has been designated as a group's source of public information. You're more likely to unearth the facts of a situation by consulting multiple sources than by even the most thorough interviewing of any one person.

Do not promise interviewees that they may read stories before publication, and be honest about a story's publishability.

Self-love is the greatest of all flatterers.   *François, Duc de La Rochefoucauld*

Reporters seem to agree almost unanimously that only in unusual cases— highly technical stories, for example—should sources be allowed to read before publication the stories in which their words are quoted. Although a source contributes to a story, the reporter is responsible for the story as a whole. Sources view completed stories from perspectives distorted by their own self-interest.

Most reporters *will* agree to call sources or write to them after a story is complete to give the sources a chance to check their own words. For beginning reporters, checking direct quotations with sources to make sure the quotations are accurate is an especially good idea. And reporters should always check with sources when the reporters suspect a quotation or fact from an interview may not be accurately stated in a story.

Reporters do not demean themselves by checking facts with the sources of their information. Beyond correction of error, however, review by sources should not be promised or allowed to influence story content.

If you are writing a story assigned to you by a publication or station whose staff you belong to, you don't need to worry about explaining chances for publication to those you interview. Freelancers, however, must give everyone they ask to interview an honest appraisal of the likelihood an article will be published. Everyone you interview gives you time, energy, and information; you should repay them by honestly telling them what to expect.

Beginning freelancers should tell sources they are not guaranteed publication, even though many sources will probably contribute less time and attention than they would if the reporter were an established freelancer or a writer on assignment.

Base your news reports on exact quotations.

The difference between the right word and almost the right word is the difference between a lightning bug and lightning.   *Mark Twain*

Reporters and PR practitioners use three kinds of fact: words used by significant sources, numbers, and direct observations. Of these three kinds of information, the words of significant sources are used most widely. Although more than half of all news reports present numbers and statistics, these reports also rely on direct and indirect quotations. The numbers, after all, come from sources and those sources must be quoted accurately. And even when reporters observe events directly, they relay what they've heard by quoting those they observe. Direct and indirect quotation, then, form the backbone of news.

A story that consisted entirely of direct quotations would be a strain to read or listen to. To vary and compress sentences and keep your audience interested, you need to include indirect quotations and statements that sum up information as well. A report including no direct quotation, or even just a few words of it, though, is powerless. Few readers, viewers, or listeners trust reports that are all, or mostly, paraphrased.

Use direct quotations to emphasize the most important points in your reports. Whatever information is most newsworthy in a report should be presented in the form of direct quotation. When an audience hears or reads the exact words a source has used, they place a confidence in those words' correctness that no indirect quotation or summary statement can earn.

Direct quotations also make news reports come alive. When an audience hears or reads exactly what a source has said, the flavor of a news event materializes. Direct quotations help re-create events for listeners, viewers, and readers; and when a source's words are worth remembering, quoting them will make your reporting memorable as well.

Whenever words are quoted in print, only the exact words a source has used may be enclosed in quotation marks. If your notes don't contain an entire statement verbatim, you must quote *in*directly, paraphrasing the source's words and using no quotation marks. You'll find that your ability to write down statements word-for-word improves with practice. Use a system of shorthand that works well for you—"w/o" for "without," "imp" for "important," and "X" for "example," for instance—and concentrate on singling out the source's most important comments for verbatim note-taking.

Some publications allow reporters to correct obvious grammatical errors in direct quotations, but many do not. As recently as twenty years ago, grammatical errors in direct quotations were routinely corrected. The president's words during a news conference in the early 1950s could not be published verbatim without his permission, and when twenty-six newspaper editors and publishers were asked during the same period whether a reporter should correct the grammar of a mayor who sounded illiterate and whose election a newspaper had opposed, sixteen said yes and six said they would instruct the reporter to use just indirect quotations. The expansion of electronic reporting, which displays a source's grammatical errors on film or tape, has affected the print media's treatment of grammatical errors by sources, leading many publications to quote grammatical errors, rather than correct them. If you work for a publication that provides guidelines for correcting grammatical errors in direct quotations, follow those standards. If the decision is up to you, standard practice is to correct grammatical errors unless there is some value to your audience in knowing the errors have been made.

If a direct quotation contains a factual error, the reporter can present the actual facts in the sentence before or after the direct quotation. Do not alter direct quotations to correct factual mistakes.

Even if your audience can tell without any doubt that someone you've already named is speaking, use at least "so-and-so said," "he said," or "she said" in any sentence that contains a direct quotation. Name the source for a direct quotation just once, though, even when a direct quotation is more than one sentence long: " 'I join the families of these heroes in celebrating their courage and mourning their deaths,' Smith said. 'They were pioneers who served us all.' " In direct quotations longer than one sentence, name the source at the end of the first sentence and not at the end of the whole quotation. And quote sentences together only if the sentences were all spoken or printed one right after another.

You can shorten a direct quotation by replacing a section of it with ellipses, but you must be careful not to distort the meaning of a comment when you shorten it. When a word or phrase is particularly striking on its own, you can also directly quote just a fragment of a sentence. (Phrases are groups of words that do not contain both a verb and a subject.)

Mix direct and indirect quotation in the same sentence or paragraph only when doing so is clearer than using just indirect quotation. When you quote just part of a sentence, make sure you do not separate words that work together—*a, an,* or *the* and the noun it goes with, a preposition and the rest of the phrase the preposition begins, or two parts of the same verb—by placing one of the words within a fragmentary quotation and the other outside it. Be sure also that the structure of your sentence remains consistent. Instead of writing "Johnson said Stevenson's resignation might change 'my decision to reduce my sales staff next month,' " for example, you should either quote Johnson's whole sentence (" 'As a direct consequence of the resignation of Beth Stevenson, my decision at this point in time is to reassess and restructure my decision to reduce my sales staff next month' ") or use just indirect quotation ("Johnson said that because of Stevenson's resignation, he will reconsider plans for reducing sales staff next month.") You should usually paraphrase rather than repeat all of a long-winded direct quotation.

When you directly quote a sentence fragment, be sure you do not continue using the subject's exact words after the closing set of quotation marks. Be careful also not to follow a direct quotation with an indirect quotation from a different source. Audiences assume that when two quotations are printed or broadcast one right after the other that the source for the first quotation is also the source for the second. Insert a paraphrased quotation by the source just quoted or a summary statement between a direct quotation from one source and an indirect quotation from another.

When you quote indirectly—to present information that is newsworthy but not striking, to pare the excess from a wordy statement, or to introduce a key fact in the first paragraph of a standard news story—be careful to echo the meaning of your source's words exactly. Double- and triple-check indirect quotations to make sure you have not used inexact substitutes for a source's words, combined sentences that weren't spoken one right after the other, or left a remark's context unexplained.

GATHERING FACTS FROM WRITTEN SOURCES

In school, you probably went to the library to do much of the research for the papers you wrote. The same is true for many college classes. When you write for the media, you continue to need to get facts from written sources, and your work will be made easier if you know what book, periodical, or electronic search system will be most helpful.

Become familiar with reference books and use them to check facts.

Diligence is the mother of good fortune.   *Miguel de Cervantes*

In addition to basic desk reference books—almanacs, standard dictionaries, thesauri, and grammar books—many writers need to have on hand a few of the reference books listed (publishers are noted in parentheses):

Bartlett's Familiar Quotations (Little, Brown).
This famous source lists sayings and writings from 2000 B.C. to the present and is a valuable reference tool.

Book Review Digest (Wilson).
This publication condenses published book reviews.

Columbia Encyclopedia (Columbia University Press).
This one-volume edition is an excellent research tool and contains a wide range of information. It is far from a replacement for the *Encyclopaedia Britannica* or the 30-volume *Encyclopedia Americana,* but its most recent fifth edition is a useful handbook.

Congressional Directory (Government Printing Office).
This is the best source for biographical information on members of Congress and their committee assignments.

Congressional Record (Government Printing Office).
The daily *Record* is set into type a few hours after the House and Senate complete the legislative day and is available the next morning.

Contemporary Authors (Gale Research).
Restricted to living authors, it includes those who have written relatively little and also those who have written in relatively obscure fields.

Current Biography (Wilson).
This monthly publication provides informal word portraits sketching people who are prominent in current news.

Editor and Publisher International Yearbook (Editor & Publisher).
This book lists daily newspapers in the United States and Canada and provides basic information about them.

Encyclopedia of American History (Harper & Row).
This book has been organized both topically and chronologically, so influential people and notable dates, events, and achievements stand out and yet the whole book can be read as a narrative.

Facts on File (Facts on File, Inc.).
Published weekly, this is a valuable encyclopedia that culls the news of the day from metropolitan newspapers.

Official publications of the state legislature.

Statistical Abstract of the United States (Government Printing Office).
This is a digest of data collected by all the statistical agencies of the United States government (and by some private agencies).

Television News Index and Abstracts (Vanderbilt University).
Published since 1972, this monthly volume is a summary of the evening news broadcasts of the three major television networks.

The Guinness Book of World Records (Guinness Superlatives).
This book is the final authority on who has the world record in almost any undertaking.

The New York Times Index (*New York Times*).
This is a valuable index to the daily *Times*.

The Times Atlas of World History (Hammond).
This fresh and instructive approach to world history from the origins of man to the present is presented visually and cartographically.

Webster's New International Dictionary of the English Language (G. & C. Merriam).
This book offers excellent definitions, careful editing, and the largest number of word entries among American dictionaries.

Who's Who in America (Marquis).
This biennial is the standard source on notable living Americans. It consists of brief, fact-packed biographies and current addresses.

Become familiar with databases, a complicated set of methods that will soon be simple.

No matter what your present condition, there's something a little better right between your reach.   *Irving R. Allen*

All databases are machine-readable files of information that are reached through a computer-telephone link. These databases can save you much time and legwork. Databases offer unparalleled convenience and speed. One librarian says that using a bibliographical database can cut research time in half. An electronic search may take less than an hour, while a manual search in a library could take days.

The coming of databases is at least a small step in the opposite direction. Databases are usually not necessary for most undergraduates; however, they are gaining ground in undergraduate research. Databases can help journalists and public-relations practitioners prepare for interviews, double-check sources' statements, and add background to stories despite time pressure. Advertising employees can also use databases in searching for facts about products, companies, and organizations that elude them in their usual research.

Searching fields.   In a database, any information in a file is in a special slot called a *field*. In a full-text database, a field might be "date," "author," "title," "abstract," and "subject."

Any user can find an information source by naming any one of the fields. In *American Men and Women of Science,* the student might specify "name," and ask for "Oppenheimer, Robert." The computer would retrieve the file for Robert Oppenheimer, and the student could then look into all other fields in the Robert Oppenheimer file (such as universities attended, awards won, address, and so on) to obtain more information. A telephone book works the same way: The searcher looks up a name to find the address and telephone number of the person.

The main difference between a telephone book and a database is that in a telephone book, the name is the only field that can be used to look up information—the only "access field." The yellow pages provide a different strategy: In looking up, say, Automotive Repair to find a mechanic, the searcher is using a subject field to look up names, addresses, and numbers. Similarly, "reverse directories," or city directories, also called "Polk directories" and "Cole directories" after their publishers, are organized by fields other than names. One Polk directory lists addresses along with the names and telephone numbers of residents; another is a numerical list of telephone numbers with names and addresses. One of the Cole directories, for example, lists office buildings with telephone numbers of tenants. All of these are simply reference books organized according to fields other than names.

In a database, though, the user is the one who chooses which field to search. Suppose the user has forgotten Linus Pauling's name, but wants information on the scientist who came up with a controversial theory about Vitamin C. The user could look up "Vitamin C" by summoning up the subject field. Print sources cannot provide that convenience.

Boolean logic and logical operators. The next step in learning to search is to understand Boolean logic, that branch of mathematics tagged with the rather intriguing name of its creator, George Boole.

Boolean logic is not difficult to learn. It revolves around three terms— AND, OR, and NOT. When a searcher uses these terms, called "logical operators," he can request information from several different fields at once, making the search more precise. A search that uses logical operators is sometimes called a multiple-level search.

To illustrate the use of AND, suppose a searcher wanted to find how many Lost Lake University graduates are Nobel laureates. The question involves looking through a database such as *Who's Who* or *American Men and Women of Science* and linking two fields, "degrees" and "awards," something like this:

Find
degrees:Lost Lake University AND awards: Nobel

Let's take another, completely hypothetical example, to illustrate some of the problems and characteristics of database searching. Suppose the searcher wants articles on "Ping-Pong diplomacy" for a paper on how it affected the later opening of trade between the United States and China. In looking through a printed index, he would probably look under "U.S. Foreign Relations," then search for the subheading "China." In a database search, that request narrows down to

Find
U.S. Foreign Relations AND China

In a Venn diagram, the request would look like this:

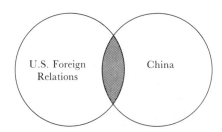

That is, the articles cover *both* U.S. Foreign Relations and China. On a computer screen, the response might look like this:

```
14506    U.S. Foreign Relations

 1278    China

   94    U.S. Foreign Relations AND China
```

The computer has 14,506 articles in the files that list U.S. Foreign Relations, 1,278 articles that list China as a subject, and 94 that list both as a subject. (Notice that each article is listed as having more than one subject.)

The results from such a request would range from statements by Chairman Mao to articles on Coca-Cola, just as they would in a print index like the *Reader's Guide to Periodical Literature*. However, in a database search, the request can be made more specific with an additional level of AND.

Find
U.S. Foreign Relations AND China AND Sports

The Venn diagram version is this:

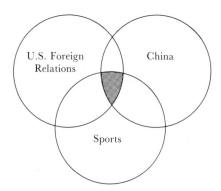

The articles encompass all three subjects.

The command OR adds another level of precision to the database search. For example, a request for "sports" narrows down the number of articles, but it still pulls in articles on the Olympics and many other topics. Yet the searcher would request "sports" because a more specific term, "Ping-Pong," would bypass articles that used, say, "table tennis" to refer to the same game. The command OR would allow the following request:

Find
U.S. Foreign Relations AND China AND Ping-Pong OR Table tennis

A particularly observant reader might notice the ambiguity in this statement: Does it mean U.S. Foreign Relations AND China AND Ping-Pong, plus an additional, totally separate subject, table tennis? That search would produce the following results:

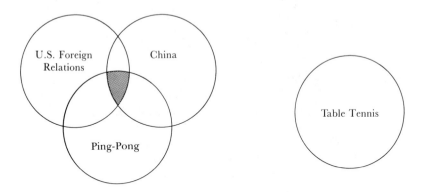

The search has just dragged in the entire gamut of articles on table tennis—tournaments in Florida, paddle-holding techniques, and all—in addition to articles on Ping-Pong diplomacy.

To solve that problem, the searcher adds parentheses, just as an algebra student would add them to "$a \times (b + c)$" to make the statement clear.

Find
U.S. Foreign Relations AND China AND (Ping-Pong OR Table tennis)

The request produces something like this:

```
14506    U.S. Foreign Relations

 1278    China

   65    Ping-Pong

  271    Table tennis

   21    U.S. Foreign Relations AND China AND (Ping-Pong

         OR Table tennis)
```

In short, using OR has both made the search more precise. The search has been expanded to include "table tennis" as well as "Ping-Pong," yet the search terms have been narrowed from the broader term "sports."

Yet another useful command, NOT (or AND NOT), can help strain out extraneous information. For example, when Ping-Pong diplomacy was at its height, there was some doubt about whether the United States was going to recognize the government of "Red China" or Taiwan as the official government of mainland China. To strain out any random articles on Ping-Pong in Taiwan, the searcher could write a request as follows:

Find
U.S. Foreign Relations AND (China NOT Taiwan) AND (Ping-Pong OR Table tennis)

You might get the following results:

```
14506    U.S. Foreign Relations

  806    China

  472    Taiwan

   65    Ping-Pong

  271    Table tennis

   20    U.S. Foreign Relations AND (China NOT Taiwan) AND

         (Ping-Pong OR Table tennis)
```

Then you can get a printout that lists the twenty articles that pertain to your topic. You may decide, from reading the titles, that only twelve of them are relevant. The time you'll spend searching the stacks will be minimal.

Index fields.   The example of searching for Ping-Pong diplomacy in a database is really quite complex—more complex than most database searches. The reason is largely that the search involves the subject of the articles, rather than the more predictable fields, like author, title, publisher, company name, address, number of employees, and so on.

But the Ping-Pong example illustrates some aspects of using databases. First, the access field used in the search is one that *describes* article subjects. The field is something like a table of contents for the article and something like an index. In fact, such a field is often called an index field.

Think for a moment of the purposes that a book's table of contents serves. First, it lists the topics the book covers. Second, it tells the order in which the chapters are arranged. If the table of contents is detailed, the reader has clues about how the author thinks about the topics, how they are organized, the emphasis that he gives to different aspects of the book, and so on. The index, though, tells the reader where to find names, specific topics, and minor points that occur in the article. In a database, the purpose of the index field is to list the many different subjects the article touches on—something like a table of contents, but one that does not clue in the reader about the organization of the article.

Remember that there are many different ways to approach research, many ways to ask questions, and many ways to answer them. Database services are merely another highly useful reference tool.

Ellen Rony, a public-relations practitioner, describes how she used a database at Stoneware, Inc.

> My first priority as public relations manager was to compile a press release list where none existed. I collected the names of editors who had received our products for review, culled the stacks of computer magazines, and sifted through the business cards I had received at [an exposition]. Since Stoneware published a software program called a database information system that stored this type of information, it was natural that I would create a computer file with my press release list. This file stored the names of publications, editors, addresses, and phone numbers, dates products were shipped and reviews published, description of the book (circulation, frequency, type of coverage). By storing it in the computer, I could print mailing labels, find all the people who had received a particular product or, say, all reviews published about our products within a particular time period. I even discovered that three review copies of one of our products (a $495 retail value for each) had been sent to different writers at one publication, and when they requested yet another, I told them exactly where to go (in their office, of course). Throughout my tenure at Stoneware, I updated and cherished this file. It became an "imaging molding" tool for the director of marketing as we added to the list the names of venture capital people, vendors with whom we worked, major dealers and distributors, and important industry personalities.

As for advertising, Scott Dailey, who has an advertising agency and music production house in Northern California, is now creating his own database of advertising agencies whose radio and television billings exceed $200,000 a year. Dailey himself is a musical expert who has produced a reel of his own songs. These songs are to be heard by broadcast and creative directors. So far, Dailey has a database of more than thirty advertising agencies in the Western states. When he completes his database—which will be about three hundred agencies—Dailey will travel to the various agencies, attempting to sell the directors on his songs.

At some point, almost all students will need at least one database, a collection of names of people, organizations, or things that will benefit almost anyone.

EXERCISES

1. Think of at least two times when you have failed to listen to directions or explanations. Describe each incident in writing and explain what the consequences were.

2. To learn to observe, take notes on what one of your instructors does while teaching. Try to capture the professor's walk, tone of voice, gestures, and mannerisms. Then write a description of the instructor in 100 words, *without* writing color of eyes and hair, or height and weight.

3. Finding facts is the first task of journalists. For each of the following questions, find the appropriate facts in the library. Write in the appropriate space the fact, source, and time it takes to determine each fact.

The sorts of books you will need to answer the questions exist among thousands of reference books, and you may be staggered by the questions. Imaginative researchers have developed techniques for finding books without knowing the books exist. One says: "When I'm looking for special information, I decide what the title of the book would be if someone had written it; then I go to the card catalog and look up the invented title. In a large library, half the time I find it."

If you obtain advice from anyone, you will learn almost nothing.

   a. When did Cole Porter, the composer, live?
     Fact
     Source
     Time

   b. Where is the capital of Iceland?
     Fact
     Source
     Time

   c. Where can one find a list of books by John Updike?
     Fact
     Source
     Time

A good journalist will find news rather than a hack. If he sees a building with a dangerous list, he does not have to wait until it falls into the street in order to recognize news.
Walter Lippmann

Writing is not apart from living. Writing is a kind of double living. The writer experiences everything twice. Once in reality and once more in the mirror which waits always before or behind him.
Elizabeth Bowen

Investigative reporters have the bias of piranha fish—they will go after anything that bleeds.
Ben J. Wattenberg

Some people read about events in newspapers. We go out and witness life in its variety. I think there's a little boy or little girl in all of us who likes to be where the excitement is, where the action is.
David Dow

When I was a correspondent in the United States for an English newspaper, I got a letter one week saying that without my work the newspaper could hardly succeed. And I got a telephone call the next week saying I was fired because I hadn't opened the door of a taxicab for one of the directors of the company visiting New York.
Leonard Wibberly

Writing News Stories for the Print Media

The good things of life are not to be had singly, but come to us with a mixture. *Charles Lamb*

NEWSWORTHINESS AND NEWSPAPERS

When the owner of Herbie's Bar in Queens, a borough of New York City, asked a patron who had become abusive to leave the bar and the patron then shot and killed the owner; tied up the other patrons; and then untied one patron, an undertaker, and directed her to cut off the owner's head, was the event front-page news for New York papers? For the *Post,* which ran the story under the headline "Headless body in topless bar," the event merited front-page coverage. For the *Times,* it did not.

Newsworthiness, the extent to which any information is worth reporting, is an audience-dependent rather than an absolute quality.

A news sense is really a sense of what is important, what is vital, what has color and life. *Burton Rascoe*

Wilbur Schramm, a communication researcher, has suggested that audiences select news for two kinds of reward: immediate and delayed. Schramm

59

Wilbur Schramm

Wilbur Schramm has earned so many honors, awards, and titles that he should be bowed by his numerous burdens. To name a few of his many achievements: Schramm was the Walker-Ames Visiting Professor, University of Washington; Howard R. Marsh Visiting Professor, University of Michigan; Aw Boon Haw Professor of Communication, Chinese University of Hong Kong; First Distinguished Center Researcher, East-West Center; Director, East-West Center; First Director, Institute for Communication Research and Janet M. Peck Professor of International Communication, Stanford University; Dean, Division of Communication, University of Illinois; Director, University of Illinois Press; and on and on.

Schramm isn't bowed by these accomplishments; he acts as though he is just another fellow who happens to be brilliant. The author of 120 papers, he has given this advice to a gathering of communication researchers: "Have the courage to write simply." These words are ignored by many researchers because they feel their work must be significant—or seem significant. Schramm illustrated the power of having the courage to write simply when he wrote:

> The field of communication research has sometimes been likened to an oasis in the desert, where many trails cross, and many travelers pass but only tarry. Because communication is a—perhaps the—basic social process, every discipline concerned with human behavior and society must pay it

said reports of crime and corruption, of accidents and disasters, and about sports and recreation, social events, and the lives of appealing individuals provide immediate reward. The reader or viewer who attends to these reports can experience dramatic situations without any of the dangers or difficulties involved in actual participation.

Schramm said that those who seek out news for immediate reward retreat from the world of reality as they read or view the news. Readers and viewers who attend to news that provides delayed reward move in the opposite direction, confronting the forces and trends that shape their lives and society. Although this kind of report may force the reader to face unpleasant truths—the mounting national debt or a rise in lung cancer among women—it provides the delayed reward of informing and preparing readers and viewers in ways that can help them in the future.

The boundaries for the two classes of news shift among individuals, Schramm said. A coach, for example, might read a report on a football game for delayed reward, and a politician might read a report on his latest some attention; and therefore a large part of all the studies we think of as constituting communication research have been done as part of psychology, sociology, anthropology, political science, or economics.

Faced with the task of describing communication research, some communication researchers (like many other researchers in other disciplines) would use gobbledygook rather than plain English. Gerald Stone, editor of *Newspaper Research Journal,* wrote this passage about researchers: "We write for our academic colleagues as if using some secret fraternity handshake:

> Of course, no one would refute Brown and Jones (1968, 1972) whose landmark work was replicated by Williams (1975; see also Smith, 1978) with findings surpassed only by Davis (1982) and Thomas (1985). The implications are obvious.

Obviously, the implications are a complete mystery unless you've been reading Brown, Williams, Davis, et al., or unless you look up the sources."

Of course, Schramm agrees with Stone. Perhaps all graduating researchers should be assigned to read a book by Schramm just before commencement. When those researchers read one of Schramm's thirty books—starting with his latest, *From Painted Cave to Microchip: The Story of Human Communication,* back to the very first book he wrote, *Windwagon Smith and Other Stories,* which won the O. Henry Prize in 1947—their writing styles will do nothing but benefit.

successful rally to relive the experience. Most publications and broadcasts provide a mixture of what will be immediate-reward news for most of an audience and news that provides mainly delayed reward. As the story about the bar in Queens illustrates, though, many publications lean more toward one category of news than toward the other. The audience that subscribes to the *Wall Street Journal* is seeking the delayed reward of financial success. Those who buy the *National Enquirer* are seeking mostly immediate reward.

Because top news for one newspaper, magazine, or television or radio station is not necessarily top news for another, the definition of news must be flexible. The late Willard Bleyer, a pioneer journalism educator at the University of Wisconsin, said news was "anything timely that interests a large number of persons, and the best news is that which has the greatest interest for the greatest number." We suggest that news is the timely report of events, facts, and opinions that interest a significant number of people. If a report does not interest at least a large minority of a publication's or station's audience, it is not news. And news has an element of timeliness;

some element of the news must be information the audience has not heard about before.

Certain characteristics make some news reports likely to appeal to a significant number of readers, viewers, and listeners. They are:

Proximity.   The Harris polling organization asked people what kind of news they read most often: local, national, or international. Seventy-four percent of those polled said they most often read local news. A municipal election is more likely to interest a city's residents than is an election in another city hundreds or thousands of miles away, and a ten-car pileup on a nearby stretch of highway will draw more attention than one that occurs in another state, unless local residents have been involved. Even stories from far away—from the state capital, Washington, New York, or overseas—can be made more interesting to viewers and readers when the impact the news may have on local affairs is explained.

The appeal of local news is especially important to today's newspapers. Some broadcast and most magazine journalists serve audiences that are geographically widespread, but most newspapers still serve particular cities and towns.

Consequence.   One of the reasons local news appeals so strongly to audiences is that it bears immediate consequences for them. Local events swiftly and personally affect the lives of those who live where they occur. If a leak of toxic gas occurred locally, it would have immediate potential to hurt listeners, viewers, and readers. The same kind of leak in India caused no immediate physical harm to American audiences. The gas leak in India was important news, though, because it had the potential to affect American lives. Because a factory with the same design as the Indian factory existed in this country, because the Indian factory was owned by an American company, and because American lawyers traveled to India after the leak to encourage injured Indians to seek compensation, the Indian disaster had potential consequence for American audiences. Because news that originates in other cities, states, and countries can often have important effects on readers and on those they care about, audiences value information about national and international events and government actions that affect or may affect their lives.

Consumer information and news about how audiences can solve their problems or enjoy life more are also appealing because of consequence. Information about how to get value for money, how to succeed in a career, how to guard and improve one's health, how to solve emotional problems and understand others, and how to have fun affects listeners', viewers', and readers' lives directly.

Human interest.   The appeal of consumer information and of stories that help audiences gratify their needs and desires shows how listeners, viewers, and readers value and respond to the personal: news focusing on the individual rather than just on an event or issue. The personal contact between television broadcasters and their viewers gives televised news particular appeal. Local columnists are popular among newspaper readers because they are people the readers can get to know, and news reports told in terms of people and with human feeling appeal in any medium.

Prominence.   When your cousin has a cancerous growth removed from her colon, the event is probably not newsworthy for any audience beyond those who know her. But when the president of the United States has the same operation, audiences throughout the country want to know. Some of the audience's interest in the president's operation is justified by concern about the condition of the federal government and the chief executive's ability to do his or her job. Some of the interest results simply from curiosity about a famous individual. Whether news about famous people has potential consequence for an audience or not, however, it is still news. Audiences want to know about the lives of prominent individuals.

Unusualness.   News is full of "firsts": the first American woman to become an astronaut, the first baby conceived in a test tube, the first patient to rely on an artificial heart. News is also full of record-setters, from Olympic athletes who break world records for their events and local athletes who break school records to people who live to be older or who have sold more record albums than their predecessors. A story like the wire service report of a woman's being struck on the head by a falling flowerpot and killed as she spoke to a relative from a pay telephone is interesting simply because it is unusual.

Conflict.   Imagine you are eating a sandwich in a coffee shop, seated between two booths, each containing a man and a woman. The couple on your left gazes dreamily into each other's eyes, and the man on your right begins angrily accusing his companion of having turned him in to the Internal Revenue Service for lying on his tax returns. Which of the couples are you more likely to attend to? Most people would pay more attention to the couple that is beginning to argue, because conflict creates interest. A fight, verbal or physical, captures more attention than does tranquillity.

Struggles between people, groups, and nations interest audiences. Conflict can lead to change, and change can affect the lives of listeners, viewers, and readers. We may also enjoy conflict simply because it is dramatic. The popularity of sports reports supports this theory, for sports are essentially ritualized conflict.

Sex.   During recent decades, sex has become an element of many news reports. Development and use of the birth control pill; an increase in couples living together before or without marriage; the legalization of abortion; an increase, until the last several years, in the divorce rate; public demonstrations by gays; and the spread of AIDS have attracted audience

interest. Like news about physical violence, news about sex can have practical consequences as well as the gut-level appeal of the forces of life and
death. Responsible journalists report news involving physical violence or
sex when doing so serves those audience interests that go beyond simple
excitement.

Fun.   Everyone enjoys laughing, and news that amuses readers, listeners,
and viewers serves their interests by alerting them to the joy in life. Ironic
and humorous events are worth reporting.

Realize that newspapers continue successfully in this time of change.

The press is like the beam of a searchlight that moves restlessly
about, bringing one episode and then another out of darkness and
into vision.   *Walter Lippmann*

A newspaper strike in the Minneapolis–St. Paul area provided a dramatic
illustration of the constancy of newspapers in American life. The strike,
against the company that owned both the *Star* and the *Tribune,* stopped
publication of the only two daily newspapers in Minneapolis.

Minneapolis residents tuned in to more television and radio news and
bought magazines in greater numbers than ever before, but doing so did
not satisfy their appetite for information. In St. Paul, next door to Minneapolis, street-corner thefts of St. Paul newspapers averaged 1,500 a day;
petty crooks picked the papers up during the early hours and sold them
in Minneapolis for premium prices. In Minneapolis itself, an advertising
executive made arrangements with a printing company, set up a skeleton
staff of reporters, stitched together a circulation network, and started is-
suing—with no wire service at all—a paper he called the *Daily Herald.* Its
circulation quickly reached 100,000.

This clamor for almost anything resembling a newspaper during the
Minneapolis strike disproved the theory that the American people, inun-
dated by the mass media, would scarcely notice the absence of one organ
of information.

Now the *Star* and the *Tribune* have merged into one Minneapolis newspaper, primarily because of the lack of enough advertising to sustain both.
The remaining paper is strong; the publisher simply had to face the economic realities that have caused trouble for many big businesses, including
leading metropolitan newspapers, over the past decade or two. Some large
newspapers have even died. Contributing to these economic pressures have
been the intrusion of cable into the market served by the news media and
the expanded broadcast times for television news.

Understand the value of the standard news story.

I grow daily to honor facts more and more, and theory even less.
Thomas Carlyle

Although newspaper writing now takes several different forms, one old form—the standard news story—is likely to be basic for some time. To learn to write this basic story, you must understand its aims, which are to present facts plainly, as part of the *informing* function of the newspaper.

Because the focus in a standard news story is on information about events or other people rather than on the writer, these stories hardly ever justify the writers' referring to themselves. Dismayed by this aspect of the straight-news formula, one bright student wrote an eleven-page defense of the first person point of view: telling a whole story through a participant's eyes rather than from a detached perspective. He cited, along with more recent examples of writers who have used the first person successfully, Henry David Thoreau as "a voice that from the woods and water of Walden Pond shouted *I.*" The student continued, "You can imagine how ludicrous Walden would sound had Thoreau chosen an omniscient, or even limited, third person; somehow the image of Thoreau calling himself 'the reporter' doesn't fit." The student ended his argument with an impassioned plea for journalists to write with "a sense of the voice that says *I.*"

Such whole-souled dedication to revolutionizing journalism has produced eloquent nonsense like this passage, written by a student:

> When I first heard of Mountain View Community Health Abuse Council, I pictured a modern, sleek building with trimmed hedges and staffed by intellectual, probing psychologists. Instead, I found CHAC to be housed in the remnants of a large classroom in the now defunct Mountain View High School Building. . . .
>
> As I was walking toward the Director's office, I imagined her to be as tired and worn as the building. Much to my surprise, I was dead wrong. . . .

In this story, the reporter is trying to focus her readers' attention on her subject, Susanne Anderson. How can the readers center their attention on Anderson, when the reporter is always in view?

If the standard news formula is designed to present the facts plainly, to provide information, then how can editors permit reporters to use "I"? Reporters' personal beliefs inevitably intrude on the facts when the word "I" appears in so many sentences. The first person has a place in writing for the media, but it is not in straight-news reporting.

The use of "I" by reporters deserves attention; it is one facet of a major attack on the straight-news formula, an attack that is especially critical of the "bare-bones skeleton that relate[s] facts instead of the truth," as one critic put it. Many who argue for first-person reporting and who hold that journalists must go beyond reporting facts to explore the meaning of events also want to junk the who-what-when-where-why form, the old formula that is indeed inadequate, or worse, when journalists blind themselves to all but its elements.

The critics, though, have not thought through how absurd reporting would become if the formula were abandoned. They appear to believe that even a two-paragraph report that the Rev. Algernon Queeble will speak to the Downtown Rotary Club tomorrow should be written with "a sense of the voice that says I" and that the ultimate meaning of his speech should be explored. Probably without realizing it, these critics are also saying a five-paragraph story on Queeble's Rotary Club speech the following day and a ten-paragraph story listing the agenda for the next city council meeting should be unmistakably personal, thoroughly analytical, or both. Absurd.

Is there a place for the personal, for the "I" in journalism? It has always had a small place, as when long ago reporter Henry M. Stanley wrote of finding Livingstone in Africa; more recently AP feature writer Hugh Mulligan reported humorously on his personal experiences in a nudist camp. Moreover, the newsroom revolution of the 1960s, during which young journalists attacked old practices effectively, convinced many journalists trained in earlier times that the place of the personal in newswriting should at least be enlarged.

The straight news formula by itself is so restrictive in its application to meaningful events that other, more flexible techniques are also necessary. In this book we emphasize the degree to which different forms of writing have elbowed their way into the media, markedly enriching journalism and public understanding. Our argument here is only that the straight news story still plays an important role. Many events are best reported by this formula.

Consider, in addition to the examples of everyday speeches and meetings already cited, the value of a formula for reporting weather information: brief items like warnings of approaching storms, forecasts, and the like. Or consider the news of film stars' divorces, local police department promotions, and results of elections to minor offices. Should journalists be expected to explore the ultimate meanings of these events? Assuredly not.

Nor should the news formula be used only for such routine items. When important news breaks, reporters must rely on the swiftly written formula story for immediate publication and broadcast. The assassination of a president or revered leader, for example, calls for instant reportage.

Reporters who tried to inject themselves into most of the stories featured in newspapers and on radio and television programs would be guilty of the worst kind of self-indulgence. Anyone who tried to find the ultimate meanings of many events would soon discover that there are none that extend beyond the trivial. Relatively little news is *worth* the attention critics of the standard news formula seem to want to lavish on it. Not that most news is worthless: In the aggregate, stories reported by formula are probably valued more highly by many readers, listeners, and viewers than is the kind of news that deserves analysis. People value routine news because the stories are so simple. Readers can understand from reading the first few sentences what each story contains. In fact, it is possible that only simple stories will be read by most subscribers. When readers attempt to understand long, analytical stories, they must read to the end. Few people have the time, or the inclination, to read for so long. Many studies indicate that a distinct minority of subscribers read complex stories.

WRITING THE NEWS STORY

Learn how to make a complicated story simple for readers to understand.

The more alternatives, the more difficult the choice.   *Abbé D'Allainval*

Imagine a county supervisors' meeting. It begins with the president calling the meeting to order. The next event is reading the minutes from the last meeting. Then the supervisors devote two hours to old business: a fire insurance plan and a construction program. Next they consider new business: a proposal to sell 25 acres of land and appointment of election commissioners. Debate on the election arrangements is heated, and two supervisors shout loudly at each other and then get into a fistfight.

Relating the events in chronological order would be a mistake. The reporter who started with the first event and described each in its proper time sequence—calling the meeting to order, reading the minutes, discussing the fire insurance plan, and so on—might find himself typing the twentieth paragraph before he had an opportunity to capture the attention of most readers. Even if the reporter never reached that captivating twentieth paragraph, it wouldn't much matter; most readers would scan the information about reading the minutes, yawn, and reach for the lifestyle section.

The key to the standard news story is presenting its most interesting aspect first. And, judging by readers' preference for stories written in standard form, even though this method for ordering information is not chronological, it is *logical*. The formula for the rest of the story relies on the same logic: Other aspects are described in descending order of importance, with the least important last. If one were to draw a picture of a news story, an inverted pyramid would emerge; at its top is its heavy base, the most interesting aspect of the story:

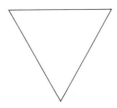

This inverted pyramid has four important advantages over chronological structure:

1. The reporter can fit events into the story rapidly.

2. The editor can select the key words that will be the gist of the headline by reading just the first two or three paragraphs.

3. The makeup editor can shorten the story to fit the amount of space available for it. Deleting the last paragraph or two will not remove important information.

4. Readers can determine in a few seconds whether or not the story will interest them.

The basic element in this formula is speed. Rapid writing and editing are not everything in this new age, but both are usually essential in newspaper work.

You can see how reporters weigh the importance to readers of various aspects of a story by considering the actions of a reporter covering the supervisors' session:

1. The president calls the meeting to order, and the reporter ignores it.

2. The minutes of the previous session are read and approved. The reporter is still idle. (Although if a supervisor challenged the minutes because they seemed inaccurate, the reporter would take notes on— and perhaps record—the ensuing argument. The reporter might even consider this dispute an important element in the story. Instances of tampering with official records are not numerous, but they exist.)

3. The fire insurance plan is discussed. This issue has come before the supervisors in an earlier session. Again, no action is taken. The reporter considers this discussion a minor matter, but takes notes, realizing that it probably won't be an important element in his or her story.

4. The supervisors devote an hour and a half to talking about the construction program. This discussion *is* important; the county has spent $90,000 on planning alone, and the program's total cost will run more than $12 million. The supervisors neither adopt nor reject the program recommended by the planners, but lines of support and opposition are obviously forming. A strong minority seems to favor a more extensive program than the planners are recommending. A slim majority objects to the costs. A final decision is postponed, but the eventual shape of the program is emerging. The reporter takes many notes, including direct quotations and numbers from the photocopied proposal. The reporter begins to think of this issue as the lead for the story.

5. The supervisors consider a proposal to sell 25 acres of land to a condominium syndicate. The reporter can do little with this topic. The syndicate's proposal is tentative; the supervisors' action must await completion of the fire insurance plan. The reporter realizes from the beginning of the discussion that only a few sentences will be devoted to the proposal and consigns them to the section of the story that reports on the fire insurance plan.

6. The election discussion begins routinely. The president announces that the usual arrangements for election commissioners are being made. But Supervisor Bud Yielding responds in a sharp-edged tone, "The usual arrangements that have always been to the benefit of President Thomas, I suppose." The president stands and shouts angrily, "Any man who buys votes by the bushel and thinks he has a right to question . . ." Yielding swings, and Thomas falls. The character of the meeting and the shape of the reporter's story have changed dramatically in a few seconds. The last section of the meeting leaps to the lead position in the story.

This story may seem to be simple to organize. The lead could run:

> One swift swing abruptly ended the county supervisors' discussion of the upcoming election and sent Supervisor Ted Thomas to the hospital last night.

This lead could be followed with several short paragraphs describing the incident. Then, to provide full context, the reporter might devote a long section to comments by the other supervisors, to the upcoming election that sparked the dispute, and to a thumbnail history of the relationship between Yielding and Thomas. Finally, the reporter could add the other, less explosive, supervisors' actions in descending order of importance: several paragraphs about the construction program, next a paragraph or two on the fire insurance plan, and last a paragraph about the proposal to sell 25 acres of land (ignoring, of course, the calling to order of the meeting and the reading and approving of the previous meeting's minutes).

A bit of reflection, though, would convince the reporter that the story should be written in quite a different order. How many readers will fail to get all the way through the paragraphs on the fight and its context? (Many readers would read all of this, but some would not.) How many will stop reading after several paragraphs, deciding the meeting must have been *all* fight? Considering such questions, most reporters would decide to interrupt the account of the fight by inserting a short paragraph or two near the beginning to summarize the supervisors' other actions. They would reason (1) that readers will discern from this short summary that there's more to the story than the first sentence indicates and (2) that those readers who are interested will know to follow the story through to the details about the more conventional supervisors' actions.

Many news stories are written in this disjointed fashion. It's not that reporters are unaware their writing is disjointed. They have simply weighed one value against another, asking themselves questions about how readers can best find the information they want, and decided that unity is not so important as wide readership.

Often, when the news is important and space is available, an editor will decide that two or more stories should be written about a single event or topic. This tactic usually solves the problem of unity; each story can be unified easily. Recognizing the advantages of smoothly flowing writing, many newspapers now make room for several stories on important governmental meetings.

One other device helps solve the problem of unifying complex stories, and there are at least a few signs that it is gaining favor: The reporter writes brief descriptions of the important elements of a news story and then switches to chronological order to spell out the details. Don Whitehead, a two-time Pulitzer Prize winner for the Associated Press, has described his version of this method: "In many cases, I find that the best way, at least for me, is to condense the news in the first few paragraphs, then go back and put the story down just as it happened."

To write readable standard news stories, know these guidelines:

1. Because reporters of news stories must be objective, they do not participate in the actions they describe, except in the most unusual circumstances (as when they are eyewitnesses to serious crimes).

2. Reporters do not refer to themselves as "I," except, again, in the most unusual circumstances.

3. Unless stories with several important facets can be divided into separate stories, all the important news is mentioned in the first several paragraphs to let readers know what information the story contains.

4. Reporters should ask themselves these questions:

    a. Does my story say or imply in the first few sentences who, what, when, where, why, and how?

    b. Have I made sure not to editorialize, even in addition to reporting facts, in my story? If others' opinions, theories, ideas, or rumors are part of the news, is it clear that they *are* opinions, theories, ideas, or rumors and that they do come from sources other than me?

5. The purpose of standard news stories is to provide facts; reporters must respect the tone of informational writing by never injecting frivolity into serious stories.

6. Read *aloud* all stories you write. Listen for disagreeable repetitions and involved sentences. Similar beginnings for more than two successive

sentences or paragraphs are monotonous. Monotony also results from series of sentences alike in length.

Begin a standard news story with a simple lead.

Have something to say and say it as clearly as you can. That is the secret of style.   *Matthew Arnold*

Students are often puzzled by what they should put in a lead, the first sentence or two of a story. Whatever information is most important to your readers belongs in your lead. In thinking, for example, about the lead of a speech story, consider what the speaker said that is interesting and important.

Here is what one student wrote as a lead in a speech story:

> The Polish change since 1974 was the topic of a speech delivered by Thomas Carleston last night.

Starting a speech story with this information is like devoting the first sentence of a basketball story to:

> UCLA played Ohio State at Columbus yesterday.

The readers want to know which team won the game and by what score; they probably knew long before the game that the teams were going to play. By the same token, the speech story's readers want to know what Carleston said. An advance story announcing that he would speak probably gave the subject of his address before he delivered it.

Here is how another student captured the essence of Carleston's speech immediately:

> The most serious problem in Poland [why] today is the remarkably deteriorated prestige of the government [what], Thomas Carleston [who] said last night [when] in the auditorium [where].

The following seven strategies for lead-writing will draw readers into your stories.

The question lead.   Some stories lend themselves to question leads like this:

> Could one man in one night at one bar on Miami Beach run up a bill of $2,400? or $3,907? or $5,109.11 at three bars?
>
> Miami liquor consultants pondered this problem. . . .

The unusualness of some stories makes a question lead work well. Student reporters should always look for something out of the ordinary in their stories, but when the information is routine, they should reject question leads.

The descriptive lead.   At the core of a story may be its setting or a person's appearance. In these cases, a descriptive lead is perhaps the most effective beginning for the story. Here is an example:

> For more than a minute today the sun hung over central Minnesota like a twinkling, slate-blue Christmas ornament as the moon moved between it and the earth.
>
> In the half-light that covered the area, hundreds of scientists and thousands of other observers had a perfect view of a total solar eclipse.

The anecdote lead.   Because newspaper editors welcome new approaches to the problem of presenting news, often they will congratulate a reporter who has written an anecdote lead. An anecdote is a small, entertaining, or gripping story like this one:

> Jim Benton motioned suddenly for silence, then loosened a four-bladed, sharpened broadhead arrow in his quiver. He had spotted a dark cave on the side of a rocky desert ravine and believed his quarry hid inside.

Reporters interviewing active people like Benton or people who share anecdotes should think of anecdote leads. Many editors welcome anecdote leads because most of them have been reading story after story with routine leads—and so have readers.

The quotation lead.   Nearly all editors will pause over the use of leads that quote speakers, because few speakers use a single sentence that sums up what they have to contribute to the news. In rare cases like this one, however, speakers do capture the essence of what they say in single sentences:

> "The press conference has become a public event rather than just a communication," said Harry Puller, a former press secretary to the mayor.

The narrative lead.   Reporters who adopt the narrative lead use the storytelling techniques of fiction writers. A narrative is made up of a continuing story. Reporters must stick to the facts but can write leads that lure readers as this one, written by a student, does:

Frank Commons is a mentalist and authority on Extrasensory Perception, but he is not a public speaker. Demonstrating "Psychic Phenomena" recently, he spoke in a halting, self-conscious voice. He even read his patter.

By borrowing the literary techniques of characterization through physical description and construction of suspense, this lead gains appeal.

The simple statement lead.   This kind of lead distills the facts into a simple sentence, which is followed by an explanation. Here is an example:

The word futurology is so new it doesn't appear in most dictionaries.

Yet people all over the country—consultants, authors, academics— are earning big money through the science of futurology.

To veteran reporters, the simple statement lead is one of the easiest to write. Those who have written many stories find that they can write simple statement leads in fifteen seconds.

The news summary lead.   The kind of lead that is probably the most widespread of all is the news summary lead. Thirty years ago, most stories began with news summary leads, made up of a short and fact-packed sentence or two. Today, many reporters prefer to experiment with different kinds of leads. Nonetheless, the news summary lead is still often the most useful device for beginning a story.

You can figure out what information belongs in a news summary lead by asking yourself the *five* "W's": "Who?" "What?" "When?" "Where?" and "Why?"/"How?" Then use the "W's" the reader will care most about early in your lead and work the others in afterward. Putting an important "W" at the end of a lead can also highlight it.

For a story about a speech Earl Butz, the former Secretary of Agriculture, gave at California Polytechnic State University, a reporter for the San Luis Obispo County *Telegram-Tribune* used a news summary lead. The reporter focused on telling readers who had spoken and on summing up what Butz had said to his audience:

Former Secretary of Agriculture Earl Butz urged Cal Poly alumni and farm management students Saturday to become more politically involved because the profit motive in agriculture is "under siege."

In a wide-ranging speech to nearly 250 on the Cal Poly campus, Butz predicted increased uses of pesticides. . . .

As you can judge, this kind of lead can be written swiftly. It also helps readers find information easily.

When you write a simple news story, reach the story's essence quickly, use concise sentences and paragraphs, and end without fanfare.

I only ask for information.   *Charles Dickens,* David Copperfield

Here is a standard news story written by a student, interwoven with comments:

COMMENTS	STORY
See how the writer tells the essence of what is happening in the first two paragraphs.	In an effort to capture two dangerous escapees who fled last Sunday, police put up roadblocks around the entire Las Vegas area last night. All highways, airline terminals, and bus and train stations have been blanketed with men on the lookout for the pair, whose escape was not discovered until yesterday morning.
Because the men are not well known, the writer waits until deep in the story to identify them by name.	The two were identified as Jim Hamden, 19, being held for attempted robbery, and William Howard Stark, 18, wanted for auto theft. They may be armed and are believed to be leaving town either in a stolen car or by hitchhiking.
Notice how short each paragraph is. Note also the simplicity of the story's sentences.	The pair escaped from a 24-man jail tank by crawling through a vent that they had pried open using parts of a wooden table. Until news of their escape was broadcast, they stayed in the house of a 14-year-old girlfriend.
The story ends plainly with a detail less important than the facts that have already been presented.	In addition to setting up roadblocks, the sheriff's office has alerted law enforcement agencies in the area and in nearby states, said Sheriff's Lt. Ray Gubser.

To reach the heart of a story quickly, you must determine its central conflict or most prominent feature and then take into account the likely consequences—the context of greatest importance to your audience. After defining these points, you can turn your attention to how you express them. Then weigh each paragraph and decide whether you should change the order of your paragraphs to help your readers.

Sentences that are easy to read and cover a limited number of ideas will help get your story's facts across. Clarify all potentially confusing references. Notice the straightforwardness and succinctness of the sentences in this annotated story about two speeches:

COMMENTS

STORY

Note again how the writer gives us the crux of the story in the first paragraphs.

Corporations cannot afford to ignore social problems because of the profits that result from solving them, two business leaders visiting the business school said last week.

"Business must take a leadership role in initiating social change," claims Bob Vöshee, Director of Executive Communications for Control Data Corp., and Gene Richeson, cofounder of ROLM Corp., who spoke at a forum sponsored by the Committee for Corporate Responsibility and attended by some 90 students.

The writer should have identified CDC by placing those initials after "Control Data Corp." in the second paragraph.

As an example of such a company, Vöshee cited CDC, which has successfully established plants in ghettos, day care centers, and consulting consortiums to solve urban and rural problems—all for a profit.

"Our stated business strategy is to address the major unmet needs of society as profit opportunities," Vöshee said.

This unique strategy was developed by Bill Morris, CEO of CDC, following racial unrest in Minneapolis in 1967. Concluding that "business cannot exist in a sick society," Morris began making plans to build a new plant in the very part of Minneapolis still smoldering from the riot's fires.

Achieving profitability for the plant, which opened in 1968, demanded some innovative changes such as simplified hiring forms, day care centers, and even bail bond attorneys to free some employees from jail.

For those who often read business stories, this is an important point.

Vöshee, a former Peace Corps volunteer, confessed that he has not always believed business can solve America's ills.

"When I graduated from college in 1966, I never would have considered going into the corporate world. It was viewed as 'boring,' 'malignant,' and 'less legitimate' than other things.

"I've obviously changed since then. I come today as a convert and as a representative of the new role that corporations must play," he said.

Notice the short one-sentence paragraphs.

That role—leading social change—is best served by business, Vöshee added, because it has the "money, manpower, and ability to respond to profit opportunities."

Vöshee contends that business must lead a "broad-based coalition with government, unions, and community organizations," because "meeting all of society's needs is an insurmountable task for any one group or company."

When asked why more corporations have not adopted this view, Vöshee asserted that only a few look beyond the return on investment in the short term.

In responding to the same question, Richeson claimed that examples such as CDC would eventually persuade other companies "that it is in their best interest to take the long-run view."

Challenging each MBA to have a far-sighted perspective and to initiate social change, Richeson said, "There is no such thing as corporate responsibility; there is only individual responsibility . . . and initiative."

Note again how the standard news story ends quietly with a minor detail.

Richeson, who left ROLM five years ago, now volunteers full-time for the Creative Initiatives Foundation.

Speech story.   Consider the excellent speech story below. The entire story is reproduced to show how much information the writer included. The comments in the left-hand column suggest how many small decisions a reporter should make:

COMMENTS

SPEECH STORY

The writer knows that the lead of a speech story must give the most interesting and important points the speaker said.

Energy self-sufficiency is a "relatively modest and wholly desirable goal," Denis Hayes, former director of the Solar Energy Institute, told students yesterday.

But the energy policies of the Reagan administration, emphasizing nuclear power, will not lead to self-sufficiency, he said. The answer lies in using the best of what we now know in an effort toward conservation.

Here, in what is called a "catch-all paragraph" by some journalists, she outlines briefly his background.

Hayes, a former student here and regent's professor at the University of California at Santa Cruz, delivered an optimistic assessment of "Post-Reagan Energy Planning" to nearly 60 students as part of the autumn series of energy policy seminars.

Energy planning is dominated by uncertainty, Hayes asserted, and while he admitted that world events can cause a dramatic shift in the energy situation, he identified the biggest and most important uncertainty as "the potential in this country for energy conservation."

Knowing that almost all news stories are only informational, the writer clings to that ancient rule: Keep most of your sentences short.

Predictions of conservation effectiveness have almost always been wrong, Hayes said, because they

Also, note the lengths of the paragraphs. By the usual standards of most writers, journalists stay with short paragraphs. In later, non-standard stories in this book, note the lengths of the paragraphs.

underestimate the response of consumers to price changes and the probability of technological innovation.

Hayes based his optimism about energy conservation on a detailed report prepared by SERI under his direction for the Department of Energy during the Carter administration.

The study found that, using the best conservation methods known today without any substantial innovation, the amount spent on energy per dollar of the gross national product would drop 50 percent by the year 2000.

The gross national product will rise 80 percent while energy use will fall from 80 to 65 quads a year, the SERI report predicted, and renewable energy resource will account for 15 to 20 percent of all energy.

Why does the writer end this sentence-paragraph without closing the quotation marks? One rule: When one person is speaking, never *close the quotation marks when the next sentence is also another of the speaker's sentences. If the first quotation marks are closed and the next sentence also carries quotation marks, that must be* another *speaker, readers think.*

In almost all paragraphs quoted so far, the name "Hayes" appears again and again. Why? A rule-of-thumb: In writing a speech story, cite the speaker's name often. Otherwise, some readers will think the writer is offering his or her own opinions.

Adding up the number of sentences in which the writer quotes Hayes, you may be surprised at the large number. If, for example, the writer never *quotes Hayes directly, some readers will suspect that the writer is*

The impetus for conservation could come directly from the federal government, Hayes said, but preferably we should work to "perfect inclination.

"Give the people the data to make the informed decision," Hayes emphasized, heralding the Carter administration's efforts to inform the public of energy-efficient products.

"Nobody wants energy," Hayes asserted, "we just want what energy will give us—food, heat, mobility, jobs."

When the price of energy rises, we need to substitute creativity, labor, and other materials, he continued. "People are smart enough to choose the most efficient energy source."

Hayes strongly criticized the Reagan administration for failing to publish the results of the SERI study, as had been planned by the group.

The two reasons the administration gave were to save money and to avoid "tinkering with the marketplace," Hayes said, and he went on to argue that neither explanation was valid and that political reasons were most likely behind the "embargo."

Political differences with the Reagan administration resulted in his dismissal from SERI, he said, despite the precedent of allowing outspoken and controversial figures to remain in national laboratories.

Hayes expressed continuing disagreement with Reagan administration energy policies. The president's creation of the strategic petroleum reserve, *fashioning these sentences out of air.*

Note especially how often the writer uses other words for "said": "asserted," "emphasized," "criticized," "quipped," and so on. Using only "said" will eventually tire the readers.

Although many of these sentences range from 20 to 30 words, note how they can be read and understood easily. Each sentence to the right is almost 30 words, but each is readable and understandable.

Most standard news stories are disjointed, but anyone who reads this story aloud will find that almost every paragraph flows smoothly into the next paragraph.

"the only thing Reagan has done," Hayes asserted, leaves the oil in a centralized location vulnerable to attack.

"What is needed," he continued, "is something that will give oil companies an incentive to store oil."

The Department of Energy is "an incredible collection of dead wood," he quipped. "I wanted to abolish it . . . you can't change the bureaucracy with anything less than abolishment."

Hayes did offer some defense for national planning agencies amid his condemnation of the Reagan administration and government bureaucracy in general.

Planning is useful "when it's updated most frequently, when it's done by bright people, and when its assumptions are tested by history, both past and present," he explained.

National planning is more efficient than state and local planning, which "fragment industry," Hayes said; " . . . it is useful for people who are going to make billion-dollar decisions."

The two most important tasks of the federal government with respect to energy planning are getting information to consumers and subsidizing bright new innovations, he suggested. "We must create a climate where entrepreneurs with clever ideas can get financing," he added.

Hayes also charged that the private sector must do more to encourage innovation, and he cited "the materialism at the heart of the American culture" as one of the obstacles to this goal.

"We've created a culture where enlightened investments are rarely made," he said. People succeed in business not by preparing for the future but by understanding the present, "the bottom line for the quarter, or perhaps at most the annual report."

Meeting story.   When beginning reporters are assigned to report meetings, they should think as professional reporters do. If the beginners do not know the names of those who will speak, they should imitate professionals by giving speakers these names: 1, 2, 3, 4, and so on. When the meeting ends, beginners should go to those speakers who said something significant and ask the speakers to spell their names.

COMMENTS

Wisely, instead of quoting only one speaker in the lead, the writer decided to focus

MEETING STORY

The decision to include informative articles about female stereotypes in *Aurora*'s next issue was one of many topics discussed by members of a fem-

her story on the most important topic.

Again, wisely, she continues her lead rather than quoting a speaker. Anyone interested in Aurora *will continue reading.*

When the writer begins quoting, she chose one of the most intriguing speakers. Good.

The writer identifies each speaker with a short description. In news stories—but not in features—these descriptions are enough.

Go back to read the first sentences and the following sentences. As you can see, each sentence is clear.

Note that her paragraphs are short. No paragraph in this story runs longer than three sentences.

Examine carefully each sentence in this story. You will find nothing that hints of the writer's beliefs.

inist magazine at their weekly meeting last Thursday.

Since the paper's inception seven years ago in an atmosphere receptive to feminist views, it has been reduced in size, but continues to receive enough funding from the Associated Student Union to publish quarterly issues.

The eight-member staff, composed entirely of females, is collectively responsible for the paper's content, advertising contracts and layout. Their weekly meetings at Theta Chi include "group brainstorming," in which members mention various types of articles and reserve them for later discussion.

Vanessa Poster, one of the more colorful and outspoken members of the group, held the interest and the respect of the other women with her intensity and self-confidence. "Other people don't see what I see when I watch commercials. They don't understand," Poster said in reference to images of women in advertising.

Jennifer Grant, a graduate in public policy, shares Poster's views as well as her apartment. After a comment by Grant on the sexist content of specific commercials, such as Huggies diapers, in which baby girls are portrayed as cheerleaders and nurses, it was decided to sprinkle the issue with short examples of biased representations of women in mass media.

Story ideas for the fall issue were as varied as the women themselves, ranging from whimsical poems to an interview with the only female member of the Out-of-South-Africa group to be arrested.

Poster, also a member of STOP, the campus anti-pornography organization, suggested an article on her endeavors to distribute an informational flier in the bookstore with copies of the recent "Girls of the Pac-10" issue of *Playboy.* Other ideas were offered by Susie Loeb, a junior majoring in political science, who suggested an expose on her domineering male professor, and Kate Wade, who discussed the images of women in children's literature.

The group remains optimistic and firm in their beliefs, despite a few obvious setbacks. "I went to the Lecture Notes office for an ad contract," Karie Youngdahl said, "but they don't seem too thrilled to have anything to do with *Aurora.*"

Regardless of this type of rejection, the group set November 10 as the deadline for interested advertisers and final story drafts. A November 25 publication date was set, in the hope that students

The writer knew that readers would be interested in the comment at the right. Also, she knew that readers would be interested in the Poster comment. Again, wisely, she realized that these comments were not *the center of her story. This is why she placed these so far along in her story.*

would have time to read the publication during Thanksgiving vacation.

The serious tone of the meeting was evident even in casual snatches of conversation. "I saw them painting over the ombudsman sign," said Kirsten Smith, last week's group facilitator. "They were changing it to ombudsperson."

Poster, however, occasionally made an effort to keep the atmosphere light; when a member suggested a story on how women feel about their bodies, Poster responded with "My stomach hurts."

At one point, Karie Youngdahl compared *Aurora*'s goals to a quilt, stating that each member brought her individual ideas, and the group worked together to make it a whole. The *Aurora* staff was so supportive of this idea that a motion was made to change the newspaper's name to "Quilts." Marta Laskowski suppressed the idea quickly, however, with the comment that the name carried a "bedroom image."

Notice especially that she ends her story with almost nothing. This is *a news story.*

No new members were present at Thursday's meeting, but the staff made it clear that they would appreciate additional support.

Rules for writing news stories.   When writing standard news stories, remember these rules:

1. Conflict, proximity, prominence (of individuals), unusual details, human interest, and consequence make information newsworthy.

2. Think of your audience: In what context do they need the news?

3. A sentence that causes you to stumble will make your readers stumble even more.

4. A sentence is not clear if you must read it more than once to understand what you've said.

5. A sentence beginning with "In other words" or "That is to say" probably follows one that needs rewriting.

6. Limit the number of ideas expressed in each sentence—usually to one and hardly ever to more than two.

7. Reduce your sentences by purging superfluous words.

8. Keep paragraphs short—usually one or two sentences.

9. End quietly, plainly presenting whatever fact belongs at the bottom of your inverted pyramid.

Name your sources for all but (1) descriptions of people and events you've seen in person and (2) the most general information.

A journalist must remain a witness, and resist the temptation to be at the same time an actor.   *Charles Gombault*

Attribute information you report to its source: a person, a group, or a document. Only two kinds of information should be reported without attribution. The first is description of an event you have witnessed yourself. The second is information so general that your audience will have practically no doubt as to its correctness and, consequently, little interest in its source. Examples of information so general it requires no attribution are the physical distance between two points and the dates and times of events. When you attribute general information, audiences will suspect that you doubt the information's truthfulness. By writing " 'Joe Quick ran 26.2 miles to complete the race in under three hours,' Quick's trainer, Amanda Wilkinson, said," for instance, you'd imply that Wilkinson's facts could be incorrect. For all but descriptions of events you've seen and information so general your audience can assume it is correct, though, you should provide a source.

Be especially careful to provide sources for allegations. If you write "Hilda Hawkins strangled her three-year-old daughter Saturday night" and don't add, "police said," you have made a mistake that endangers the rights of both the suspect and the public. Hawkins may be innocent. (For about one of every four felony arrests, the charges are dismissed.) Or if Hawkins did strangle her daughter, she may become more likely to escape conviction because she has been labeled guilty in the news and argues that as a result she can no longer receive a fair trial.

Do not assume that just because you have a source for some piece of information, you're justified in broadcasting or publishing it. Sources do sometimes distort the truth and even lie to interviewers. Consider whether a source has any reason to twist facts. Check the facts you intend to report and then, if they appear to be truthful, attribute them to their source. Name the source wherever in the story you use its facts, even if you need to name the same source over and over.

Most news stories require that you name sources sentence after sentence; and stories based on interviews, speeches, reports, surveys, and other documents require that you attribute many pieces of information to the same source. Consequently, you need strategies for dealing with the problem of monotony: sentence after sentence ending with "so-and-so said." Three ways to vary sentences that contain attribution are placing attribution at the beginning of or in the middle of a sentence rather than at the end, inverting "said" or its synonym and the source's name, and using another word instead of "said." Each of these approaches has limitations, but each is also useful provided you remember when it aids rather than hinders your audience.

Attribution should usually go at the end of a sentence, because that's where it sounds most natural and interferes least with the audience's ability to digest information. In all media, though, you should attribute at the beginning of a sentence whenever *who* a source is matters even more than what the source has said. If you need to name your source right away to make information believable or if the significance of the news depends on who is being quoted, attribute at the beginning of the sentence.

Writers in the print media can attribute direct quotations in midsentence, and midsentence attribution works for indirect quotations in all media. Use this device sparingly, though, as it can easily jar readers and make your sentences sound forced. When you do attribute in the middle of a sentence, be sure the attribution is placed at the end of a phrase or clause, where there is a natural pause in the sentence, and not in the middle of a pair or group of related words. (A phrase is a group of words that works together but does not contain both a verb and a subject; a clause contains a verb and a subject working together.)

You should use the second method for varying sentences, inverting "said" or its equivalent and the source's name, only when a source's name is followed by identification more than a word or two long: ". . .said Donna Lee, head of Arts Unlimited's marketing division." Other inverted constructions sound unnatural. An audience expects to hear or read ". . .Johnson said" rather than ". . .said Johnson," for example, or ". . .the head of the company's marketing division announced" rather than ". . .announced the head of the company's marketing division." Any sentence departing from the natural word order an audience expects interferes with the audience's ability to understand the information the sentence presents.

Type your stories in the form editors expect.

Ascend above the restrictions and conventions of the world, but not so high as to lose sight of them.   *Richard Garnett*

Type on only one side of regular 8½-inch by 11½-inch white typing paper. Use a black ribbon and double-space between lines.

On the first page, in the upper left corner, type a slug consisting of your name on the first line and, on the second line, the name of the story in two or three words: "Reagan Speech," "Student Council Meeting," etc. Begin typing at least one-third of the way down the page to leave room for the editor to give instructions to the printer. If your story is longer than one page, put "more" at the bottom of every page except the last one. When the story ends, type -30- or the mark # and circle it.

On all succeeding pages, put your slug in the upper left corner and then start typing just below the slug. Leave margins of about an inch and a half on all sides.

To show a dash, use two hyphens without spacing before, between, or after them. To insert marks that are not on your typewriter like mathematical symbols and accent marks use a pen.

The preceding guidelines probably still apply to your class assignments and campus newspaper. More and more, however, news stories are written and edited on computer terminals. Only the final version is ever printed out—in the newspaper.

EXERCISES

1. Count the words in the first sentence of each major story in the nearest local daily newspaper. Is each sentence easy to understand? Are the longer leads necessarily the most difficult to comprehend?

2. Read the front-page stories in any metropolitan daily. How many can be described as objective? Does the writer of any of the stories seem to be advocating, or is he or she just explaining?

3. Choose any speech on campus and cover the speech. Take notes while listening. Finally, write a story of at least 400 words.

4. Attend any formal meeting on campus. Take notes while listening. Finally, write a story of at least 500 words.

5. Attend an address on campus and take notes on the speech. The following morning, read carefully the speech story in the campus newspaper or the local professional paper. Matching your notes to the newspaper story, decide whether the story is accurate or not.

6. Read again the paragraphs that explain Proximity, Consequence, Human Interest, Prominence, Unusualness, Conflict, Sex, and Fun. Then decide for yourself which two of these eight kinds of stories are most likely to lure your interest, write the names of the two kinds on a piece of paper, and take them to class. The instructor may find it useful to tally the class's preferences. Then ask someone who is not a student what two categories he or she finds most appealing. Bring your findings to class and compare them with your classmates. What sorts of people seem to focus on what elements of news interest?

The best time for planning writing is while you're
doing the dishes.
Agatha Christie

Good writing, like a good house, is an orderly
assortment of parts.
Mortimer Adler

If I didn't know the ending of a story, I wouldn't
begin. I always write my last line, my last
paragraphs, my last page first.
Katherine Anne Porter

Every writer, by the way he uses the language,
reveals something of his spirit, his habits, his
capacities, his bias.
E. B. White

The last thing that we find in writing is to know
what we must put first.
Blaise Pascal

Genius has been defined as supreme capacity for
taking trouble.
Samuel Butler

The worst cynicism: a belief in luck.
Joyce Carol Oates

4

Newspaper Features and Magazine Articles

America is *par excellence* the land of magazines.   *Frederick Lewis Allen*

In the *New York Times Magazine* on February 21, 1982, Diane McWhorter published an article called "The *Atlantic:* In Search of a Role." Although the *Atlantic* magazine was the focus of her article, midway through her piece she wrote,

> Meanwhile, in response to the growing sophistication and immediacy of television journalism, newspapers of the 1970s turned into daily magazines, with fat feature sections and slick designs; their long, investigative pieces were not simple reactions to events, but magazine-like analyses of the forces behind the news. Papers like the *Wall Street Journal* and the *New York Times* assumed that national editorial mandate that was once reserved for weeklies and monthlies.

Although McWhorter's observation is not quite true—only the metropolitan papers have adopted this new role—smaller newspapers are also beginning to publish magazine-like articles. Grant Dillman at the United Press International headquarters in Washington, D.C., has said, "At least 25 percent of our effort now goes into in-depth, magazine-type stories."

WHAT IS A FEATURE OR AN ARTICLE?

Many newspaper editors, accepting the encroachment that television news has made on their circulation and advertising revenues, are looking for a new way of reporting. The more they seek alternative approaches to presenting the news, the more they find their job resembling that of the magazine editor. Reporters also are taking more and more time on their stories. David Shaw of the *Los Angeles Times,* for example, does not write a story for a daily, weekly, or monthly deadline. He writes eight stories a *year.* His is a special case, but indicative of a trend.

Understand the difference between news and features.

A journalist must remain a witness, and resist the temptation to be at the same time an actor.   *Charles Gombault*

Palmer Hoyt, former publisher of the *Denver Post*, became convinced while he was judging newspaper-feature contests that the newspaper world should try to settle on a definition of feature writing. It seemed to him that veteran newspaper people tended to consider everything not in the news category— including editorials—as feature material. He asked his assistant, Alexis McKinney, to define the feature. McKinney offered this definition:

> A newspaper feature story is an article which finds its impact outside or beyond the realm of the straight news story's basic and unvarnished who-what-where-when-why and how.
> The justification, strength and very identity of the feature lie in its presentation of the imagination—not, however, in departing from or stretching the truth, but in piercing the peculiar and particular truths that strike people's curiosity, sympathy, skepticism, humor, consternation or amazement.

This distinction should have meaning for the beginning feature writers. They are to use facts, McKinney points out, but the writers' primary aim is not the simple presentation of fact. It should be helpful to consider exactly how newspaper features differ from other forms of writing.

The feature differs from the short story in that it is factual, not fictional. The feature writers may, however, use the devices of the short story, especially in narrative features, and they can feel justifiably proud if someone says that their feature "reads like a short story."

Features differ from editorials, reviews, and most columns in their approach to opinion. It is the difference between making reasonable judgments and advocating. Feature writers often judge; they should never advocate. They aim not at persuading but at illuminating. It is dangerous for beginning feature writers, however, not to recognize the subtle difference between features and most opinion pieces. Feature writers never attempt to persuade. They inform and entertain.

The feature differs from the straight news story in many respects. There is no standard form for features; the middle and the end should be as compelling as the beginning. Feature writers should not ignore the hallmarks of good newswriting—simplicity is as important in some feature writing as it is in most newswriting—but the terse statement of fact characteristic of the informational news story is seldom useful in feature writing. Feature writers must think of their writing as thematic, with the sentences and paragraphs tied to each other in such a way that a unified, flowing story is produced. Although many feature stories are quite as timely as news stories, feature writers must not depend on timeliness for reader interest. The simple presentation of facts growing out of recent events is not for them. Instead, the facts that they use must be informed with color and life, background and interpretation, imaginative perceptions of people and situations, and sharp, bright phrases. Some notion of the different flavor of features is apparent in the difference between most news leads and these feature leads (the first of which emphasizes the value of *twisting* a cliché):

> In the spring a young man's fancy may lightly turn to thoughts of bilking a housewife out of her pin money with a door-to-door sales racket.

> O say can you sing "The Star-Spangled Banner" without mumbling the words and petering out on the high notes?

> Stoneacre is being demolished. Three red chimneys jut from the rubble. In a slope of debris, a bathtub is caught like a boat in jagged ice.

To introduce an article on the difficulty of writing science news for an uninformed audience, one feature story began: "Somewhere between the satellite and the synonym, a lot of words are being lost."

The subjects as well as the language of features depend on creativity and imagination—always based in fact. Here are ideas for features and magazine articles suggested by students:

> 1. "St. Petersburg's Wild Gabooners." (This is a race between various sailboats in which *all* captains will cheat.)
> 2. "The Riotous Professor." (This is a profile about a professor who ignores the rules of a faculty member.)

3. "Writing to the Wrong Author." (A student wrote letters to various authors, asking whether they have had praise for writing books they never wrote. The student was right.)

4. "Americanization of the French Bourgeoisie." (This student went to France on a vacation and used much of her time visiting shopping centers and interviewing people.)

Memorize the following guidelines for magazine articles before you begin to write.

The root of all bad writing is to compose what you have not worked out for yourself.   *Alfred Kazin*

Almost all magazines need articles from freelancers, and some newspapers need such articles with increasing frequency. We will refer in these guidelines only to magazines, but nearly all of them also refer to newspapers.

1. Is the article you're planning one you can complete? Many student writers have had what they consider a precious idea for an article, think of pursuing it, do a little research, write the article—judging that their weaving wonderful words will sell it. It won't. Be ruthless with your idea. If a vital part of the article isn't researched, it almost surely won't sell.

2. Can you document the facts, interview the principal subjects, obtain and read the necessary material, understand technical jargon (in some instances), and, if necessary, travel to the place where you need to go? Make a list of the things you need to write the article: facts, subjects, material, and, in some cases, travel.

3. Does your article argue for or against something? If so, many student writers stress the points they want to make, ignoring counterarguments. The editors have, almost surely, read articles that stress the opposite. Always take into account the fact that some writers or speakers will have argued against something you're for, and vice versa. Include the basis of at least one argument against your article, and defeat it—if you can.

4. Is your proposed article suited to the audience of your magazine? Barry Golson, who was once the managing editor of a magazine called *World View,* said, "Some guy sent us an unsolicited manuscript on beauty aids for children. Others deluge us with constant hot tips, ambitious political essays, revolutionary tracts—none of which have the slightest bearing on 'Best from the World Press,' our clearly marked subtitle." Read carefully any magazine you're considering as a home for your article.

5. Has the magazine you're writing for published an article like yours in the past five years? If so, you have hardly any chance of publishing your article in this magazine. Always read back issues of the magazine and consult the *Reader's Guide to Periodical Literature* to determine whether your article has a chance with this magazine.

WRITING THE STORY

Use vivid quotations to illuminate unfamiliar events or circumstances when writing features.

Successful living is a journey toward simplicity and a triumph over confusion. *Martin Marty*

Many news features depend on the interview: the information a reporter can gather from talking to people, expressed in a lively, true-to-life fashion.

The reporter often becomes an interpreter between a particular world and the public. Writers in this position must explain all jargon and ambiguous references without sacrificing their stories' flavor. In the following story, the writer attempts to use quotations to present and explain the world of cocaine users:

COMMENTS

FEATURE STORY

This is a good beginning; starting with a quotation doesn't usually work, but here the quotation implies so much and arouses such curiosity by comparing cocaine to champagne that it will make readers want to read on. The speaker doesn't know what "stigma" means—a mark of shame or discredit. The writer should have rewritten this paragraph, using a quotation just as interesting but without misused language or, if this quotation absolutely must be used, briefly pointing out the word's misuse.

"It's the champagne of the drug world," says one student who deals cocaine. "If you can afford it."

"It's a social stigma. If someone comes to my room, instead of offering him a cocktail, I offer him a line," says another dealer.

Cocaine is expensive and illegal—and can be fatal if abused. Yet one dealer estimates that "there

This paragraph provides information about the cost of cocaine that's valuable to the outsider, but the reader is left wondering what a "decent deal" is.

This quotation is excellent. It leaves the reader with no unanswered questions and provides unconventional information.

Will readers know Niemeyer is captain of the campus police? Few reported cases of cocaine use or of sale of cocaine? Will readers in a general audience all know what "narc" means?

Again, the writer is quoting someone who doesn't know the meaning of a word he uses. "Myth," which implies imagined rather than actual history, is misused. "Trafficking" should be defined. Many readers will not know the difference between trafficking and "intent to sell."

are about 100 dealers on campus. About 15 percent of the students use cocaine. Almost 40 percent of all my friends use it."

Known on campus as "coke," the drug costs $150 to $200 per gram. When one freshman user was asked if his dealer had given him a fair deal, his immediate response was, "Yes, he's a friend of mine. He gets me a decent deal. Accessibility is good, and he always has some stuff."

A senior who has been dealing for three years explained how he uses cocaine to meet the rising costs of college life: "I usually defer my tuition. I go into the City and can usually find an ounce floating around.

"Sometimes I can get rid of all 28 grams in one day. It depends on the clientele. It's like the stock market. I develop clientele and BAM! I close the deal, make the profit, and pay my tuition. But it's not the safest business in the world. I worry about the police."

Police Captain Raoul Niemeyer said, "There are no narcs actively working on campus. There have been few reported cases of cocaine." He said he had no idea how many students use the drug. Only when a case is reported to the campus police is it actively pursued, he said. "We know guys smoke grass. Are the cocaine dealers students? Maybe I better tell Narcotics to get up here." Niemeyer added, "We've had very few cocaine arrests on campus, and one was a juvenile from high school."

"There's an old myth around here," said a campus dealer. "A long time ago, the police walked into the Alpha Delt house and told them to turn down the amount of 'traffic' in the house. We don't worry about the police too much."

Trafficking cocaine with intent to sell is a felony. Conviction for a first offense costs 15 years in jail and a possible $25,000 fine. Conviction for a first offense with intent to sell cocaine leads to 5–15 years in jail. Possession of cocaine for personal use carries a penalty of 2–10 years in jail for a first offense.

A powder made from the dried leaves of the coca plant, which grows in Andean valleys, cocaine is usually smuggled into the United States by Colombians and Chileans, often sponsored by the Mafia. Smugglers also include independent workers, often college students, who while touring South

America may pick up a few kilos to sell when they get home.

"In Bolivia it's only about $6.50 per gram," says one dealer. "But if you get caught, sometimes the only way out is to bribe the police. It can cost you anywhere from $600 to $1000." People have tried smuggling coke into the U.S. in their children's clothing, a bottle of whiskey, toothpaste tubes, and even the cage of a boa constrictor.

There are a number of ways to eat cocaine. In 1886, Coca-Cola was made by mixing cocaine and caffeine in a syrup called "the intellectual beverage." Today, cocaine can be sprinkled into cocktails or smoked with tobacco or marijuana. Some people enjoy "frosties": a friend puts a small portion of cocaine on a piece of paper and blows into the back of their mouth. Most often, cocaine is inhaled through the nose from a vial or a "line" after being chopped into tiny pieces with a razor blade and then, for a line, scraped with the blade into thin rows on a smooth surface like a mirror's. Through a straw or rolled-up $100 bill, lines of cocaine are inhaled via the nostrils.

The drug has a fairly quick but short effect, usually lasting 10–15 minutes. After it is inhaled, it combines with the mucus and drips down the back of the throat, producing a numbing effect. Cocaine is a stimulant. It does not cause blurred vision or memory lapse, but rather a feeling of confidence and assurance.

"I like to use it in conjunction with alcohol," says one user. "Alcohol slows you down. Coke does the reverse. I'm in total control of what's happening."

Cocaine does not produce physical addiction. Dr. Lester Grinspoon, a Harvard psychiatrist, says cocaine use *can* produce psychological dependence. For moderate users, the risks are few: sniffles and inflamed nasal tissue, which usually heals itself after a couple of days. For heavier users, the risks can be more serious. The drug constricts the blood vessels, cutting down the supply of blood that reaches the

---

The quotation used at the beginning of the paragraph is a good one—clear, interesting, and coupled with a source. The last sentence in the paragraph, though, may leave the reader wondering where its facts came from. Who was the source? "Eat" cocaine? "Ingest" would be a better word, given all the methods listed. The $100 bill is an intriguing detail that could have been expanded on. Look also at the beginning of the paragraph: Very few readers would be attracted by its initial sentence.

Readers could conclude from these two paragraphs that cocaine will improve their performance in whatever pursuits they engage in. To give a more accurate picture of the pleasures and nonmedical drawbacks of the drug, the writer could work in information here about the significant number of professional athletes who have publicly discussed the detrimental effects habitual cocaine use has had on their performance.
Readers need more information here: When a hole cuts through the cartilage between nasal passages, what happens? Is it serious? The writer also endangers readers by leaving out other information in this paragraph. Al-

though nearly all moderate cocaine users escape serious medical problems resulting from their cocaine use, case studies have led some doctors to believe cocaine can cause fatal respiratory failures, strokes, heart attacks, and seizures. Dr. Mark Gold, the director of research at Fair Oaks Hospital in New Jersey, for example, says, "We have no way of predicting who'll die from the drug and who won't. It could be a regular user or it could be a first-time user."

nose. Users sometimes develop sores, bleeding, and eventually a hole cutting through the cartilage dividing the nasal passages.

Emilia Garfield, project director of a drug education problem at the medical school here, said, "Coke is not good or bad. It's the uses to which the drug is put, who uses it, and for what reasons. There is nothing wrong with coke if it is used by an eye doctor as a local anaesthetic."

Cocaine, which does have medical usage, is legally sold to druggists who supply hospitals. "There are 27.5 grams in one ounce," says one dealer. "If it's good stuff I can sell it."

The reader begins this paragraph expecting it to have something to do with legal sale of cocaine. Instead, he finds a paragraph about an unrelated idea.
How does one have it analyzed?

Another dealer said, "I can usually add about four grams of bullshit. I cut my stuff with manita (a baby laxative) or manacol (sugar). The purity of the stuff floating around the country is terrible. Sometimes people buy coke that has been cut with speed or No-Doz. It's hard to tell with coke unless you try it or have it analyzed."

One university student said her only problem with dealing cocaine was that most of her profits went right up her nose.

Having a captivating beginning and ending for a feature is important. No less important, though, is meeting the readers' needs in between. They should know that in 1986 two outstanding athletes in their early twenties died from using cocaine.

In writing stories that require you to interpret your subject to an uninformed audience, follow these three rules:

1. Prepare for interviews by learning as much as you can about your subject, your interviewees, and their circumstances.

2. Use conversational techniques to both control each interview's direction and elicit natural responses.

3. Scrutinize your material for references that could leave questions or confusion in your readers' minds.

Use imaginative language within a unified framework when re-creating an event for a color story.

My task is to make you hear, to make you feel—it is, before all, to make you *see*.   *Joseph Conrad*

Occasionally, you may be assigned a story showing the atmosphere of an event: a party, an election, a game, a seasonal celebration. Color stories like these provide a sensory experience through words, evoking for the reader the flavor and excitement of the actual event.

Truman Capote appealed to his readers' senses in this sentence:

> Though mud abounded underfoot, the sun, so long shrouded by snow and cloud, seemed an object freshly made, and the trees were lightly veiled in a haze of virginal green.

Like Capote's sentence, the color story should combine graceful writing and imaginative description. Avoid the strictly factual quality of a news story, but at the same time be aware that your audience is a newspaper audience: Simplicity of language should be your goal.

A color story often consists of disparate elements. Writers may have trouble tying them together into a unified story unless they look for a pattern—anything that links the elements. Because a solid framework is important, avoid trailing off at the end of a color story as you do in a standard news story. Each paragraph should grow out of the last, and the middle and end of your story should be as compelling as its lead.

Describing significant details.   In some color stories, general judgments will appear: The crowd at the football game was boisterous and enthusiastic; the halftime show was an exercise in precision. Some general observations may be necessary, but be careful not to let subjective impressions crowd out significant details.

The following story was written by Carmel Derecho, a student:

COMMENTS

COLOR STORY

*The writer knows that the
primary purpose is description. Of course, she need not
make each phrase memorable.
Note how often she attaches
just the right adjective to the
noun. She is intelligent
about writing, which is why
she does not attach two or
three adjectives to each noun.
She ignores opportunities to
quote her subjects. Quotation
is usually necessary, but she
writes so winningly that the
instructor ignores her failure
to quote.*

*Observation is necessary
when a writer is attempting
to describe. Perhaps if this
writer were merely there, not
writing, she probably would
come away with about 10
percent of what she described
here. For most beginning
writers, they should say to
themselves, over and over,
"Observe, observe, observe,"
and take notes.*
Note how often she describes
things *as well as* children.

Stern Hall's Casa Zapata is not quite the
haunted-house type. Although it has a few cobwebs
and its bathrooms exude an embalming smell, its
functionally rectangular shape, its cement walls, and
its creak-proof metal doors belie the dorm's true nature. The institution's mundanity did not, however,
prevent the children in the Barrio Assistance program from enjoying an eerie time as they trembled
through Casa Zapata's rendition of a haunted
house.

Waiting in the dorm lounge for the haunted
house to open its doors was like awaiting the deliv-
ery of a first baby: indecision abounds as to whether
one should be thrilled at the prospect of parent-
hood or scared stiff that the baby's hair might exactly match that of the mailman. The dark Mexican
children displayed their mixed feelings about enter-
ing the house as they fluctuated between asking
wide-eyed questions about what they should expect
and preparing themselves to look their scary best.

With the fuss over preparation came a subtle
division of society into two classes: the "costumed"
and the "uncostumed." The former pompously
pouted about how they would *ever* get all that paint
off their faces; the latter declared that it was child-
ish, no, babyish, to dress up on Halloween.

Retracting their earlier statements, the uncostumed discovered that painting their faces was just
as good as having a costume. This precipitated a
mad rush for the watercolors—one that led to the
conversion of the bathroom counter into a kalei-
doscopic masterpiece. Speaking in frenzied Spanish,
the young picadors battled it out, with one face
emerging a triumphant black, the next one remaining an untarnished brown.

The pacifists who refuse to engage in such
senseless savagery chose instead to chase each other
around the lounge. They grabbed, pulled, and
ducked as they tumbled through the obstacle course
created by the furniture. If a chair or a table proved
to be too much of a hindrance, the children kicked
and pushed it around with the surety of professional interior designers. Underneath it all, the aging carpet quietly bore the beating of the children's
feet, complaining only occasionally by tripping one
of them unexpectedly.

Sitting oblivious to the tempest surrounding
them were the two bigger boys, who considered

themselves to be in a class different, and presumably higher, than the rest. With a mixture of contempt and utter superiority scrawled on their faces, they turned their grown-up attention to the television set in front of them, and for thirty minutes stared with adult eyes at a Donald Duck Halloween cartoon . . . yet another Halloween mystery never to be solved.

Donald Duck's garbled ebullience combined with the children's wild raucousness served to drown out the usual dullness of the Casa Zapata lounge. The splotchy green carpet that looked like the remnants of a squashed giant avocado was still there. The four perfectly perpendicular walls topped by a square slab of cement were still there. Although still impeccably normal, they all took on an eerie glow as the children prepared for their descent to the haunted house.

Throughout this story, she makes each paragraph as important as any other paragraph. Unlike the standard news story (in which the writer grades the paragraphs in descending order of importance), this kind of story must be as interesting at the middle and at the end as at the first paragraph.

The haunted house.

Going through the haunted house was like having a prolonged epileptic attack. The convulsive shivering began when the guide told the group that most of the monsters were not real (what about the rest?). The children entered the first room to find themselves in a universe of dead people which had a stroboscopic light for a sun. During the intermittent flashes of light, the absolute panic on young faces could be seen, thus providing visual accompaniment to the high-pitched screams that filled the room.

Again, go back to the beginning of this story and note how she ties each paragraph to the following paragraph.

The screams, as well as shivers, persisted until the group reached the last room of the haunted house. Here, revulsion overcame any emotion that was being experienced. A mad scientist with unblinking, bulging eyes was eagerly sawing open the leg of the victim, and in a moment of sheer ecstasy, pulled out a piece of meat from the mutilated man's knee and proudly thrust it toward his audience. It was then that the barrio children ran up the cement stairs, past the metal doors, and settled back in the comfort of the easy-to-clean vinyl furniture.

This last paragraph is a triumph for the writer. It begins with screams, is pitched higher with the mad scientist, then ends with children being safe. It is a wonderful paragraph.

Remember these guidelines for writing color stories:

1. Use your senses to observe closely.

2. Look for a pattern in the details you observe and use that pattern to unify your story.

3. Focus on sensory detail rather than on generalization in your writing.

4. Listen to the rhythms of your sentences to make sure they are graceful.

Feature or article?   At the beginning of this chapter, we stressed that newspapers were becoming more like magazines, at least in part. The following feature-article could have been written for a newspaper or a magazine. As it happens, the writer, Judy Mikacich, aimed this article at *Sunset*, a magazine. Shortly after writing this article, she became an employee of *Sunset*.

COMMENTS

This is an intriguing lead. The writer thought of what would interest readers. After three tries, she came up with this beginning.

Although she uses the formal name, note that all other words are clear and provocative.

Here, in a brief history, the writer tells her readers about where kiwis came from.

The writer introduces the person who brought kiwis to the U.S. Note especially that she does not linger with how kiwis are introduced. Instead, knowing that general readers are more interested in other facets, the writer continues this interesting story.

GROWING KIWIS: FRUIT OF THE VINE IS WORTH THE WAIT

Some say they taste like a lime crossed with a banana. Some say more like a cantaloupe mixed with strawberries. But whatever the taste description, kiwis seem to have won over the taste buds of many Westerners. Beyond their unique and refreshingly tangy taste, kiwis are also used extensively for decorating and garnishing—their bright-green flesh and tiny edible purple seeds make any dish, be it entree or dessert, look like something special.

Though most Americans have already discovered the taste and charm of kiwifruit, it is still somewhat a secret that the vines, formally called *Actinidia chinensis,* can be grown easily in one's own home garden. And not only do the kiwi vines produce fruit, but their large, fig-like, fuzzy leaves can provide shade for a backyard patio from March through October.

Called the Chinese gooseberry or yang-tao in many parts of the world, kiwis are actually native to mainland China and Taiwan. For years, kiwi were imported into the U.S. from New Zealand, where they were introduced in 1906 and are still commercially cultivated. New Zealand was at one time the principal producer of kiwifruit, harvesting 4 million trays annually. Now, though, New Zealand's production is being closely rivaled, if not surpassed, by U.S. production.

In 1962, Freida Caplan, a Los Angeles broker of specialty produce, brought kiwi to the United States. By the late 70s, thin, round slices of kiwi could be seen adorning nouvelle cuisine of all types on magazine and recipe book covers. Now, kiwifruit sold in the U.S. is grown almost exclusively in California's Sacramento and San Joaquin valleys—but anywhere west of the Sierra-Cascade divide plants can be grown easily and will bear fruit. Last year's harvest was 4.3 million trays, each tray weighing seven pounds. The fruit yields $12,000 an acre, more than any other fruit in the country. The retail price of one kiwi ranges from thirty-five to seventy cents—making it the pricey-est fruit in the produce section.

For just that reason it is nice to know that the fruits can be grown in the home garden. In the last decade or so, many have figured that out and have started their own crops, but for those who haven't, here are some easy instructions on how to join the backyard kiwi-farmers of the West.

In these easy-to-read instructions, the writer makes certain that almost anyone who can read can understand this guide.

In order for kiwi vines to bear fruit, there must be at least one male and one female plant. Most full-scale nurseries have male and female plants available in either one- or five-gallon containers. Prices range from about ten dollars for the smaller to twenty dollars for the larger-sized plant. Some nurseries will suggest planting six females to each male plant to ensure optimal pollination and production. Once planted, the two vines will intertwine, and male blossoms will provide pollen for female vines. Reddish fuzz identifies new growth, followed by blossoms, which resemble small white or buff roses. You can plant them anytime, though perhaps fall is best so that the soil is still warm and rains are on the way. The plants should be leafy and blossoming by spring.

Again, rather than go into dry information, she gives facts while she writes in a way that will intrigue anyone who is interested in kiwis.

Kiwi vines grow feverishly, and veteran kiwi-farmers suggest giving them plenty of room to grow: a single plant can easily spread to 30 feet. The plants do need support for their travels, though. A fence could work or, of course, a metal or wooden trellis. If using a fence, sturdy wire should be used to train the twining vines. To provide shade and sun control over a deck or patio, a grape-like arbor can serve as an anchor for the vines.

Full sun is most pleasing to kiwi plants, though you may want to provide shade for young plants their first summer. The young plants will also need wooden stakes and plastic ties in the beginning to train them and prevent wind damage. After the first year or so, the plants should be hardy and pest-free. Plants must be pruned regularly to keep them winding along their way.

The writer's grandfather, a home kiwi grower, gave much of this information to her. Nonetheless, to gain a wider perspective, she consulted these publications: Encyclopedia Americana, Harper's *magazine, and* Sunset *magazine. Then, to make certain that her information was correct, she interviewed a nursery clerk at Tree Farm. Her persistence is what many magazine editors seek.*

It may take four years for the vines to fully cover a large arbor, but at the end of that time, the result should be more than worth the wait. Plants will bear fruit after three years, and your first heavy crop will come two or three years later. A fully developed female can provide up to 200 pounds of fruit each year.

The fuzzy, brown, egg-shaped fruits will hang from the vines beginning in mid-October. Before you pick the kiwis, though, check them for ripeness: a slight squeeze should cause fruit to indent. If you pick them early, let them sit out at room temperature for a few days to ripen, then refrigerate them. After all fruit has been picked (late November), plants will become dormant, and should be pruned as you would grape vines to encourage fruiting the next season.

Though the actual harvest runs only from mid-October through mid-November in California, growers can still be eating kiwis long after. Kiwis can be stored up to six months in a refrigerator for use in the off-season.

Note how this writer plotted her article: From the very beginning to the end, you'll find that nearly all of this article is chronological, from introducing kiwis, describing them, giving a bit of kiwi history, instructing those who might like to grow them, and ending with eating kiwis.

To prepare kiwis, you must first remove their thin, fuzzy brown skin. A new type of kiwi with no fuzz on its exterior has recently been developed. Plants are still hard to come by, but extensive nurseries should have them. The best way to remove the skin is to pare the fruit gently with a very sharp knife. This will leave you a full fruit to cut crosswise, producing the beautiful emerald green slices with soft centers framed by tiny, edible seeds. If you don't need a round kiwi slice for your purposes, and just want a refreshing treat, cut the fruit in half length-wise and scoop out the center carefully with a wide spoon, as you would an avocado. A large kiwi has only 60 calories, making it a delightful snack for people of all ages and waistlines.

Kiwis are most commonly used in fall fruit salads, mixed with pineapple, grapes, bananas, and other tropical fruits. They are also used in rings or swirled on tarts or pies. Many make kiwi ice similar to the Italian ices that have become popular in the U.S. Other uses include skewering thicker slices with other fruits for a garnish on a plate or in a fruity tropical drink. Kiwis go particularly well with rum drinks. Beyond desserts, kiwis add a tangy, sweet accent to chicken salad or other light poultry dishes.

Look for unconventional ways to describe people or events when writing from observation.

Genius has been described as a supreme capacity for taking trouble.
Samuel Butler

The late Walter Lippmann made a point about observing in the excellent chapter of *Public Opinion* where he explained how stereotypes shape our view of the world:

> For the most part, we do not see first, then define; we define first and then see. In the great blooming, buzzing confusion of the outer world we pick out what our culture has already defined for us, and we tend to perceive that which we have picked out in the form stereotyped.

Recall the exercise in Chapter 2 that asked you to describe a professor without citing eyes or hair, height or weight. One student wrote this:

> He brings to mind Woody Woodpecker. That cowlick that will never lie down creates the impression, and the bright eyes and sharp nose add to it. Finally, the slightly zany quality of the man makes the impression stick.
>
> The zaniness is hard to pin down. Everything he says seems normal, perhaps even serious. He doesn't walk funny or make odd expressions when he talks. Somehow, though, he isn't convincing as the staid professor.
>
> Perhaps he appears mildly "touched" because he makes even firm statements with a quizzical air. Questions seem to momentarily surprise him, as if he's being called back to earth from somewhere far away. He needs time to mull questions over, and probably reconsiders most answers. He'll say goodbye, walk slowly away, and then pause and turn around, one more thought having occurred to him.
>
> Not everything about him is tentative, however. When he does get back to earth, he is very much back, concentrating on the matter at hand. Thus, he seems intent on and concerned with students, even if he's not always easy to reach.

You can see why it's not surprising that when writers observe a subject *minutely,* they can unearth unique and accurate descriptions. Many students have said after performing exercises like this one that they have, at last, learned to observe in a way they had never considered possible.

When you write from observation, remember these two tips:

1. Work at seeing the person or event with a fresh eye, holding all preconceptions in abeyance.

2. Find unusual images or striking metaphors to describe what you see.

Walter Lippmann

Walter Lippmann was not a reporter in the conventional sense. Being first with the news did not interest him, but his most direct and measurable influence on Washington and the world came from his writing. He conceived of his column, he once said, as an effort to keep contemporary events in such perspective that his readers would have no reason to be surprised when something of importance occurred. Thus, although he had no effect on news gathering, his impact on interpretative reporting was profound. Those correspondents who sought to establish the meaning of events usually looked to Lippmann for a useful approach. In James Reston's words: "He has given my generation of newspapermen a wider vision of our duty. He has shown us how to put the event of the day in its proper relationship to the history of yesterday and the dream of tomorrow."

It was not just that Lippmann took the long view, and it was not only that his words seemed to carry, in the phrase of another journalist, "the authority of the basic intentions of the American political system." What Lippmann did, in essence, was to bring to bear on the questions of the time a powerful mind, a simple style that was shapely rather than staccato, and an absolutely relentless concern for disciplined thought and language. Thus, during the 1964 Presidential campaign, when Senator Barry Goldwater charged the Democrats with planning an economy in which "no one is permitted to fall below the average," Lippmann icily wrote that "there cannot be an 'average' if no one is below it." No doubt many another journalist who knows how an average is derived might have made the same point had he only thought to analyze Goldwater's words. Lippmann thought and analyzed. Similarly, Lippmann seemed to have been pretty much alone in thinking through the central implication of Senator Goldwater's "extremism in defense of liberty is no vice." To justify this to General Eisenhower, the Senator told him, "The most extreme action you can take in defense of freedom is to go to war. When you led those troops across the channel into Normandy, you were being an extremist." According to all accounts, the point seemed to register with Eisenhower. But Lippmann wrote: "The crucial truth is that when General Eisenhower went to war, he was not a private individual. He was not a member of a private and secret society. . . . The essence of the matter is that to be an extremist is to encourage and condone the taking of the law into unauthorized private hands. It is in truth shocking that the Republican candidate for President is unconscious of this sovereign truth. For the distinction between private violence and public force is the central principle of a civilized society."

No one could have foreseen Lippmann's future. By the time he was four years old, in 1893, Walter was already politically aware: President

Grover Cleveland was to him "a sinister figure," and William Jennings Bryan was an "ogre from the West." Lippmann remembers, as a seven-year-old, "waiting for the election returns of 1896 with a beating heart."

According to his childhood friend Carl Binger, who met Lippmann in 1896 in Dr. Julius Sachs' School for Boys in New York, he was a wonder child in other ways: "I don't suppose he ever got less than an A on any examination in his life. This habit began in Miss Estvan's class in 1896 and continued until we graduated from Harvard in 1910. He could recite the names of the states and their capitals in less time than anyone in the class. He could point out where the Guadalquivir arose and emptied and also the Guadeloupe. He knew his French irregular verbs so well that our goateed teacher, M. Jean Pierre Auguste Porret, preened himself when his prodigy of a pupil recited. He could translate Ovid at sight, and all the efforts of Mr. Douglas to teach us Greek met with success with Walter only."

Lippmann's standing after a short time at Harvard was indicated by what happened on his visit to a meeting of the Western Club. John Reed, who was later to write *Ten Days that Shook the World,* leaped to his feet as Lippmann came in, bowed sweepingly, and cried, "Gentlemen, the future President of the United States!"

Before Lippmann died in 1974, he lived serenely, as always, following his own prescription:

> Every man whose business it is to think knows that he must for part of the day create about himself a pool of silence. . . . So long as so many jobs are an endless, and, for the worker, an aimless routine, a kind of automatism using one set of muscles in one monotonous pattern, his whole life will tend toward an automatism in which nothing is particularly to be distinguished from anything else unless it is announced by a thunderclap. So long as he is physically imprisoned in crowds by day and even by night his attention will flicker and relax. It will not hold fast and define clearly where he is the victim of all sorts of pother, in a home which needs to be ventilated of its welter of drudgery, shrieking children, raucous assertions, indigestible food, bad air, and suffocating ornament.

Draw on substantial interviewing, close observation, and good background research when writing profiles or other long stories.

No man is an island; every man is a piece of the continent, a part of the main.   *John Donne*

Saul Pett of the Associated Press, a great feature writer, gives this excellent advice:

We can no longer give the reader the fast brush. We can no longer whiz through the files for 20 minutes, grab a cab, spend 30 minutes interviewing our subject, come back to the office, concoct a clever lead that goes nowhere, drag in 15 or 20 more paragraphs like tired sausage, sprinkle them with four quotes, pepper them with 14 scintillating adjectives, all synonymous, and then draw back and call that an incisive portrait of a human being.

Today, the reader wants more in his features. Over his second or third Sunday cup of coffee, he wants to be drawn in by substance. He wants meat on his bones and leaves on his trees. He wants dimension and depth and perspective and completeness and insight and, of course, honesty.

Although Pett is talking about profiles, stories that flesh out a personality, his points apply to many other kinds of long stories. His words should be heeded; sharply written, probing stories bring new vitality to newspapers. The fat and successful *Los Angeles Times* is one of the best newspapers at featuring long profiles. The *Times* carries many features that run longer than 5,000 words.

Increasingly, the long profiles that used to be printed only in magazines are appearing in newspapers. What is the difference between the old-style newspaper profiles and profiles in magazine style? Usually an old-style newspaper profile could be researched and written in two or three hours, while a magazine profile could be researched and written in, at the very least, days and sometimes weeks or months.

Here is what the writer of a good magazine-style profile writes about:

1. *What the subject says in interviews.* The writer cannot interview a subject in an hour or two and be satisfied. He or she must interview the subject at least twice and preferably three or more times. Important revelations will emerge when the interviewer and subject become accustomed to each other.

2. *What the subject says spontaneously.* The writer must not just talk with the subject. The subject must be observed and quoted, preferably both at work and at leisure.

3. *How the subject looks and what he or she does.* The writer should note not only routine facts such as height, weight, and color of eyes and hair, but especially more vivid details like how the subject walks, talks, and gestures. The writer must observe closely and often enough to record anecdotes that show the subject's personality.

4. *History of the subject.* What the subject is like *now* is most important, but failing to color in personal background in at least a few paragraphs may suggest he or she was always this way—never in the process of *becoming*.

5. *What others say about the subject.* The writer should interview detractors as well as friends of the subject.

6. *Has the subject been involved in anecdotes?* Almost nothing is more valuable to a writer than an anecdote about the subject. In fact, the more anecdotes the writer discovers, the better his or her writing will become. When readers come upon an anecdote, very few of them can stop reading until the anecdote is done. To give an example of a good anecdote: James Barrie, a British journalist and playwright, was sitting next to George Bernard Shaw, an Irish playwright, at a dinner party. The vegetarian Shaw had been provided with a special dish of salad greens and dressing. Eyeing the unpleasant concoction, Barrie whispered to Shaw, "Tell me, have you eaten that or are you going to?"

To write about people, observe them closely.

The eye of the master will do more work than both his hands.
Benjamin Franklin

This sentence was written by Katherine Anne Porter:

> She hated being pale, and had the habit, while reading, of smoothing her cheeks round and round with two fingers, first one cheek and then the other, until deep red spots would burn in them for a long while.

Here is another sentence by Porter, describing a different woman:

> Eva, shy and chinless, would sit in corners watching her mother.

These sentences work because they enable readers to *see*.

Use these guidelines to describe people, as you would to describe events, in order to bring what you observe to life for your readers:

1. Instead of telling, *show*.

2. Make certain to use anecdotes and examples.

3. Reach for visual words and turns of phrase.

4. Use metaphors and similes.

5. Note revealing details that will appeal to your readers' senses: sight, hearing, smell, taste, and touch.

6. Personalize experiences you observe by using good quotations, especially when they heighten drama.

Memorize the main points in these guidelines for writing magazine articles and newspaper features.

The two most beautiful words in the English language are: "Check enclosed."   *Dorothy Parker*

1. Does your lead take your readers into the article quickly and in an interesting way? Does the lead relate to the body of the article?

2. Does your article flow from the beginning sentence to the last? Look especially for disconcerting changes of pace. Have you provided smooth transitions that link paragraphs?

3. Does your conclusion offer readers a reward for their efforts? Does the conclusion grow logically from the body of your article?

4. Have you supported your assertions with visual details?

5. Anecdotes are valuable in almost all articles. Check your work for good anecdotes.

6. When you check the material you have gathered, it should be *much longer than your article.*

7. Is your article tightly focused? Have you eliminated irrelevant observations and unworkable ideas?

8. Is your article the proper length and style for the magazine or newspaper to which you are submitting? *Always* check the lengths of sentences and paragraphs.

EXERCISES

1. Examine several newspaper features for evidence that a writer is offering—consciously or unconsciously, overtly or subtly—his or her own opinion. Do you find phrases or sentences that would not be allowed in a standard news story? Check the feature stories for particularizing adjectives ("nearby," "little," and the like) and for evaluating adjectives ("pretty," "menacing," and the like).

2. Considering the differences between newswriting and feature writing, what qualities should a good feature writer have that are not necessarily shared by a good news reporter? Write a 200-word response to this question.

3. To write the best feature story you can, choose a professor who teaches you. The professor is the easiest person to write a profile on because you can see him or her at work. Also interview the professor in his or her office—observing the office, as well as the professor. Interview several of the professor's students. Finally, write an 800-word (or more) feature story.

Writing and rewriting are a constant search for
what one is saying.
John Updike

What is easy to read has been difficult to write. The
labor of writing and rewriting, correcting and
recorrecting, is the due exacted by every good book
from its author, the easily flowing connection of
sentence with sentence and paragraph with
paragraph has always been won by the sweat of the
brow.
G. M. Trevelyan

An editor, Katharine White inspired her writers,
down to the dash.
Patricia Holt

The life of every man is a diary in which he means
to write one story and writes another; and his
humblest hour is when he compares his story as it is
with what he vowed to make it.
James Barrie

"Where shall I begin, please, your Majesty?" he
asked. "Begin at the beginning," the king said
gravely, "and go on till you come to the end: then
stop."
Lewis Carroll

C H A P 5 T E R

Revision

Everyone excels in something in
which another fails.   *Publilius Syrus*

The late Truman Capote, a noted writer, wrote slowly, largely because he weighed and tested each word. The late Robert Ruark, who was a fast and slovenly writer, one evening boasted of his own speed and teased Capote with, "Truman, I'll bet you spent all day writing one word." Capote responded, "Ah, but it was the *right* word." If all other writers were always to use the right words, there would be no need for rewriting. But nearly all writers must rewrite.

The writer who writes a piece in a single draft is usually saying little and saying it poorly. Say something substantial, and say it well. Revising, rewriting, reorganizing, polishing—call it what you like, it is often essential in producing the kind of work that can be described as unified.

WORDS AS WORDS

Centuries ago, Philip of Macedon, a powerful king, threatened Laconia with this message: "If I enter Laconia, you shall be exterminated."

The Laconians responded with one word: "If." They used the power of a common word.

Studying a single language, your own, can be a delightful adventure or hated drudgery. Thanks to Charles W. Ferguson who wrote *Say It with WORDS:* First, think of Abraham Lincoln's Gettysburg Address, in which he did *not* say "a people's government," nor did he say "government of, by, and for the people." Instead, he said "of the people, by the people, and for the people." You have undoubtedly been warned against repeti-

107

tion, but observe why repeating "people" three times worked wonderfully well for him. Although a word was repeated in Lincoln's passage, each use of the word is preceded by a different, one-syllable word: "of," "by," and "for." Moreover, note especially how he achieves rhythm here by using only "of the," "by the," and "for the," all followed by "people." Such is the power of common words if you think of them as Lincoln did.

Note especially that Lincoln did not use repetition again in his speech. Instead, read *aloud* this Lincoln passage, also from his Gettysburg Address. The verbs are italicized: "our fathers *brought* forth on this continent a new nation, *conceived* in liberty, and *dedicated* to the proposition that all men *are created* equal. . . ." Lincoln knew that verbs are like hinges in sentences, so he took special care about selecting verbs. Observe how his verbs beat a regular time and mark the cadence.

In using verbs, almost always choose the active voice over the passive. For example, *He knows the story* shows the subject in mental action. *The story is known by him* unfolds a picture of the subject being acted upon.

Examining each word you select is always necessary. In the following excerpt from a student's paper about a professor, try to decide what is wrong with the second sentence before you read the explanation:

> Her pale white skin, untouched by the intensity of the sun's rays, wrinkled in patterned lines at the corners of her mouth as she attempted to comprehend the mutterings of her student. Her right arm grew strength and touched the limp hand of the student in a simple gesture of compassion.

If you are one of those who like description—as many people do—you may overlook the bad choice of words in the second sentence. The student writes of the professor's gesture, "Her right arm grew strength and touched the limp hand. . . ." Has anyone ever seen someone touch another person's hand with her *arm?* Certainly not. All the writer has to do is think of her choice of words, and substitute the word "hand" for "arm."

Moreover, another error follows. After "Her right arm," the student wrote, "grew strength." We suppose that this is wildly possible, but not likely. How could the writer have watched her right arm grow strength?

The last two words in the next sentence show that the writer bows too low toward alliteration: "Her deep eyes then formed a penetrating stare as she realized she must gently push the perplexed student into a higher level of philosophical thought to achieve unified understanding." The words "unified understanding" are a striking way to erect an image, but what does it mean? Neither before nor after these words is there an explanation of what they mean.

Alliteration is a powerful arrangement of words because the phonetic effect can relieve humdrum language. But be careful to make alliteration understandable to the readers.

VISUAL WRITING

Captivating writing, which begins with visual phrases, does not begin with overpowering words. Here, for example, is an exhausting sentence: "Today, the monstrosity which sunders the City of Berlin exemplifies the incarnated East-West standoff in the heart of Europe while at the same time adding stimulus to the already electrified emotions of a severed nation." True, there is visual language here, along with self-conscious vocabulary, but this sentence is like background music that submerges all the foreground. Also consider, "The Americans cannot plant the seeds of social unrest, nourish and fertilize them, and then leave them to pursue their own course." Note the mixed metaphor, which begins with agricultural images and ends with nautical ones. It would have been far better had the student written: "The Americans cannot plant the seeds of social unrest, nourish them, then leave them to grow untended." This second example may seem a minor correction, but it illustrates the ease with which a writer can enhance a mixed sentence.

To practice making visual phrases, make it your own personal assignment to observe games—football, basketball, baseball—parties, or any event where many people gather, and attempt to see what almost all people fail to observe.

Here are some phrases written by students:

FOOTBALL GAME

The home crowd grumbled out of the stadium.

The visiting band lined up in neo-Nazi formation.

jeer leaders

The crowd began to seep out of the stadium.

Crowds jammed each gate, squirting files of fans.

She hugged someone who looked unexciting enough to be her husband.

The high school bands looked like children playing dress-up.

so hot that everyone is getting runny around the edges

examines the crowd through beer-bleared eyes

A shirt comes off as one rooter surrenders to the sun.

GAMBLING

Dealers pause only to reshuffle the cards as marksmen at a mass execution reload.

$100 bills as common as confetti

signs that discourage the financial flyweights

PARKS

the foul breath of suburbia's early-morning yawn
The dawn had grown too old.
Redwood trees stretched their limbs and fanned away the clouds.
The campground had already transformed itself into the setting for the daily rape of majestic calm.

HOSPITAL

contrary-to-nature colors, too perfect, too manufactured
worn body and clothes slouched crow-like and defeated
bird-like limbs exposed, legs hanging from her chair ironically

When students are attracted by phrases they have created, they may use the same phrase over and over again, perhaps in the same paper. On page 2 of a student's paper, she wrote of a professor's appearance and fell in love with this sentence:

He looks like a teddy bear stuffed into a smaller doll's clothing.

Then, near the top of page 5 in the same paper, she wrote:

His large, teddy bear-like body . . .

Finally, six lines down from her last use of "teddy bear," she wrote:

his looming, overstuffed teddy bear physique . . .

Readers who were attracted by the first reference to the professor's body no doubt smiled in appreciation at the writer's clever use of this image. Later, though, when they again came upon "His large, teddy bear-like body," all of them remembered her first use of "teddy bear." Perhaps many readers shrugged, but some must have wondered why she used "teddy bear" again. Finally, when readers ran across "his looming, overstuffed teddy bear physique," most probably were irritated.

Instead of repeating much the same phrase, she should have arranged her words this way:

He looks like a teddy bear stuffed into a smaller doll's clothing.

Next:

His large, bear-like body . . .

Finally:

> his looming, overstuffed physique . . .

When you have created a new phrase, *never* repeat it in the same paper. Isolate your creation; it will draw more positive attention than if you had repeated it. What will you do when you are tempted to use it again? Instead, make up a new phrase. This isn't work; it is *agony*. But nothing can be compared to creating still another original phrase. Another inventive set of words will bring you only joy.

For example, when you face the necessity of using "as smooth as," perhaps the first phrase that comes to your mind is "as smooth as glass." Don't pause over this dismal cliché. Instead, try again. Your next phrase may be "as smooth as borrowing your prospective mother-in-law's knife at dinner to pick your teeth with." This phrase, in addition to its many faults, is much too long. Trying again, you may think of "as smooth as Nixon's pardon." This phrase may have been the proper choice twenty years ago, but you must try again. Perhaps, after much thinking, you may have made these two phrases: "as smooth as a con man's manner" and "as smooth as an innuendo." By all means, use your "innuendo" phrase.

Again, you may find yourself using "as fast as," with no other words to round off this phrase. Almost certainly, you'll probably think of "as fast as an antelope," which, of course, is another cliché. Like most college students, you may think of a negative phrase, like this: "as fast as five o'clock traffic." Try harder. Perhaps you may come up with two phrases, like these: "as fast as a keg gets tapped at a fraternity party" and "as fast as a greased rumor." Choose the latter.

If your class should vote on the best phrases, remember these rules of thumb:

1. In many cases, the phrases that win will be shorter than the others.

2. In college circles, negative phrases have a head start on the positive ones.

3. Phrases that show originality are better than most of the others because they surprise all readers. Notice especially the combination of "as smooth as an innuendo." Smoothness seems to call for something material to complete the simile, but this phrase doesn't provide it, which makes the phrase entirely original. This same rule of thumb applies to "as fast as a greased rumor." Again the simile calls for something concrete, but the combination of "fast" and "greased rumor" surprises the readers.

4. Alliteration in a phrase will almost always draw votes. For example, consider this phrase that emphasizes alliteration: "As colorful as a colony of Puritans."

All students who are interested in phrase-making can find good phrases in the better newspapers and magazines. Consider these phrases, all from the *New York Times* and *Time* magazine:

THE *NEW YORK TIMES:*

He settled down in a wooden armchair and began turning the golden sunlight blue with the ruined stump of a cigar.

A defense alert in New York City was like a telephone ringing in an empty room.

It was like trying to tell where the wind went.

A blind boy's horizon is at his fingertips.

TIME MAGAZINE:

Like a Polaris missile, the great fish roars out of the water, sometimes jumping twelve feet or more as he goes raging and tail-walking across the ocean.

It was like trying to drive a tack into a marshmallow.

To sit through the film is something like holding an elephant on your lap for two hours and fifteen minutes.

You can hardly measure what you have there, but it leaves a definite impression: big, warm-hearted, and tons of fun for the kids.

Spain is a land of mystery where the dust of isolation has often settled on men's work and obscured their lives.

Making phrases is not the center of your work, but attempting to make phrases will free almost anyone of lazily writing sentences. It could be that you will never put together an excellent set of words, but trying will improve your writing.

MAKING SENTENCES

About trying to make music with words, the late Stephen Spender wrote:

Sometimes when I lie in a state of half-waking half-sleeping, I am conscious of a stream of words which seem to pass through my mind, without their having a meaning, but they have a sound, a sound of passion, or a sound recalling poetry that I know. Again sometimes when I am writing, the music of the words I am trying to shape takes me far beyond the words. I am aware of a rhythm, a dance, a fury, which is as yet empty of words.

Like every professional writer, Spender thought often of writing—not of words, but of the magic of music that can at times transcend the mere carpentry of a writer. From the standpoint of a reader, S. I. Hayakawa wrote:

> We stop being critical altogether and simply allow ourselves to feel as excited, sad, joyous or angry as the author wishes us to feel. Like snakes under the influence of a snake charmer's flute, we are swayed by the musical phrases of the verbal hypnotist. . . . Some people never listen to *what* is being said, since they are interested only in what might be called the gentle inward message that the sound of words gives them.

Spender's and Hayakawa's dreams describe what many students aspire to; a few student writers come close to these visions, even when dealing with hard facts. Here are two sentences about *Stars and Stripes* written by a student:

> In the closed world of the military, the need for such a publication as *Stars and Stripes* becomes increasingly evident. An unreported and unresolved dispute can flare up into an open conflict; an unwatched general can claim increasingly arbitrary powers; an unseen deficiency can signify a military weakness.

Students who don't pay attention to words often write sentence-paragraphs like this:

> His dry wit is scattered throughout the lecture to keep everyone watching.

What are the students watching? Is it "wit" that floats on air for others to admire? No, of course not. This writer apparently has paid no attention to the precision of words that round off his sentence. More importantly, the worst error in this sentence-paragraph is that the writer thinks that *saying* that the professor is witty is enough to invite applause from his readers. No, to prove that the professor actually *is* witty, the writer must give an example—perhaps two or three examples that will help define for the writer and his readers the professor's degree of humor.

Here is another sentence that suffers from lack of precision in using words:

> He decides that he has been over-enthusiastic and quiets down again, giving his observers the impression that somehow a hurricane has passed over them, but they were not aware of it at the time, and now they wonder where it went.

This student writer used "hurricane" to describe his subject's excessive enthusiasm, apparently not knowing that "hurricane" might be chosen by anyone over the age of twelve. To define *exactly* how his subject and the audience reacted, when he thought of "hurricane"—an important word—he needed to use, not a word that invites "cliché," but rather a word of some originality. Moreover, the words after "passed over them" are not merely valueless, but they also leave the readers not quite knowing what these words mean and pausing to wonder, and thus the words ruin reading. No other words in this story make it apparent what the writer was trying to say.

Another student wrote the concluding sentence of her six-page paper using "I" for the first time:

> After talking with most of Rod's friends, I am convinced that he developed his motto, "Always be prepared," through a long, painful process.

Readers are accustomed to the third-person voice, and many are jarred by the sudden appearance of an "I" at the end of the story. In some pieces of writing, you can use an "I" many times, but think always of its effect on the readers.

In the following sentence, you will find good writing that is submerged in too many words:

> Deep in the primal chaos of Gate H, spectators arrived endlessly from being strained through the ticket booths.

This was written by an able writer, who perhaps knew too well that he can describe vividly. In this sentence, the writer observed people closely at a football game, then created the above sentence, with these pivotal words: "primal chaos," "arrived endlessly," and "strained through." Using all three in a short sentence is far too much. At least, he should have written his sentence this way:

> Deep in the primal chaos of Gate H, spectators were strained through the ticket booths.

If he were still proud of his creation, he could have used "arrived endlessly" in another sentence.

Here is another sentence that must be purged of a few words.

> Strings of approaching people wended their way like hoards of wandering Visigoths through the interstices of the parking lot.

The image of "wandering Visigoths" is so striking that the writer should not drown it in words. The words "through the interstices of the parking lot" hang on at the end of this sentence and dilute the effect for readers of "wandering Visigoths."

If you can make images, one after another, never weave words in a way that will have your readers choking on too much sweetness.

Simplify the sentences in your writing.

Perhaps of all the creations of man, language is the most astonishing.
Lytton Strachey

A newspaper's readers generally range from those with little formal education to society's most competent readers. Even in a magazine or newspaper serving a highly literate audience, simplicity is a sign of respect for readers: Conveying ideas and information in easily readable form allows readers to focus effortlessly on an article's content.

Use ordinary words.   Winston Churchill, who used words at least as effectively as he did weapons and strategy, said, "Short words are best." Illustrating his point, he restated this sentence:

> The information obtained from our sources in France of the general picture there indicates that the situation there is deteriorating.

Churchill's version read:

> The news from France is bad.

Following Churchill's example will make you a successful writer.

Sentence after sentence of choppy "Dick and Jane" simplicity would irritate readers and should, of course, be avoided, but those of you who have large vocabularies must resist the temptation to make writing seem important by clothing it richly and showing off words. The true measure of vocabulary is not the length of words chosen, but the number of words used effectively.

Eliminate meaningless words and phrases.   Some meaningless expressions are so widely used we write them without thinking. We have all read and heard the phrase "needless to say" hundreds of times. But if something really is needless to say, why say it? "Remains to be seen" is also familiar, but the phrase has no meaning worth its words; aside from events that have already run their course, *everything* remains to be seen.

Guard against reading through meaningless phrases without rewriting to improve conciseness. Readers should not have to waste time reading phrases that mean nothing.

Eliminate redundancy. One way to achieve simplicity is to eliminate redundancy—saying the same thing twice or using more words than necessary. The words at the left and the words at the right say the same thing:

REDUNDANT	CONCISE
exact same	same
free gift/free pass	gift/pass
personal friend	friend
sudden explosion	explosion
sufficient number of	enough
at the present time	now
at this point in time	now
invited guests	guests
in the immediate vicinity of	near
in the near future	soon
in the not-too-distant future	eventually
all of	all
in case	if
in most cases/in most instances	usually
as in the case of	like
at the intersection of Second and Spring	at Second and Spring
consensus of opinion	consensus
entirely destroyed	destroyed
despite the fact that	although
due to the fact that	because
during the period from	from
for the purpose of	for
repeat again	repeat
past experience	experience
knots per hour	knots (which measure the speed per hour)
new innovation	innovation
present incumbent	incumbent
reason why/reason because	reason
future plans/future developments	plans/developments

REDUNDANT	CONCISE
advance planning	planning
both agreed	agreed
equally as	equally
in excess of	more than
in back of	behind
in order to	to
advance reservations	reservations
the city of Los Angeles	Los Angeles
the sum of $22.50	$22.50
a triangular shape	triangle
most unique/completely unique	unique
in a dying state	dying
in the year of 1981	1981
traditions of the past	traditions
old adage	adage
lift up	lift
Sierra mountains	Sierras
the hour of midnight	midnight
made out of iron	iron
the subject of charity	charity
dead body found	body found
throughout the entire day	throughout the day
perhaps it may happen	it may happen
for a period of ten days	for ten days
during the course of the day	during the day
reported to the effect that	reported
for a short space of time	briefly

This list is far from being exhaustive, but it does show how common redundancy is in American speech and writing. To understand the burden redundancy places on a reader, read this sentence:

> Brown commented to the effect that in the not-too-distant future, the consensus of opinion of his personal friends would be that due to the fact that noise from traffic at the intersection of Sycamore and El Camino was increasing he should change his place of residence.

The sentence could have been:

> Brown said his friends would soon think he should move because of the increasingly noisy traffic at Sycamore and El Camino.

Dead words—words that serve no purpose—should not be allowed to stand unrevised, even if they increase the gracefulness of a story by varying sentence length. As a writer, you must eliminate all redundancy in a story and then rewrite any sentences that have become choppy.

Use the best one or two modifiers or rewrite.   A pile of adjectives or adverbs debilitates even a skilled reader. Consider this sentence:

> Vivacious, inquisitive, perplexing, pretty, and perverse, Friedheim is seldom ignored.

Each of the five adjectives at the beginning of the sentence forces the reader to work to determine exactly what it says. Having considered the meaning of each adjective, the reader must remember *that* meaning (and the meanings of up to three other adjectives) while considering a new one.

Ordinary verbs and nouns demand little work by readers. The reader of the sentence about Friedheim would, for example, have little trouble understanding that Friedheim is difficult to ignore. Voltaire said, "The adjective is the enemy of the noun." Likewise, the adverb can be considered the enemy of the verb. Voltaire exaggerated, of course—a carefully chosen modifier or even two can clarify or intensify a noun or verb's meaning.

More than one or two wisely selected modifiers, though, cripple nouns, verbs, and readers. When you find piled-together modifiers in your drafts, either select the one modifier (or two, at most) that seems best or devote several sentences to saying what the reader would have choked on in the unedited sentence.

Rewrite to eliminate jargon.   *Jargon* is an exclusive vocabulary of over-used terms and phrases adopted by a specialized group (an academic discipline, a profession, a religious or political sect) to express the ideas and technical information the group needs. Jargon is usually unintelligible to those outside the specialized group and so must be translated for a general readership. Jargon also sounds self-important.

Break apart overwritten sentences.   Turning to her typewriter after struggling through an article made up of long, complex sentences, an instructor inserted the back side of her student's final page and typed period after period until the page was almost filled. Then she added this message at the bottom of the page: "These interesting objects, which apparently you have never encountered, are known as periods. You will find them most helpful, and I urge you to use them—often."

The problem of interminable and overly complex sentences faced by this instructor is common. Even newspapers, which pride themselves on their short, readable sentences, are sometimes guilty of overloading their sentences:

> The records show that the recruiter made calls from his Austin, Texas, office to the police department and the Angelina County district attorney's office in Lufkin, Texas, November 12, 1979, according to the Marines, who also say a third call was made to the county sheriff's office but there was no telephone receipt to prove it.

This sentence's problem is not as much due to its length as to its content. Very long sentences can be perfectly direct and clear. The problem in this example is the amount of information crowded into a single sentence. The reader cannot possibly comprehend or retain all this information in one reading and must stop and start over several times to understand the sentence.

R. J. Cappon, general news editor of the Associated Press, has described two major causes of unwieldy sentences. The first cause is failure to limit a sentence to a single idea. A writer who crams more than one idea (or set of closely related ideas) into a sentence is forced to overcomplicate the sentence with *who, that,* and *which* clauses:

> The King of Spain, *who* had been a favorite of the Falangist Party, *which* had ruled Spain for the 30-odd years *that* intervened between the Spanish Civil War and his coronation, told the President of France, *who* . . .

This kind of sentence is a linguistic traffic jam.

A second cause of unwieldy sentences, Cappon says, is reckless use of conjunctions like *and* or *but.* This sentence shows how overuse of conjunctions can lead to confusion:

> The reaction was not a common one and it was undoubtedly well justified because Deputy Chief Engineer John Kozack of the Toll Bridge Authority committee had announced that the bridge construction could begin within a month, consultation and research at the local level had been practically ignored, and the community was quick to respond with suits.

This sentence seems as if it will never stop, and is typical of the sentences produced by writers who have not learned to limit a sentence either to one idea or to the simplest possible presentation of two or more *closely* related ideas. Overburdened sentences like this one seldom occur in speech. Yet writers unaware of the sound of their sentences mount idea upon idea, making a chaotic, unreadable jumble.

Good sentences follow the simple pattern of speech. As a writer, you must group and relate your ideas thoughtfully. Precision may require that a single sentence include a relative (*who, which, that*) clause or the connection of several related ideas. But thinking that writing is unworthy unless it is more long-winded and complex than ordinary speech is a mistake the writer and copy editor cannot afford to make.

Use synonyms and vary phrasing to prevent monotony.

Life is just one damned thing after another.   *Frank Ward O'Malley*

A writer covering a narrow topic may repeat the same words again and again. Some repetition is good, of course: the writer cannot refer to the topic of a story once in the first paragraph and then as nothing but "it." The reader needs repetition of important and unique terms to keep ideas straight.

Repetition of the same word, sentence after sentence, though, makes the reading of an article numbingly monotonous. A good writer would, for example, change

> New York seemed overwhelmingly noisy to him. He had never heard noise at 2 a.m. Trying to sleep in New York, he heard noise at two in the morning for the first time.

to

> New York seemed overwhelmingly noisy to him. Trying to sleep in Manhattan, he heard the pulsing of traffic at two in the morning for the first time.

Substituting synonyms for "New York" and "noise" in the edited sentences increases their variety and readability.

Use copy editor's marks to show where and how copy is to be changed.

I stand a wreck on Error's shore.   *Adah Isaacs Menken*

Copy editor's marks indicate changes without wasting words. Copy editor's marks (unlike proofreader's marks, which appear in a story's margin) change copy at the points where errors occur. Almost all these symbols are used throughout the world of journalism.

Copy Editor's Marks

Insert this letter or word	torado the destructive storm
Insert these several words	tornado was the storm of the decade.
Delete this letter	judgement
Delete this word or group of words	four new recruits
Insert a space	but the or but the
Close up this space	up right
Spell out if abbreviated here; abbreviate if spelled out here	62 California Az Governor
Transpose these letters/ words	recieve his bony five fingers
Capitalize this lowercase letter	Archibald Macleish
Capitalize these lowercase letters	Paris
Make this capital letter lowercase	two years of Science
Insert a comma here	
Insert an apostrophe here	
Insert a quotation mark here	
Insert a hyphen here	the twelve-pound penguin
Insert a dash here	which except when
Insert a period here	
Start a new paragraph here	In Miami, robbery
	or
	In Miami, robbery

(continued)

Copy Editor's Marks *(continued)*

Do not start a new paragraph here	the witnesses.
	Ron Jorgenson, a police
	or
	No # (write this in the margin)
	or
	[Ron Jorgenson, a police
Center this	] Five Diplomats
	Asked to Leave Washington [
Move this line over to the right margin	98.20]
	200.28
	117.04
There's more of this story	Los Angeles residents (more)
Ignore the editing mark I used here	(stet)
	concerns that increasing
Make this italic	Los Angeles Times
Make this boldface	Beethoven Festival

Preserve copy as you edit.

The obvious is better than obvious avoidance of it.   *H. W. Fowler*

When you delete, cross words out with a single line so that edited copy can be compared with the original. If more than a word has been deleted, draw a curving line from the beginning of the deletion to its end, like this:

> Most of the miners, however, chose to make the
> decision to cross the picket line, ducking.

Never destroy or throw away any copy; it may be needed later.

Be aware of the differences and similarities between magazine and newspaper editing.

Errors, like straws, upon the surface flow;
He who would search for pearls must dive below.   *John Dryden*

A copy editor working for a medium-sized daily newspaper edits about twenty stories a day, including shorts and fillers, in addition to writing about twenty headlines. On a busy day, the fastest newspaper copy editors may handle up to three times that amount of stories and headlines—sixty of each. Much newspaper copy, then, gets only light editing. Newswriters need to be good at editing their own copy.

Because a magazine is published less frequently than a newspaper, magazine copy editors usually have time to thoroughly refine the copy they edit. And because magazine stories ordinarily cover a subject much more fully than newspaper articles do, magazine copy editors must emphasize story organization and especially use of transitions. If you write for a magazine, however, you still need to edit your own copy. A story that is not well-written won't be accepted. If you haven't been careful to choose the right words and to make your sentences clear and concise, an editor trying to do that for you might change your meaning.

PARAGRAPHS AND BEYOND

Make paragraph length correspond to the complexity of the idea a paragraph presents.

A dwarf standing on the shoulders of a giant may see farther than a
giant himself.   *Robert Burton*

Twenty years ago, a newspaper editing instructor would have taught that paragraphs in newspaper stories should be only one or two sentences long. He or she might have explained that the format of small print and narrow columns makes a single sentence fill several lines in a newspaper column and that long, multisentence paragraphs would turn newspaper pages into uninviting, unreadable gray.

Newspapers are changing, though. Nearly all large metropolitan newspapers have shifted from an eight- to a six-column format, which gives editors more room for long paragraphs. In many stories that appear in the *New York Times, Washington Post,* and *Los Angeles Times,* paragraphs run much longer than one or two sentences. Although many smaller papers still use the old format and one- and two-sentence paragraphs, smaller papers, too, are using wider columns and longer paragraphs. In-depth reporting and newswriting are becoming more common too, and this interpretive form tends to lengthen paragraphs.

Paragraphs—although not always miniature essays composed of topic sentences followed by supporting statements—do consist of unified statements about one point. The more complex the point, the longer the paragraph that presents it must be. Every paragraph should be self-contained in its development of a single idea.

The break between the end of one paragraph and the beginning of another allows a reader to rest. The kind of rest a reader gets between paragraphs does not slow the pace of reading, but quickens it. In an article made up of fairly brief paragraphs, readers regularly apply an idea to the idea that follows it as they progress from one paragraph to the next.

The writer must be aware of this thought pattern—presentation of an idea alternating with brief rest and preparation for considering a related idea—and shape paragraphs that correspond to it.

Any writer should also consider how paragraphs will sound and look to the reader. Paragraphs should be as brief as possible, and the appearance and tone of paragraphs should be balanced and consistent throughout an article to produce an attractive and fairly uniform block or page of text.

Passages of dialogue cannot be edited to change paragraph length. To distinguish one speaker from the other, each change of speaker in a dialogue is indicated by the beginning of a new paragraph:

> "The school district may have to institute double sessions," Eikenberry said. "We just don't have the classroom space we need." His turquoise ring glinted as he combed tan fingers through his gray hair, over and over.
>
> "That's simply not an acceptable option for us," Shepherd replied.
>
> "Double sessions are certainly not what we would *choose*," Eikenberry retorted. . . .

Report numbers in ways that (1) allow readers to understand them easily and (2) reflect the truth.

[The writer] has the urge, first of all, to order the facts one observes and to give meaning to life.   *Aldous Huxley*

Columnist James Kilpatrick has said, "If I were teaching journalism, I would require my students to take one year of statistics for every semester of newswriting, and I'd turn out better reporters." Some colleges require journalism students to learn how to understand and report numbers; at Michigan State University's School of Journalism, for example, learning how to conduct public opinion polls has been part of reporting classes since 1975. Even if your journalism training includes some instruction on how to use and explain numbers, however, you should include extra courses in statis-

James J. Kilpatrick

James J. Kilpatrick is staunchly conservative, but he also realizes that millions of people are relying on *him* for his view of the truth. He proves himself a responsible and courageous reporter.

Even Kilpatrick's journalistic beginnings were conservative. A native of Oklahoma City, he went to the University of Missouri, then got his first full-time job as a reporter with the *Richmond News Leader* in Virginia in 1941. "I have been covering politics since I was 20, and I was pretty naive at the time. I suppose I once believed that all politicians meant to fulfill all their promises. One matures."

In Richmond, in a time when civil rights were at issue, he learned the lessons of conservatism from the general manager, John Dana Wise, an aristocratic South Carolinian. When Kilpatrick asked him to publish a liberal columnist to balance Kilpatrick's conservatism, this formal colloquy ensued:

> "Well," said Wise, "I am perfectly agreeable, Mr. Kilpatrick, perfectly willing to authorize the expenditure for this purpose if I could justify it. But do you believe you're propounding the truth as to, say, civil rights?"
>
> "Yes, Mr. Wise."
>
> "And the columnist you would propose to buy would take the opposite view, correct?"
>
> "Yes," said Kilpatrick.
>
> "Then you would be taking for our paper what you conceive to be in error?"
>
> "Well, in a sense, Mr. Wise, I would say so."
>
> "Well, then, how can you justify to me your wishing to carry in our editorial section what you honestly conceive to be error? Is this the function of your editorial section, to deliver error to your readers?"
>
> "Well, er . . . ," Kilpatrick would begin.
>
> Wise would then say, "Oh, but you certainly have been expressing yourself very sincerely in your editorial pages in these matters."
>
> "Yes, Mr. Wise."
>
> "You believe you are speaking truth, do you not?"
>
> "Yes."

Kilpatrick later said, "We never hired a liberal columnist. I accepted that, as I had to be editor of the paper. To be truthful, I didn't argue very fiercely. He was persuasive."

In 1964, he continued as editor of the *News Leader* and began writing a column three times a week at the invitation of *Newsday*. He was one of the few right-wing columnists at that time, and he was joyously and fiercely conservative. The column was picked up by so many newspapers that, the following year, the now-defunct *Washington Star* offered Kilpatrick a base in Washington. He took it. The number of papers that

(continued)

James J. Kilpatrick *(continued)*

are publishing him have increased from three hundred to nearly four hundred. Significantly, some papers claim that they have begun to publish Kilpatrick because he has changed his tone slightly and has become less conservative.

In fact, his columns show evidence of a centrist tendency. In a column headlined "Who's to Watch the Watch Dogs," he wrote of someone he had supported strongly:

> J. Edgar Hoover, for all his good qualities, was a man of obsessive prejudices. As FBI director, he had massive powers to pursue them. He dealt with a succession of presidents, attorneys general and congressional leaders who had weaknesses of their own. Hoover's skill was to understand these weaknesses and to capitalize on them.

At an earlier time he had congratulated the new U.S. Postal Service on moving into private enterprise. In 1976, he began a column:

> More than four years have gone by since the old U.S. Post Office Department became the new U.S. Postal Service. The idea at the time—and it seemed such a good idea at the time—was to get the mail out of politics. A dismal conclusion has to be voiced: We had better get the mail back into politics again.

Kilpatrick is one of the best of the writers in Washington. His style is sprightly and compelling. John Leonard of the *New York Times* wrote, at the twentieth birthday celebration of the conservative *National Review:* "James Jackson Kilpatrick, the antebellum Oscar Levant, was the master of ceremonies. He wore a kilt. He spoke entirely in heroic couplets. They rhymed, they scanned, and they were clever."

Kilpatrick's passion for language was particularly marked in a column he wrote about California Governor Jerry Brown, who at the time was running for the Democratic presidential nomination. Kilpatrick said that "in the jaded world of the Washington press corps he is a bright-plumed bird of passage," then ended with:

> What was that word again? In my dingo shorthand, the symbols for "r" and "l" look pretty much the same. I thought he had said "placatory," a nice $2.95 word, but I ran after him down the sidewalk to check. He had said, "precatory," a three-dollar word if there ever was one. That was when I started wagging catty-wampus. I'm skeptical of Brown; but I'm impressed.

How did this star become so influential? Kilpatrick has intelligence and persistence. Because he is persistent, this star is influential.

tics, computer science, accounting, and public finance in your training. Numbers are the bedrock of fact upon which much of reporting and public awareness stands. You must be able to understand the significance of numerical information and to test the validity of numerical conclusions to inform your audience responsibly.

Although numbers can add clarity because they mean the same thing to everyone, they can confuse and mislead as well as inform. To report numbers effectively, follow these guidelines:

TO KEEP NUMBERS FROM CONFUSING YOUR AUDIENCE:

1. Express numbers in terms your audience can visualize.
2. Supply the English equivalents for metric measurements.
3. Make sure numbers add up correctly.
4. Put all numbers in the same form when you draw comparisons.
5. Be careful not to place many numbers close together within the text of a news report.

TO KEEP NUMBERS FROM MISLEADING YOUR AUDIENCE:

1. Put numbers in context.
2. Evaluate, explain, and collect statistics.
3. Beware of exaggeration.

ONE STUDENT'S REWRITING

An instructor required his students to hand in their early drafts as well as their final draft. Here is what one student did: After typing each paragraph, he would read it over and over, then use his typewriter to cross out words:

ROUGH DRAFT I

Black, close fitting pants. Immaculate white turtleneck.

Sitting, he looks like a prim, straight, lean man, ~~cat-like~~.

                                           his

~~When-he-moves,-Juan-Valenzuela-comes-alive.~~ In ~~the-office,~~ cramped

but tidy office decorated with tasteful art prints and pictures

drawn by grade-schoolers, he talks quietly of his life and thoughtxs.

    When he moves, Juan Valenzuela comes alive. ~~Donning~~ In tights

& leotard, he commands a gym full of raptly attentive dance students.

This is his domain/kingdom/turf/place/.

The dance students sweat and grimace as they ~~obey-Juan's-command.~~

stretch stiff joints ~~on-Juan's~~ in time to/pounding drum. "Bend those
                                          Juan's

backs; I want you to be sore tomorrow," Juan says, effortlessly

touching his touching head to his knees.

"Keep smiling," he says, flashing his own 100-watt smile....

After ending his first draft, he read it again, and groaned.

Rough Draft 2

"Don't _think_ about it, feel it!" commands Juan Valenzuela,

and 31 amateur Baryshnikovs strive to obey. For four hours a week,

the gentle, nut-brown man ~~in-charge~~ at the front of the studio

is their benevolent master, and he demands   ~~every-ounce-of-effort~~

~~they-possess-excellence~~ of them only what he demands of himself

~~absolute-devotion-to-dance~~ devotion of body _and_ soul to dance.

~~In-class~~ "When you come to class, I want _all_ of you, not just

your bodies; I want your spirits as well," Juan says. "You are

also to enjoy this class. If you aren't then something is wrong.

"Smile! Isn't this _fun_?"

"I hate the blank faces I see in professional dancers today.

They're like Xerox copies of each other. If I can't see emotion,

joy, then I'd rather go watch a tree growing.

"If all you have is a physically beautiful body, you are

only half a person. I might see you create beauty on stage, and then

when I go backstage and meet you and you don't feel what you danced,

then that beauty on stage is destroyed.

Not that the body is neglected in Juan's classes. He is notorious ~~the-hardest-worker~~ for working students hard. Grunts &

"Martha Graham," he says with a touch of pride, "taught me to work with my body instead of against it. She taught us to be scientists using our instruments skillfully. Once I blacked out doing pirouettes, fell and broke groans when Juan says,

"touch those heads to

those knees. Smile! Isn't

this _fun_!"

my ankle. Talk about panic! I thought, "Now

I'll never be a dancer,' and I urged my body

to heal."

In reading his second draft, he is pleased with the opening quotation, but not with the rest of his profile. Here is the beginning of his final draft:

Final Draft

"Don't _think_ about it, _feel_ it!" commands the
lean, nut-brown man at the front of the dance studio, and
31 amateur Baryshnikovs strive to obey. Moving with the
soft-footed grace of a deer, he pauses to gently straighten
a student's slightly bent leg, then glides back to the huge
tom-tom to pound out the next routine. As the dancers prance
past, he studies them intensely, shouting "Yes! That's it!
Now turn! Keep smiling!" He flashes his own mega-watt
smile, eyes sparkling.

His smooth, Indian features, jet black hair and
sinewy frame suit a man of 30. His freshness and unflagging
zeal are those of a delighted child. Juan Valenzuela is
61 years old.

Juan lays down the law the first day of class.
"I want all of you, not just your bodies. When I call roll,
your mind and spirit had better be here too."

EXERCISES

1. The following story is so flabby that it has no place in a newspaper. Read again the sentence in this chapter that Winston Churchill corrected to become, "The news from France is bad." Adopt that method to reduce the

following story to at least half its length. *Make certain that the information the reporter wrote is contained in your version:*

U.S. Senator George Johnston, who spoke to a joint session of local civic organizations here Tuesday night, in summing up the work of the current sessions of Congress, pointed to the improvement of foreign relations as one of the bright spots in the picture. This, he said, was the result of cooperative action between the President and the Democratic leadership in Congress, and it came despite prophecies of doom emanating in some quarters during the political campaign last fall.

Acting in cooperation with the President, Democratic leadership stood fast with Peace Through Strength policy, thus warning China that the United States would take quick action to stop further aggression in Asia. Since last January, the picture has continued to brighten, and today the danger of immediate war appears remote. It was not so last January, Senator Johnston said.

2. The writer of the following paragraph is not a quantitative expert, but he began his article in a national magazine with the paragraph below. He wanted to emphasize a real estate boom in Florida. Decide for yourself whether this paragraph is clear or too loaded with numbers. In the next class, state your reaction to this paragraph:

Forty thousand Florida realtors are selling three million homesites so rapidly to the seven million tourists who visit the state every year, to the three thousand new residents who arrive every week, and to the hundreds who mail in ten-dollar checks every day that Florida is hard put to hold onto all this business: One development is technically in Alabama. This is the little island of Pineda, a few miles west of the Florida border in Mobile Bay, which will soon be sliced into 2,148 waterfront lots. It is distinctly Floridian, however, for three Fort Lauderdale men are putting millions into it, and a sizable portion of the money will be spent to raise eight hundred acres safely above high tide.

If you can keep your head when all about you are losing theirs, it's just possible that you haven't grasped the situation.
Jean Kerr

Your manuscript is both good and original; but the part that is good is not original, and the part that is original is not good.
Samuel Johnson

It was loud in spots and less loud in other spots, and it had that quality which I have noticed in all violin solos, of seeming to last much longer than it actually did.
P. G. Wodehouse

"Sing Until Tomorrow" had two strikes against it. One was the fact that you couldn't hear half of it. The other was the half you could hear.
Walter Kerr

This novel is not to be tossed lightly aside, but to be hurled with great force.
Dorothy Parker

I have knocked everything in the show except the knees of the chorus girls, and God anticipated me there.
Percy Hammond

I never read a book before reviewing it; it prejudices a man so.
Sydney Smith

C H A P 6 T E R

Writing Opinion

WHAT IS OPINION WRITING?

For our purposes, opinion writing includes not only editorials, but also public affairs columns, humor columns, and reviews.

Opinion writing offers journalists more freedom to express their ideas than standard reporting does.

Comment is free but facts are sacred. *C. P. Scott*

"The trouble with the Baptists is that they aren't held under water long enough," wrote editor William Cowper Brann.

"Heywood Broun is a one-man slum," wrote columnist Westbrook Pegler.

"Tallulah Bankhead barged down the Nile as Cleopatra last night—and sank," wrote drama critic John Mason Brown.

Listen for phrases like these in any small-group conversation: "I think . . ." "But the way *I* see it . . ." "Let me tell you how it *really* is . . ."

Like anyone chatting with others, journalists enjoy stating their opinions. Why do reporters aspire to write opinion pieces? Many editorial writers, columnists, and critics bask in the company of the famous—and some opinion writers are themselves famous. Moreover, most writers of opinion pieces are specialists, and specialists are usually better paid than generalists. Even so, some editorial writers, columnists, and critics practice the craft of opinion writing because they are so convinced of the value of public affairs, or literature, or the arts that they want to share their understanding and involve others. Certainly, whatever complex of reasons draws them to this field, writers of opinion pieces are among the most dedicated journalists;

133

William Cowper Brann

Texans had gulped down a strong dose of civilization by the 1880s—barbed wire held cattle, booster clubs were booming, and religion had set in—but the hard-knuckle scene in the office of the *San Antonio Daily Light* on the morning of July 29, 1884, was not unusual; William Cowper Brann was involved.

A skinny, tall-standing six-footer, Brann was aflame in his fashion, dictating a story for the next day's paper. In walked W. H. Brooker, a local lawyer, hugely built from his shoulders to his hips. Brann, wiry and unafraid, hadn't a chance. Brooker had only one arm, but he weighed 225 pounds to Brann's 150. As they closed, Brooker bludgeoned the lean editor down. Every time Brann pushed up to rise from the floor, Brooker raised his hard fist above his head like a sledge and hammered him down again. Then, triumphantly, he warned that the editorial Brann had printed the day before must be retracted or Brann's brains would be blown out.

Rather than retracting, Brann stuffed a pistol into the waistband of his trousers the next day and went hunting. Watching from his office as the slender, beaten Brann walked the streets with the purposeful air of a butcher, Brooker was unnerved and sent two friends to withdraw the threat.

Brann was probably the world's worst fighter, but he would battle anybody, anywhere, with anything. Among his antagonists were three college students, three newspaper editors, and an old man who thought his daughter had been insulted—all of whom won. There is no record that Brann ever bruised anyone in a fight, or backed down from one. He always came battling back like an animated sponge, drawing strength from the taste of his own blood.

In fact, it was clear from his birth in 1855 that Billy Brann was spirited. Noble H. Brann, a Presbyterian minister in Milton Station, Illinois, was unable to raise the boy when Mrs. Brann died in 1857. The two-year-old was turned over to foster parents, but Preacher Brann kept a dismayed eye on him. Once, long after his son had become notorious, his father reminisced: "Well, Billy, you always was a mighty bad boy. I kind of calculated you'd go to hell some day, but Praise God, I never thought you was bound for Texas."

On Brann's way to Texas, he had close-clipped, dark brown hair; the erect, easy figure who was job-hunting in the *St. Louis Globe-Democrat* office in 1883 appeared to be anything but a rabblerouser. One look at the firm, kind face inspired liking in Editor Joseph McCullagh. Brann was hired.

McCullagh admitted to a faint uneasy feeling, however. This Brann not only seemed to have read everything but he also talked about music, art, and theology with the loving respect of a professor. It would be good to have an educated man around, but a mannerly reporter? He'd need some stiffening to get by in the brawling world of St. Louis journalism.

Wanting his new man to succeed, McCullagh gave Brann two warning bits of advice: "Journalism is knowing where hell will break loose and having a reporter on the spot," and "When I tell you to go after a man, you can't just pour a barrel of vinegar over him; you've got to put a drop of vitriol on him."

Brann was a learner; he reversed the counsel, *causing* hell to break loose wherever he was, and pouring a barrel of vitriol over his opponents.

One of his first *Globe-Democrat* items gave this estimate of a windy politician:

> Nature plays no favorites. When she gives a man a lower-case brain, she makes amends by supplying him with a display-type mouth.

After several such bites at the body politic, Brann was hastily assigned to a less explosive area, society, but he dealt body blows even at the elite:

> That Annual intumescence of anthropoid idiocy known as the Veiled Prophets Ball. Everybody who entered that Circean Circle was required to personate an ape—to wear a full-dress suit. I hid behind a fat man who resembled nothing so much as Mark Twain's frog with his belly full of bird shot. I took a brief survey of the assembled imbeciles, beat a hasty retreat and threw my borrowed plumage in the wood-box.

Fired by the *Globe-Democrat* for laying open too many of St. Louis' more elegant hides, Brann reached Texas. He was an editorial writer for the *Galveston Tribune*—just long enough to insult that paper's sacred cows—and lasted five months with the *Galveston News*.

Moving to Austin, Brann announced publication of *The Iconoclast*: "This magazine will not pander to the prejudice of any creed, class or calling, but will tell the truth as I understand it—as long as men can be found who have the stomachs for it."

The first issue kept the promise. There were articles entitled "The American Press—Its Hypocrisy and Cowardice," "The Criminal's Pards— Legislators and Lawyers," "Female Chastity—What Is It?," and "Playing the Pimp—The Personal Column in Newspapers."

The reactions were invariably spirited. One reader stopped Brann on the street and said: "Mister Editor, I found a grammatical error in your paper." Brann snapped: "The hell you say! What else did you find—any ideas? Or would you recognize one?"

His single-minded assaults on sham made Brann the literary love of many an intelligent man ("Brann is an intellectual buzzsaw," a Harvard professor told his classes), and the verbal fire that burned through every issue made delighted readers of the uneducated. Even those who gritted their teeth and wanted to throttle the editor were magnetized by *The Iconoclast*.

(continued)

William Cowper Brann *(continued)*

Called the "Apostle of the Devil," Brann had almost given up trying to explain that he was not an atheist but a deist, who rejected revealed religion but believed in God and immortality. He went far out of his way to bait the unbelievers.

"I don't believe anything I can't prove," an atheist exclaimed to Brann.

"Then why," he replied, "do you take such a lively interest in your wife's children?"

The name Apostle of the Devil trailed him when he moved to Waco to publish *The Iconoclast,* and Brann helped promote his magazine by making the most of the title. "I admit a personal fondness for Satan," he said, "because he sat into the game with a cash capital of one snake and now he's got half the globe grabbed and an option on the other half."

On a lecture trip to St. Louis, the editor admitted to his friend William Marion Reedy, editor of the *Mirror,* that even though the circulation of *The Iconoclast* was now more than 100,000, he was losing faith in his approach to reform. "But I've got to attack personalities to get the people to consider principles."

Reedy answered that if Brann attracted attention by shocking readers, he could hold them only with continued shock treatments. Brann became despondent. "I'm only a fad. I'll pass away when my vogue is done."

Brann's last day came on April 1, 1896. At four o'clock in the afternoon, Brann went to town to get a shave. He was returning after five with his business manager, W. H. Ward. A few feet past 111 South Fourth Street, the office of a lawyer named Tom Davis, Brann and Ward heard a shout: "You damned son of a bitch, were you looking for me?" As Davis spoke, he drew his revolver and fired once. The bullet slammed into Brann's back. Ward leaped, grasped the muzzle of Davis's revolver, and the second bullet ripped through Ward's hand.

As the first shot hit him, Brann began a staggering turn, pulling his revolver as he wheeled. He gunned Davis down with one shot. Davis raised himself on his elbow and fired twice more, unsteadily. Brann, who was standing again after the shock of the first bullet, felt the slugs tear at him, but he continued to fire. Every bullet hit the prostrate Davis.

Only the shot that had hit Brann in the back proved to be a serious wound. It had clipped a large bronchial artery as it went through his body. Lying in the hospital, Brann began to improve, but as his pulse grew stronger, the injured vascular wall gave way and hemorrhage began. Brann died seven hours after the fight.

Brann's enemies breathed more easily; it was said that it had been God's will that the dark spirit of *The Iconoclast* had been gathered up. Waco and Texas could go back to civilizing now that the Apostle of the Devil was traveling to the place he called "Satan's celebrated winter resort."

their commitment is reflected in records showing that they often work happily in the same positions for decades.

The prospect of writing opinion pieces lures many reporters, at least partly because the ideas permitted in editorials, columns, and reviews can make news stories seem to be bound in straitjackets. Unfortunately, some reporters find that they need more than the talent they have developed for research to help them in opinion writing. The style of opinion pieces is quite different from that of standard news reports. Most excellent opinion pieces are probably written by expressive essayists who have also mastered the perceptive reporter's fact-gathering techniques.

All opinion writing can take a variety of forms: It relies on evidence to support criticism and on fresh, appealing language; it should be balanced and unified.

Criticism comes easier than craftsmanship.   *Zeuxis*

Editorials, columns, and critical reviews differ in many ways, some of them subtle. First, though, consider the qualities that characterize *all* opinion pieces:

1. *No opinion piece follows a set formula.* Effective opinion pieces take many forms, and we will present some in this chapter. The writer need not search desperately for *the* formula for an editorial, a column, or a critical review; it does not exist.

2. *Always support all critical comments.* Everyone knows that to win in a debate, one must give examples to prove one's case; yet the most common weakness in opinion writing is the lack of illustrative examples. Too many writers are content simply to make charges and pronounce opinions, apparently on the theory that only lowly reporters concern themselves with facts. Merely stating that a governmental or school policy, an actor, a book, a movie, or a ballet is good or bad is never enough. Show why; offer proof. The drama critic who laments that dialogue is limp or cheers that it is lively, the editorial writer who pontificates on the stupidity or wisdom of legislation—both are writing ineptly if they fail to support their contentions with evidence. Not even the most respected editorial writers, columnists, or critics can convince their readers with bald opinion.

3. *Sparkling, appealing language should be part of critical opinions.* Another failing common among opinion writers is laying out facts in the form of a news report and then concluding that those responsible for the situation have either produced pure gold or don't know the difference between gold and peanut butter. Criticism should begin where an opin-

ion piece does. It should not consist of a critical sentence grafted on the end of each paragraph or of a scathing paragraph plastered on at the end of a piece; commentary should pervade the writing. Although opinion writers need not criticize in every sentence, they should use graphic, flavorful words at every opportunity.

Opinion pieces written in the faceless style of most informational news stories do not interest readers. Coin captivating new phrases; vary your sentences. Demonstrate that you know how to use analogies—how to show that *this* is like *that* in such a way that the reader who knows one will come to understand the other.

You need not make your piece a collection of literary pyrotechnics. But few writers ever weave in too many new phrases, too many novel analogies and ideas. The fault lies in the opposite direction: in using words and ideas that have long been decrepit. Any phrase or idea that calls attention to itself and has become worn by years of handling is trite. Avoid it.

4. *The word "criticism" means praise as well as slurs.* One may criticize with praise. Perhaps most important, the writer may sneer and praise in a single piece—and perhaps most often should. Few works are entirely good or entirely bad. Positive or negative aspects will usually prevail, but only in rare instances is there no reason to be both negative and positive to some degree. Mature writers often upbraid "collegiate writers" for "excessiveness," meaning lack of balance.

5. *An opinion piece must be tied together.* Ideally, any piece of writing should consist of sentences and paragraphs that are so smoothly linked to one another that the perceptive reader has a distinct (if subconscious) experience of following a connected line from the first sentence to the last. Most opinion pieces are so short that there is no excuse for a lack of unity. Unity results, however, only from careful organization and close attention to transitions and is nearly always the result of rewriting.

WRITING EDITORIALS

Editorials today tend to be more temperate than those of the past, but the best editorials still convey genuine intensity or humor.

To be caught up in the world of thought—that is to be educated.
Edith Hamilton

Editorial writers themselves complain that editorial pages have come down with a wasting disease. One of the best of these writers, the late Alan Barth of the *Washington Post*, commented, "Most newspapers were started by men who had something to say, but many of them are carried on today by men who merely have something to sell." In the view of former editor James Kilpatrick, however, the principal blame goes to the editorial writers. "We write, all too often, like butchers' apprentices, or Congressmen," he said. "What it is that comes over the editorial writer, when he puts his belly against the Underwood, I cannot say. I feel it often enough myself, God knows. It is a sort of pomposity, trying not to be pompous, a straining after dignity—high school principals addressing the parents and teachers. If there is a hard way to say something and an easy way, nine times out of ten we will pick the hard way. . . ."

Most of the critics of the editorial page, including some editorial writers, seem to lament the death of the vigorous, even violent, prose of old-time writers like H. L. Mencken, who commented, fairly typically, "American women are like American colleges; they have dull, half-dead faculties."

Much of the rich vigor of the Menckens, the Branns, the James Gordon Bennets, and the Horace Greeleys has certainly disappeared. One wonders, however, whether their more vivid slashes would even be effective today. The rising level of education in the United States seems to have led readers to demand that editorial writers do more than present their quirks and prejudices. Unfortunately, too many editors have recognized that readers have new demands without understanding quite what those demands are or how to satisfy them.

The late Arthur Brisbane joked that the editorial aims at "saying in a commonplace and inoffensive way what everybody knew long ago." Some of the caution that characterizes editorials today, however, is praiseworthy. Now, unlike a century ago, most editorial writers recognize that the world contains few absolutes and that many situations have both positive and negative aspects.

Editorial writers explain the news, fill in background, forecast the future, and pass moral judgment.

Thus I live in the world rather as a spectator of mankind than one of the species. *Joseph Addison*

The late Paul C. Edwards of the *San Francisco News* was one of the great editors of this century. As he was about to speak to some of the leaders of his city, he had a highly original thought. Edwards said:

> I have a neighbor and friend I have come to value, respect, and appreciate very much. He moved into my neighborhood some time ago and I was at once impressed with his friendliness. He has a business downtown and we formed the habit of walking to our work together.

Each morning he would greet me with a smile, give his guess as to the weather, comment intelligently on local and foreign news, tell me a funny story perhaps, make some estimate of the value of a fellow citizen to the community, etc. Usually we would fall into discussion of local issues, and invariably he would have clear-cut, positive views, based on broad knowledge of the subject, views with which I did not always agree, but had to respect because of the fine spirit in which they were offered. He was not intolerant or vindictive. He did not hesitate to express himself without equivocation.

My neighbor is only a figure of speech for the newspaper. Newspapers are intensely human institutions, probably more so than any other institution of relative importance that civilization has devised. The editorial is the expressed personality of the newspaper, or should be.

As if having listened to Edwards, the National Conference of Editorial Writers issued this Basic Statement of Principles:

Journalism in general, editorial writing in particular, is more than another way of making money. It is a profession devoted to the public welfare and to public service. The chief duty of its practitioners is to provide the information and guidance toward sound judgments which are essential to the healthy functioning of a democracy. Therefore the editorial writer owes it to his integrity and that of his profession to observe the following injunctions:

1. The editorial writer should present facts honestly and fully. It is dishonest and unworthy of him to base an editorial on half-truth. He should never consciously mislead a reader, distort a situation, or place any person in a false light.

2. The editorial writer should draw objective conclusions from the stated facts, basing them upon the weight of evidence and upon his considered concept of the greatest good.

3. The editorial writer should never be motivated by personal interest, nor use his influence to seek special favors for himself or for others. He should hold himself above any possible taint of corruption, whatever its source.

4. The editorial writer should realize that he is not infallible. Therefore, so far as it is in his power, he should give a voice to those who disagree with him—in a public letters column and by other suitable devices.

5. The editorial writer should regularly review his own conclusions in the light of all obtainable information. He should never hesitate to correct them should he find them to be based on previous misconceptions.

6. The editorial writer should have the courage of well-founded conviction and a democratic philosophy of life. He should never write or publish anything that goes against his conscience. Many editorial pages are the products of more than one mind, however, and sound collective judgment can be achieved only through sound individual judgments. Therefore, thoughtful individual opinions should be respected.

7. The editorial writer should support his colleagues in their adherence to the highest standards of professional integrity. His reputation is their reputation, and theirs is his.

Keep these principles in mind when you review the following attempt by a student to write an editorial. The student's attempt is at the left; a professional editorial writer's edited copy is at the right:

DRAFT—INCENTIVE
TO INNOVATE

The rift between high-tech innovators and politicians veers sharply.

To keep scientific innovators and their business sponsors safe from the rumblings of politicians, the House Republican Task Force on High Technology Initiatives issued its 1985 legislative agenda.

The package is the Republican answer to the Atari-Democrats' proposals.

Instead of targeting industries, as would a planning board of labor, management, and government officials, approved last month by the House Banking Committee, the Task Force would target a process: innovation.

Rather than funding planners' decisions through a special bank, as the House Banking Committee bill proposes, the Task Force recommends creating an economic and social environment to encourage risk-taking, investment, and trade.

EDITED—INCENTIVE
TO INNOVATE

Some House Republicans think the best way the government can help high technology innovation is to stay out of the way.

To keep scientific innovators and their business sponsors safe from the rumblings of politicians, the House Republican Task Force on High Technology Initiatives has developed its 1985 legislative agenda.

The package, released last week, is a Republican alternative to the Atari-Democrats' proposals.

Rather than direction from government, the task force proposes incentive through the market.

Instead of targeting industries, as would a planning board of labor, management, and government officials (a plan approved last month by the House Banking Committee), the Task Force would target a process: innovation.

Rather than funding planners' decisions through a special bank, as the House Banking Committee bill proposes, the Task Force recommends creating an economic and social environment to encourage risk-taking, investment, and trade.

Government's role should be confined to providing incentives for and removing barriers to innovation, Republicans argue. Otherwise, it should leave innovation to the innovators.

The Task Force rests its table of recommendations upon four legs: promoting basic research, providing incentives to investors, innovators, and entrepreneurs; broadening and deepening education and training; and expanding domestic and foreign markets for high-tech products.

Specifically, Task Force members propose altering anti-trust policy to promote joint research, giving corporations tax breaks to fund university research, strengthening patent protection for innovators, easing immigration rules to let foreign students whose technical skills are in short supply stay here, and promoting high-tech exports.

The Task Force recommendations make good sense. We support the plan's general approach. Like the Republican members, we're uncomfortable with the House Banking Committee's idea of letting a government council target industries. We also share a basic suspicion of lawmakers' efforts to pass judgment on issues of science and technology.

Congress, in particular, has not distinguished itself in dealing with long-term, complicated technical problems. Part of the trouble is that lawmakers are too used to picking winners and losers—in the short-term, on the basis of who best persuades. When the nature of winning and losing is not at all clear—as is the case with new industries—Congress can't foresee the consequences of its actions, and falters. The market is the place to impose discipline on technological innovation. Congress is best placed to protect interests of a related but non-market and general nature, such as health and safety.

Government's role should be confined to providing incentives for and removing barriers to innovation, Republicans argue. Otherwise, it should leave innovation to the innovators.

The Task Force rests its table of recommendations upon four legs: promoting basic research; providing incentives to investors, innovators, and entrepreneurs; broadening and deepening education and training; and expanding domestic and foreign markets for high-tech products.

Specifically, Task Force members propose altering antitrust policy to promote joint research, giving corporations tax breaks to fund university research, strengthening patent protection for innovators, easing immigration rules to let foreign students whose technical skills are in short supply stay here, and promoting high-tech exports.

The Task Force recommendations make good sense. We support the plan's general approach. Like the Republican members, we're uncomfortable with the House Banking Committee's idea of letting a government council target industries. We also share a basic suspicion of lawmakers' efforts to pass judgment on issues of science and technology.

Congress, in particular, has not distinguished itself in dealing with long-term, complicated technical problems. Part of the trouble is that lawmakers are too responsive to immediate pressures. Moreover, they simply lack the technical expertise to pick winners in a race with changing players and shifting rules. The market is the place to impose discipline on technological innovation. Congress is best placed to protect more general interests, such as health and safety.

The Task Force recognized that high-tech enterprises are especially hard to regulate. They involve a different time frame and a more secret process than lawmakers might like. Moreover, such endeavors promise less-than-certain outcomes. The Task Force on High Technology Initiatives creatively adapts to these special characteristics. Steering Committee Chairman Ed Zschau especially deserves credit for acquainting Congress with high technology issues and shaping the legislative initiatives.

Several, such as making permanent the R & D tax credit and providing a tax break for business contributions to university research, already are included in the Senate tax bill.

Two others got a boost last week. The full House agreed to loosen antitrust restrictions on joint R & D, and the House Judiciary Committee strengthened protection against semiconductor design theft.

We commended last week's House votes and support the Task Force package. It's a step in the right direction as Congress learns to adapt to the special kind of progress that high technology brings.

The Task Force recognized that high-tech enterprises are especially hard to regulate. They involve a different time frame and a more secret process than lawmakers might like. Moreover, such endeavors promise less-than-certain outcomes. The Task Force on High Technology Initiatives creatively adapts to these special characteristics. Steering Committee Chairman Ed Zschau, R-Los Altos, especially deserves credit for acquainting Congress with high technology issues and shaping the legislative initiatives.

Several, such as making permanent the research and development tax credit and providing a tax break for business contributions to university research, already are included in the Senate version of tax legislation making its way through Congress.

Two others got a boost last week. The full House agreed to loosen antitrust restrictions on joint R & D, and the House Judiciary Committee strengthened protection against semiconductor design theft.

We commended last week's House votes and support the Task Force package. It's a step in the right direction as Congress learns to adapt to the special kind of progress that high technology brings.

The editor made only a few changes to the student's editorial, but note what they are. The first paragraph, for instance, is made more specific.

The effective editorial need not thunder to make a memorable point, a fact that is emphasized by this quiet piece written by Richard S. Davis of the *Milwaukee Journal:*

AFTER THE CONCERT

Last night in the Auditorium, one of the great artists of the day, a tall, handsome woman with sorrow in her face, sang for an audience of thousands, who whispered to themselves: "There simply couldn't be a lovelier voice than that one. Nor could there be a greater gift for singing."

And that was right.

Last night in the Auditorium, the tall woman with the almost tragic face—yes, of course, she was Marian Anderson—stood as she sang beneath a huge American flag. People commented: "There's meaning in that, her singing there against the background of the flag."

And that was right.

Last night in the Auditorium, when the woman sang the "Ave Maria" of the tender Schubert and the hall was as hushed as a house of prayer, there were tears on hundreds of white cheeks, and tears on scores of black cheeks, and when the last golden note had floated away, the listeners said: "No song by any singer was ever more beautiful."

And that was right.

Last night from the Auditorium, the people poured into the crisp night and every face was lighted. The great majority hurried every which way to their cheerful homes, but those who belonged to the race of the incomparable singer had to carry their soaring pride into the ramshackle, tumbledown district where neither pride nor hope can long survive.

And what was right about that?

Other editorials may provide *evaluation* of an event. In contrast to explanation—which presents objective, verifiable facts—evaluation is subjective and necessarily the expression of a point of view that cannot be independently verified and must remain indefinitely a matter of opinion. Note how the following editorial by Rob Elder evaluates by interweaving fact and opinion in the *San Jose Mercury:*

A REGULAR ROYAL QUEEN

"Oh, 'tis a glorious thing, I ween,
To be a regular Royal Queen!
No half-and-half affair, I mean,
But a right-down regular Royal Queen!"
W. S. Gilbert, The Gondoliers

In the fairy tales, queens are beautiful or brave or cruel. They wear jeweled crowns and velvet gowns, and they never carry handbags. They may have the occasional problem with ogres or sorcerers, but they don't have to trade chitchat with loony intruders in their bedchambers. Their sons, handsome princes all, get into plenty of scrapes with girls—girls with dwarves, girls with dragons, girls in towers, girls in enchanted castles, and even goosegirls—but not with porn stars.

Queen Elizabeth II of England is a wealthy middle-aged woman, of average face, figure and fashion, with an unemployed husband, a disagreeable daughter and an uncontrollable younger son. She's never been dwarfed, bedragoned, entowered, encastled (not in an enchanted one, anyway) or even goosed in her whole life, though she's a grandmother.

She's also a descendant of Queen Victoria, George III, Henry VIII, Richard III and William the Conqueror, inheritor of the history, majesty and jewelry of her illustrious predecessors. In a world of imitation margarine and non-dairy coffee creamer, in a world where Suzanne Somers is a superstar and Anna Maria Alberghetti is a celebrity, Elizabeth is the real thing, a "right-down regular royal queen."

So, it's not surprising that many Californians are longing for a chance to see the queen or eat in the same room with the queen or say a few words to the queen or show a semiconductor to the queen or read about other people seeing, eating, talking and showing to the queen.

The briefest association with the queen confers elite status on those who made the guest list at reception and dinner in San Francisco and lunch at Stanford—either because of social standing, political contributions, British origin or luck. Hewlett-Packard, chosen for the queen's tour of Silicon Valley industry, may not style itself "Electronics-maker to the Queen" in the future, but even that eminent corporation gains an added eminence from the royal touch.

On the other hand, the queen's visit may not do so much for the state's image. She'll go back to soggy old England and tell them that California is plagued by rain, wind, tornadoes and earthquakes. Perhaps it's just as well the White House rejected a royal tour of San Jose's sewage treatment plant; floodwaters are surrounding it like a moat anyway.

Editorial writers need to remember that their paramount responsibility is to seek the truth.

The crucial role of journalism in a democracy is to provide a common ground of knowledge and analysis, a meeting place for national debate: it is the link between people and institutions.
William A. Henry III

As our examples should have made clear, there are no restrictions on the form an editorial may take. There is also no restriction on editorial subject matter. Most issues are treated in the straightforward fact-plus-opinion essay style of *New York Times* editorials, but editorial writers can present their commentary in any form, including the dramatic. Or they can make their editorials open letters, addressed, ostensibly, to a single reader. This form was used in the most famous editorial ever published in a newspaper in the United States. Written in 1897 by Francis Church and published in the now-defunct *New York Sun*, the piece responded to an eight-year-old girl who had asked whether there really is a Santa Claus. Church's editorial ran, in part: "Yes, Virginia, there is a Santa Claus. He exists as certainly as love and generosity and devotion exist, and you know that they abound and give to our life its highest beauty and joy."

Still another form is illustrated by an ironic takeoff on the famous "Yes, Virginia" editorial. When the commonwealth of Virginia displeased an editor, he wrote, simply, "Yes, Santa Claus, there is a Virginia."

WRITING PUBLIC AFFAIRS AND HUMOR COLUMNS

Public affairs columns are much like editorials, but unlike editorials, which are the voices of institutions, columns take on their writers' personalities.

This overwhelming impulse is to gyrate before his fellow man, flapping his wings and emitting defiant yells. This being forbidden by the police of all civilized countries, he takes it out by putting his yells on paper. Such is the thing called self-expression.   *H. L. Mencken*

What is the difference between a column and an editorial? Walter Lippmann, probably the most distinguished "thinkpiece" columnist in the history of American journalism, doubted the difference was much more than slight. Writing in the *American Society of Newspapers Editors Bulletin,* Lippmann noted: "No doubt because I started life in the newspaper business as an editorial writer, I always think of a columnist as primarily a writer of signed editorials. There are differences, of course. But even if the two jobs are not identical twins, they are certainly near cousins."

Lippmann's chief concern as a columnist was public affairs. Most editorials are concerned with similar issues. In fact, columns on public affairs would fit comfortably into some newspapers in the space given over to editorials.

In tone and substance some columns are indistinguishable from well-written editorials. The editorial-page editor would find it necessary only to remove the bylines and substitute the editorial "we" for "I." The signature and the pronoun often represent the only real difference between these two kinds of opinion writing. Consider, for example, these excerpts from a column and from an editorial:

THESE FIFTY STATES

A ceremony performed in Washington yesterday afternoon would have

CENTRAL BANKERS

In the ancient Altieri Palace in Rome for four days recently, about 120 astounded the statesmen and politicians who successfully proposed in 1787 the union of these states. There were thirteen then. There were fourteen when the independent republic of Vermont consented to join with the others in 1791.

The Old Thirteen clung to the Atlantic seaboard, looking west into the wilderness that wise men believed . . .

of the globe's most powerful men conferred behind closed doors on ways to stem the outflow of gold from the United States, erase this peril to our currency's stability, and thereby maintain the U.S. dollar as the pivot for the currencies of the free world.

Among the 120 were the top central bankers of Europe and the United States. Heading our delegation . . .

It happens that the excerpt on the left is from an editorial, the one on the right from a column. The important point is that nothing in either would have prevented its being published as the other type.

Several vague differences do separate the great majority of editorials and many individual columns—including some on public affairs—but there is one overriding distinction: the viewpoint of the institution in most editorials as opposed to the viewpoint of the person in most columns. This can best be observed by classifying and examining columns—and by recalling the impersonal tone that informs so many editorials.

One columnist with a distinctive voice is James Reston, who writes on public affairs for the *New York Times*. Reston seldom uses "I," but his personality comes through, especially when he reports on imaginary presidential press conferences to point up unstated truths or makes himself an official of the Society for the Exposure of Political Nonsense to "translate, decontaminate and summarize wordy official documents." The tone of many of his columns is suggested by this lead:

> The Capitol is now engaged in the usual quadrennial diversion of hanging political labels on the Presidential candidates and dividing them into heroes and villains.
>
> This labeling operation is part of the story-telling and myth-making industry in Washington—a vast enterprise—and it is a great convenience because it enables the voter to avoid thinking or dealing with the facts.

Incongruity is the source of humor.

Brevity is the soul of lingerie.   *Dorothy Parker*

Humor is difficult to discuss and describe. Reading the box called Humor Columnists might make you laugh, but it might not move you any closer to understanding humor. If you try to answer the question "What is humor?" you might turn to a dictionary, which will define the word something like this:

Humor Columnists

Andy Rooney, one of the most popular syndicated columnists, has a disarming way of writing about everything. He finds new angles from which he focuses on ordinary aspects of his life, which is not so different from the lives of millions of other Americans. Here he describes typical feelings about a new car:

> If it weren't for the fact that new things are so satisfying to buy, it would be depressing how soon they start to deteriorate after you acquire them.
>
> When I buy a new car, which isn't often, I always wait with a feeling of dread for the day I put the first scratch or dent on it. Sooner or later it has to come. Once I scraped the side of my car on the green paint of the garage door when I was hurrying to put it away during a rain storm.
>
> One new car I had got its first dent in the parking lot of a supermarket. Some guy parked too close to me and the edge of his door banged into mine when he opened it. It wasn't much of a dent, but it doesn't take much to change your attitude toward a new car. . . .

Rooney focuses on one small aspect of owning a new car (or stereo or bicycle)—that calamitous moment when it suddenly is no longer new. It's a feeling we all know. Rooney uses much the same approach in the high-rated "60 Minutes," where his common-man attitude lures viewers as much as it does readers. The experiences he writes about have happened to almost everyone. Nonetheless, his writing is not easily imitated. "My knack," Rooney says, "is for observing something everyone knows about, but from a different angle. I'll take something, say a pencil, and put down everything I can think of about it, what it means to me, what it's meant to history. It isn't hard to type out two pages of notes about the pencil."

Rooney also says, "I'm angered that the things I've done often on television are considered expendable, or not really important. I would match the importance of the pencil to mankind with that of the war in Lebanon or anywhere else."

Rooney's prose may be simply written, but he is a hard worker, in his office at CBS at 8 A.M. many days. "When I'm working on something, my mind is really turned on to it," Rooney emphasizes. "When I did a piece on hotels, there wasn't a thing about a hotel I wouldn't see."

Anyone who wants Rooney's job should know that Rooney does not see himself as primarily a television journalist. "I don't have any great desire to be on camera," Rooney says. "It's not unpleasant, but I'm a writer first. When I'm not turned on as a writer, I'm just the average guy on the street."

Art Hoppe, a humor columnist for the *San Francisco Chronicle,* usually writes his columns in one draft and in less than two hours. Here is a typical Art Hoppe performance.

> Just when employment opportunities in his field were beginning to sky-rocket, the nation's top nude male model, Rock Swett, quit in a huff.
>
> "I'm sick and tired of being thought of as nothing but a sex object," Swett bitterly told a press conference. "How would you like knowing that millions of women under hair dryers all over the country were drooling and giggling and making jokes about you?"
>
> With all the new sex magazines for women now coming out, Swett admitted he was giving up a lucrative career. *Playgirl* magazine is claiming a circulation of one million: *California Girl* has gone national; and a half dozen more similar publications—all featuring nude males—are due on the newsstands by fall.
>
> "Money isn't everything," growled Swett. "It's gotten so I can't go to a nude beach or a sensitivity awareness encounter group without being recognized. Every female thinks this gives her a right to paw and pinch me.
>
> "If I try to discuss Sartre or SEATO, they don't even listen. All they want to do is jump in bed with me. I've got a mind, too, you know."
>
> Swett, described by Swinging Single Gal as "a 6-foot-4 gorgeous hunk of flesh," got his start as second runner-up in the Mr. Cosmos Contest in Atlanta City, where he received a standing ovation in the talent competition by kicking a homosexual into the orchestra pit. . . .

Hoppe, who is less widely known than Art Buchwald, Russell Baker, and Erma Bombeck, may be the nation's best political satirist. Although Buchwald—a genuinely funny man whose column misses almost as often as it hits—is better known, he seems bland compared to Hoppe. Russell Baker is the most gifted writer of the four, but he is primarily a moralist. Bombeck has a clear field in competing with the other three; she is a family humorist. Hoppe has more ideas, and richer ideas, than any of his rivals. Hoppe is also much more a political animal than Buchwald, Baker, or Bombeck. There is an acid quality in much of his political whimsy.

Until one tries to imitate it, Hoppe's method seems ridiculously simple. He observes the foibles of humans, especially those in government; focuses on one of their more dubious enterprises; and then imagines in print that it has been carried to its most absurd extreme and to an absurd conclusion. The result is political commentary that both penetrates and sparkles.

Hoppe's description of his motives is slightly less noble: "I just do it because I like it." However, when he gets his ideas by "reading through the paper until I come to an item that I don't understand—then I explain it to everybody," he indicates that he, too, feels an obligation to educate the public.

Humor is that quantity that makes something funny or fanciful. It includes satire, a work in which vices, stupidities, and follies are held up to ridicule. It also includes wit, which is the ability to make clever or ironic remarks, usually by expressing them in a surprising or epigrammatic manner.

If that definition seems imposing, back up a bit and look for the common denominator that underlies it. *All* humor starts with incongruity. That is, anything incongruous—deviating from the usual—is potentially humorous. For example, if someone you know nearly always wears jeans, you'll become so accustomed to seeing him or her that way that the day he or she shows up with one leg of the jeans cut off, that's *potentially* humorous. It may not seem humorous to you, but someone will consider it funny.

The incongruity that leads to the humorous is usually based on one or two possibilities, or both: *exaggeration* or the *pairing of unlike elements*. Most humorists exaggerate.

Most humor columns focus on the writer's experiences.

Humor is emotional chaos remembered in tranquility.   *James Thurber*

The leisurely informal essays that were once almost as characteristic of journalism as they were of literature are now easier to find as travel articles than as public affairs columns. Most editors seem to prefer that columnists use the little space they have for commentary that makes its point immediately.

The work of Buchwald, Baker, and Hoppe can certainly be classified as humor rather than as public affairs writing. But their columns are devoted more often to government and politics than are those of most humor columnists. This light piece by Bill Vaughn of the *Kansas City Star* (who, like a few other columnists, uses the editorial "we") is more typical of most humor columns.

If you have ever had the feeling that you have failed someone who depended on you, then you have some idea of the way we feel about David Forrest, who works for *Fortune* magazine.

"After going to considerable effort," he wrote to us the other day, "to winnow your name and some others from the great mass of names available, I sent you a letter (transcript enclosed). It included, and this letter repeats, a very good *Fortune* subscription offer—good, that is, if you are indeed a logical but, so far, only a prospective reader of *Fortune*.

"As the earlier letter points out, we're almost sure you're the manner of man who most enjoys *Fortune*. That's because we believe you're in bidding for a business position where the thoughts and facts this magazine provides are likely to pay rich dividends. But now and again we do miss. . . . My apologies if we're similarly off the beam with you."

The first letter (transcript enclosed), which honest, Dave, we don't remember getting, told how we had been selected for this fine bargain:

"We may have made note of you because you recently spoke before a management group, or got promoted or transferred. More likely, your name was chosen for us by one of the better list houses, who are pretty good at putting together such factors as your neighborhood, your company, your title, the books and magazines you order, your alma mater and civic interests—and inferring that, at the least, you're a bona fide man-on-his-way-up."

Look at the position we're in. Here we are going blithely about our business throwing away ads unopened. And all the time the *Fortune* people were winnowing our name, at considerable effort, from the great mass of those to whom they could have made this offer. True, we didn't ask them to go to considerable effort to winnow us, but that's no excuse—they did, and we're sorry.

We had noticed a man, earlier this year, lurking behind a tree across the street, and we guess now he was from one of the better list houses, putting together such factors as our neighborhood, our alma mater and our civic interests, all of which must have given him a pretty good laugh. If that was who he was, he probably figured we were a man-on-his-way-up, having no other place to go.

We are not conscious that we ever, in word or deed, led *Fortune* on to think that we are anything we aren't.

It's just about to get us down, thinking of Dave Forrest going home after a hard day at the *Fortune* office and telling Mrs. Forrest, assuming there is one, "Well, dear, I'm afraid I was off the beam on Vaughn."

"But," she cries, "you were almost sure."

"I know—his alma mater, his civic interests, his neighborhood—I don't know where I missed."

"And after you had gone to considerable trouble winnowing his name," she comforts him.

"If I ever meet the four-flushing little so-and-so I'll winnow something besides his name," he says forcefully.

We hope she had a good dinner that night—pot roast, or something else he especially likes. Perhaps time will heal the pain.

Meanwhile, next time we're in New York we're not accepting any invitations unless we're darn sure in advance Dave Forrest won't be there. We couldn't look him in the eye.

Vaughn's writing is better than that of most columnists, but the kind of column he writes is typical of a great many others; he uses ordinary events as a basis for comment and wry, mock-serious insights to gain wide readership.

Anecdotes rely on conciseness.

Three stagehands saw me naked. One threw up and the other two
turned gay.   *Joan Rivers*

Most columns made up of anecdotes are cousins of a very old journalistic
form, the editorial paragraph, and related to a relatively new one that is
nonetheless fading, the gossip column. Anecdotal columns usually differ
from gossip columns in that the anecdotes are full-fledged little stories about
people, whereas gossip items sometimes consist of only a few words about
well-known persons.

Herb Caen of the *San Francisco Chronicle* sometimes describes himself
as the "last of the breed" of gossip columnists, but his work is seldom like
that of the long-time epitome of the gossip columnist, the late Walter Win-
chell. Instead of producing a series of quips by and about celebrities, he
combines anecdote, paragraph, and gossip in a way that San Franciscans
and visitors to San Francisco find addictive. Although Herb Caen writes
almost exclusively about his city and its people, he has many readers scat-
tered around the world.

Explaining Caen's appeal is difficult, but certain qualities in his writing
are obvious. Nearly all of it is lean.

No matter how frothy his subjects, Caen's columns suggest an active
intelligence at work. Judged by the kind of column he produces—the ultimate test of any journalist's work—Herb Caen is an excellent writer. These
items from his column indicate the reason for his appeal:

A NEW YORK TV CREW, filming a children's show at Hillwood
Day School's campus near Muir Woods, came upon Solomon Ets-Hokin
and Suzanne Walker, both seven, seated on a log. "Why does Suzanne
keep trying to kiss you?" the interviewer asked Solomon, who replied,
"Because she loves me." "Are you going to marry her when you grow
up?" "No," Solomon said, "there are two problems. First, I'm Jewish
and she's not, and second, she loves me and I hate her."

CULINARY ARTS   Candi Wolf of the Beltz Travel Service, guid-
ing a tour around Taiwan a couple of weeks ago, picked up the phone
in her Taipeh hotel (an American one) and ordered breakfast from
room service, as follows: "I'd like orange juice, half canned and half
fresh with the pulp and seeds left in. Then I want two eggs with the
yolks hard and the white runny with undercooked bacon, very fatty.
The toast should be burned on one side and soggy on the other, with
hard butter, and make sure the coffee is bitter and cold."

"That's going to be a difficult order to fill," grumbled room service,
at which Candi observed, "Why? You did it yesterday."

WRITING REVIEWS

"Critic and author bear the same relationship as the knife and the throat," wrote Clifton Fadiman, who should know; he is both a critic and an author. Fadiman was writing about literary criticism, but the antagonisms are so rich throughout the world of criticism that he might have referred to the arts in general.

Anyone who aspires to become a professional critic should not assume that it is necessary to always maintain a tough stance—to live a professional life of challenge and response.

Reading good criticism can help you write good criticism. Some sources of intelligent and well-written criticism include the *New York Times, Los Angeles Times, Washington Post, Chicago Tribune, New Republic, and Atlantic Monthly.*

For literary critics, the great trick is neither to outline the plot nor to ignore it. Let us consider as a guide one talented student's review, in which he grasps contextual reviewing.

COMMENTS

REVIEW

Although some reviewers prefer to color in the context of a book at a later point, this is an excellent example of the value of context. These first paragraphs build a framework for considering the book; the book does not sit there; it has meaning beyond itself.

The sun never sets on American anxiety. Throughout the world, we are defending, imposing, offering, or degrading our national culture. Perhaps the main motive power of this incredible involvement is an amalgam of fear for our national security and a naive desire to export the blessings of our way of life. Certainly the main characteristic of our effort is its mind-boggling size.

Note how the analogy is carried through—"arms . . . encircling . . . clutching . . . grasp . . . holding." One or two more such words would ruin the effect—would call too much attention to the device. This is the kind of thing a writer must *wrestle with: "arms" is the word that goes with "encircling," but "hands" will fit with "clutching" and "grasp." But I can try. . . .*

Minds do boggle. The American public, historically unaccustomed to the immediacy of foreign affairs, reacts by placing unprecedented faith in the executive branch of its government. Our administrative arms encircle the globe, clutching at each crisis, hoping that significant pieces of our influence will not slip through the grasp. But there is so much that we seem intent on holding.

Everything is happening so fast. In the rush of events, milestones can be lost in the commotion. We clear our heads of Korea, the Cuban missile crisis, an unfamiliar road in Southeast Asia or the Russian menace.

Observe especially the smooth transitions—stressed through repeated words between paragraphs 1 and 2 and 4 and 5, natural between other paragraphs—which unify the review.

"interesting" is such a tired word. Consider "rich," "arresting," and "extravagant."

"understood" and "view" could be coupled: "events as he saw them despite an American mission with a radically different perspective."

If we agree on anything in our national debate, it is that nobody likes to be where we are. And as we search for the best alternative from an ever-diminishing number, we hear the most disconcerting cry of all, "I told you so."

David Halberstam's *The Making of a Quagmire* adds volume to that cry. It is a well informed, often first-hand account of tortured years. It documents with interesting detail and dramatic direct quotations, and clearly reveals the position of a journalist faced with reporting events as he understood them despite an American mission with a radically different point of view.

The book is of more than historical interest, however. It is, above all, an account of how a reporter lives, the respect he must have for the anonymity of sources, the alertness and receptiveness he must demonstrate, and the sense of humor that is part of the game. While the land is in a crisis, it is still inhabited by people. And the stories of these people make up the book.

This is a nice, smooth series. Consider: ". . . sense of humor essential to sanity."

Think of this stronger transition: "Halberstam lived these stories. He arrived in . . . "

Halberstam arrived in the war zone by way of 15 months in the Congo, ready to take over for the previous *New York Times* correspondent. It was not long before he found that the role of a reporter had its special problems: "The split between the American press and the American officials continues. . . ."

The rest of this review adroitly uses quotations and examples.

Good literary critics do not outline the plot of fiction; the same general rule applies to reviews of feature films. In the following review, observe how deftly the student, Natalie Beauchene, merely refers to the plot and, at the same time, note her wonderful way with words:

"Kiss of the Spiderwoman" is an absorbing tale of transformation, a tribute to the power of fantasy. Escapism is a way of life for Molina (William Hurt), an aging homosexual window dresser with an eight-year prison sentence for "corrupting a minor." He spends his hours flouncing around a prison cell in some anonymous South American country, re-creating scenes from old movies as his cellmate, Valentin (Raul Julia) looks on, at first with disgust, then with wonder. Valentin is sour and arrogant, a beaten bourgeois revolutionary who is as dominated by his cause as Molina is by his fantasy world.

They are two outcasts from wholly different worlds, thrown together in a single putrid cell. It's a perfect set-up for a story about friendship and respect, learning to give and take—and that's exactly what "Spiderwoman" is. Yet there's more to this movie than that. The themes and morals aren't so clear cut and obvious as to be trite, and their development is subtle enough to allow for unpredictability.

Screenwriter Leonard Schrader (co-author of "Mishima" with brother Paul) manages a retelling of Manuel Puig's 1976 novel that is both sensitive and delightful. Brazilian director Hector Babenco carries his first English-language film off with grace, yet without any certain special touch that could have made the magic of this movie a bit more pervading. It borders on tedious at times, but the strength of the characters and the intrigue of the storyline keep the film on safe ground.

The most fascinating part of the movie is its alternating between reality and fantasy, with flashbacks and, specifically, with Molina's lapses into the slow motion re-creation of his 1940's movie, "Her Real Glory." The two thus escape the boredom, pain and unpleasantness that encompasses their daily lives. But Molina more than retells the movie for Valentin. He lures his cellmate inside it along with him until the movie world is as vital as the other, "real" world for both men. Filmed in pseudo black-and-white, Molina's movie is like a tinted photograph, a somewhat romanticized reality in both appearance and action. For even before Molina says "I always identify with the heroine," we can already see that the heroine of his movie, Leni Lamaison (Sonia Braga), is a romanticized version of Molina himself, and the events and emotions in Molina's life continually draw closer to Leni's.

Such parallelism could be laughably obvious, but here it's not. It's almost surprising, in fact, and certainly pleasing. The comic melodrama of Molina's movie prevents it from suffocating the audience with meaning, and instead allows them a delightful escape along with Molina and Valentin. Braga is wonderfully purse-lipped and waxen as Leni, "the foremost diva of French song." She is a pure and devoted (yet exotic) French patriot who falls in love with an Aryan bigwig from the invading Nazi army, played properly stiffly by Herson Capri.

At first, Valentin is offended by the shallow phoniness of Molina's movie, evidenced as he peers outside his cell and yells, "They're killing one of my brothers and I'm listening to your f——ing Nazi movie!" But gradually Valentin begins to open up and learns to indulge himself in the romantic side of the movie and of life, at least momentarily rising above his narrow-minded politics. Molina is unqualified in his kindness and generosity, sharing his food with Valentin and nursing him when he's sick and debilitated. Through Molina, Valentin learns humility and becomes more of a man. Raul Julia makes Valentin's transformation subtle, yet believable, and though his tenderness near the end is not quite as passionate as it might be, the stiffness is inherent in the character, not the actor.

Molina is also transformed through the course of this encounter. The love and happiness he shares with Valentin lead him to a new self-respect. He gradually sheds the heavy theatrical make-up and vivid queenly gestures so dominant in the beginning of the movie, and begins to develop a natural glow and quiet reservedness. Valentin's open criticism of Molina's lack of seriousness ("Your life is as trivial as your movies") strengthens Molina, and by the end, when Valentin says "Never let yourself be humiliated again," we feel confident that he won't.

In playing Molina, William Hurt has successfully overcome a challenging role, very different from his other recent roles ("Body Heat," "The Big Chill"), and one in which many have called him miscast. Granted, his large, masculine form creates a certain awkwardness as Molina acts the role of his movie heroine, but that only adds to the humor of the character. Hurt, who took the Best Actor award at Cannes for this role, is an unlikely queen, yet manages to make Molina real—real enough to evoke a full range of emotions, from disgust to delight to sympathy. He is charming and charismatic, and really the star of "Spiderwoman" in more ways than one.

The film's one major flaw is near the end of the movie, when Molina is attempting contact with Valentin's group outside of the prison. In spite of his realization that he is being followed by the police, Molina foolishly neglects to abandon his mission, threatening himself as well as Valentin's associates. Instead of admiring Molina's determinedness and loyalty, one wonders at his stupidity. The behavior is out of place and out of character.

Although overall this movie merits much praise, again, it is slightly lacking. Lacking what, it's hard to say, but somehow even the ending sequence where Valentin finally escapes in his own "movie" fantasy with the woman of his dreams misses the powerful punch it should have delivered. The missing emotionality and wonder may be the fault of Babenco, and it may not. But if "Kiss of the Spiderwoman" is indeed a tribute to fantasy, then the feeling one is left with is not quite fantastic enough.

In the following review of a musical, note especially how Lisa Dray, a student, adroitly describes the many actors and actresses. The ability to describe is essential in anyone who hopes to become a professional reviewer.

COMMENTS	REVIEW
Observe how this writer chooses her words. She wrote this final copy after writing three drafts.	In the quiet of a Los Angeles theatre, small green cat eyes darted like fireflies though the blackness of the audience. From the crevices of the stage, decorated with the trash of a musty Brooklyn alley,

cats began to appear; not genuine felines, but humans elaborately decorated as cats, walking on two legs and clawing at the air. One by one they darted onto the stage in brief flashes, then mystically retreated to the security of the junkpiles.

Here she uses vital information, but it does not dominate this paragraph.

Thus begins the production of the Broadway musical CATS. From the first musical score that cuts through the air in a dynamic collage of notes to the final twang of a high pitched piano key, the company of CATS dances and sings its way through one of the most provocative and entertaining musicals of the 80's.

Again, more information, but the writer makes this a pleasing paragraph with more description.

CATS, adapted from T. S. Eliot's *Old Possum's Book of Practical Cats,* was set to music by Andrew Webber in 1977. The company, comprising 35 young talented artists, tells the story of the hypersensual, cold, warm, elastic and mysterious life of cats. The narrative verses of song and dance are intended not only to depict the tragic, yet lyrical world of the feline, but are also intended to parallel the lives of humans and cats.

CATS stages the production in a darkened alley, lit only by the dulled reflection of street lamps. Everything in the feline playground is constructed to a cat's scale. Enormous metal garbage cans, massive tires, bicycle wheels, broken Christmas decorations and even an abandoned car decorate the stage. The lots of garbage enable the cats to tell the story from the pieces of trash they find lying around. The stage itself stretches out like fingers into the wings and sides of the theatre and gives the illusion that the whole audience is an active participant in the story.

Describing the actors' and actresses' costumes becomes a necessary part of this review. Now the readers can see *the performers.*

The first cliché: "cut through the air like a machete."

The ornate costumes of the cats combined both human and feline characteristics, and added to the audience's fascination with the musical. Each cat had an individual personality, as seen through the costume. The hair of each cat was spiked out into angular formations and sprayed in earth-tone stripes. Each cat wore an elastic suit which made body movement precise. The bulging muscles of the dancers could be seen through these leotards as they struck cat-like poses. Each cat was also equipped with a long slender tail that cut through the air like a machete cutting through a thick jungle. The faces of the cats were painted to highlight the slanted eyes and narrow cheeks of the cats. Wiry whiskers jutted from their faces and moved in rhythmic pattern as they danced. Brilliant colors of orange, red, brown, and black blended to form geo-

Again, the writer is describing. This description is vital.

metric shapes similar to those found on the faces of felines.

Dancing was another aspect of CATS that projected the musical's dynamic personality. The dancers contorted their bodies into forms that moved through space with expression and power. From behind a pile of rubbish, a cat leaped fiercely onto center stage and began to dance with authoritative and exaggerated motions as if to show supremacy. One meek female feline shyly began to dance in the blackness of the stage with only a single spotlight to illuminate her motions. Her slow, rhythmic dancing gained momentum as she gained confidence. Then suddenly, the orchestra exploded into a forceful coloration of sound. The entire company of CATS appeared on stage and moved in synchronized beauty.

Rather than continuing with general description, the writer chose to single out one performer. This helps almost all readers to continue reading.

Then as suddenly as the music began, it ceased, and silence filled the theatre. On stage, the spotlight highlighted an old cat, dressed in shaggy grey fur, who began to mimic the dancing of the younger cats, but tripped and fell to her knees in desperation. The old cat began to dance and sing with the emotion of a small child about her memories of youth, in what was the most moving and touching scenes in the musical. As her despair became nulled by the sweet words of her song, she slowly began to rise and dance with grace and splendor. The 35 voices of the company then combined effort with the old cat in her sentimental song about distant memories. The impact of their voices shook the audience like a thunderbolt and echoed in every corner of the theatre. Thus CATS concluded with all the power and force that was evident in the first magical scene.

A fine conclusion.

CATS has been a Broadway production for five years and continues to stun audiences with its creative theme and electrifying antics. In describing CATS, Lloyd Webber, the producer, commented that CATS is "Nothing short of magic" and has "an enthusiasm for the musical theatre bordering on insanity."

EXERCISES

1. To make certain you know that there is no formula for an opinion piece, cut from a big daily newspaper three editorials, three columns, and three reviews. Rank each of them in the order that is most pleasing to

you: 1, 2, 3. Be prepared to explain in class why you liked the pieces you ranked first and how the three pieces in any one of the three categories differed in form.

2. Choose a topic that is making your campus come alive with controversy. Write an editorial of at least 400 words. Would you have approached the topic differently if you had been writing a public affairs column? Explain.

3. Choose a subject, preferably a campus-oriented subject rather than a municipal, national, or international topic. Write a column in about 700 words.

4. Attend a movie or a dance performance, or read a book. Write a review of the subject you have chosen in at least 500 words.

The message of the medium is the commercial.
Alice Embree

Radio, the great syllabic storm of the age.
Edwin John Pratt

Radio sets are like continuously firing automatic pistols at silence.
Max Picard

No one can write a script for a spontaneous demonstration.
Anonymous

If there had been television cameras at Gettysburg, this would be two countries; the carnage would have caused the North to let the South go.
George Will

Children spend so much time watching TV that they are changing from irresistible forces into immovable objects.
Jack Paar

Being natural beats any performing skill and on television, being a bit ugly helps.
John Updike

Will the day ever come when a newscast ends without the anchorpeople shuffling all their papers into a pile? Does neatness count, or what? And since most of these worthies read "thuh news" off a Teleprompter, what's on those papers?
Herb Caen

7
C   H   A   P   T   E   R

Writing for the Electronic News Media

Writing news stories for the broadcast media is much like writing news stories for print. On the other hand, even those newspaper readers who hurriedly glance at the day's headlines and skim the leads can review, reread, and decipher the words used to describe events; listeners and viewers cannot. The difference is crucial for writers and editors.

TELEVISION

When Serena Wade and Wilbur Schramm of Stanford University studied the mass media, they came to this conclusion: "Television is more likely to be the more major source of public affairs information for females, non-whites, and farm and blue-collar workers with little education than for others; whereas the print media are more likely to be the major source for the highly educated groups; white, male, professional, managerial, and white-collar workers; and high-income groups than for others." This study is now twenty years old. Some educated people, who once chose only print, are now turning to television news as well.

Most working-class Americans rely on televised news, which is shorter and shallower than reporting in the print media.

If the idea of democracy should ever be invalidated, it will be because it came about that more and more people knew less and less that was true about more and more that was important.   *Willard Wirtz*

161

At television's beginning, some viewers were disappointed because televised news reports were so short. Local news and network news programs were all limited to fifteen minutes. A story would run one minute and fifty-eight seconds or even fifty-four seconds. On occasion, a story ran as long as two minutes, and very occasionally one would run almost three.

Then television news programs were lengthened to thirty minutes, which seemed to give broadcasters plenty of time to devote more reporting to each story. The thirty-minute news program works out to about twenty-four minutes of news with six minutes given to commercials. Even though television news programs had become longer, though, stations continued to restrict their broadcast stories. They included many more stories. As a consequence, television reports so little about each subject covered during a news program that too-simple stories are usually inevitable.

Now, though, television executives have gradually learned the power of news that can be shown. This is why Ted Koppell's "Nightline" started airing every weekday after prime time. This is also why David Brinkley designed a Sunday program in which Brinkley, George Will, and Sam Donaldson shared thoughts with many viewers. On many television stations, some morning and afternoon hours are given over to programs named "People," "People Are Talking," and "Magazine Show."

Another aspect of television news is encouraging. Although network news has much the same time limit that local stations have—almost as though the executives were saying, "You can't give it two minutes; the span of the audience attention is *short*"—there are excellent specialists in network news. Some concentrate on trials and report on justice, and there are also many able political reporters. Such journalists have developed a range of expertise that enables them occasionally to report brilliantly in spite of crushing time limitations.

In television news, pictures of news events overshadow words.

Every medium has to live with its weaknesses and exploit its strengths. Television's strengths are, of course, its immediacy and its ability to deliver both picture and sound to a very wide audience. Its weakness is that it cannot deliver anything like the volume of news found in good metropolitan newspapers, that it cannot be laid aside and perused at a more convenient time. . . . But that is what we are, an orange, and it would be pleasing if our critics would stop complaining because we are not an apple.   *William McAndrew of NBC*

In one thoughtless paragraph in an otherwise perceptive article about depictions of violence on television news, Henry Fairlie, who writes knowledgeably about the mass media and American politics, reveals that he is

David Brinkley

It is doubtful that television commentators will ever be able to swing with all the freedom of the newspaper columnists, but that is not likely to affect David Brinkley. For although he, too, is an ex-reporter (Wilmington, N.C., *Star-News* and United Press) and is sometimes impatient with the superficial scope of television, he is one of the few newscasters who range widely enough to be considered a commentator—one who expresses attitudes. It is a measure of Brinkley's subtlety that his commentaries are broadcast by ABC, which was long notable for neutral tones. And they are subtle expressions indeed, for Brinkley seldom uses "It seems to me," "My opinion," and other baldly editorial lead-ins, and he never betrays elation or outrage.

He never identifies gods and devils as explicitly as did radio commentator Fulton Lewis, Jr. But anyone who watches him regularly can visualize his gods and devils—and venture confidently that Brinkley and Fulton Lewis wouldn't get along very well. More to the point, watching Brinkley, once you have watched one of the more conventional television newsmen—say, Dan Rather—makes it clear that Brinkley's presentation is a network of nuances. He reacts, often with a tone of irony and the facsimile of a smile.

Although many television critics have hailed the Brinkley style as a refreshing new phenomenon, it has been developing for more than forty years. Leaving United Press in 1943 to write news scripts for NBC in Washington, Brinkley was encouraged by News Manager William McAndrew to go on radio—"in the early mornings so that nobody would hear me." In 1953, NBC tried him on television, but again at a time (Sundays at noon) when only news addicts would know about it. However, McAndrew and others who considered Brinkley talented were soon high in the NBC councils. In 1956, Brinkley and Chet Huntley, who was already taking shape as the fluent answer to CBS's Ed Murrow, were sent to the national political conventions. Assigned to spell each other, they decided instead to work together. "I did what I'd been doing for years," Brinkley says, "but now people were paying attention."

The nation was so attentive to Brinkley's relaxed irony and so taken by his chemistry with Huntley that NBC immediately set up the "Huntley-Brinkley Report." It built such a strong following that when Huntley and Brinkley returned to the conventions in 1960 they spread-eagled the field, winning 51 percent of the audience to 36 percent for CBS and 13 for ABC. In 1964, their audience was nearly double the combined audiences of CBS and ABC.

One of the more astute television critics, Robert Lewis Shayon, held that the "Huntley-Brinkley Report" owed some of its popularity to the

(continued)

David Brinkley *(continued)*

fact that Huntley and Brinkley were essentially moralists. Wry commentary was only the frosting; the program was distinctive for the revelatory footnotes that gave flesh to facts.

Thinking of Brinkley as a moralist is a great improvement on a more widespread belief; that he is a topical humorist who just happens to be working at ABC on a weekly news program rather than on a comedy show. A light edge is often visible, but the stark difference between Brinkley and the wisecrackers is apparent.

The thrust of Brinkley's appeal is not waggery; it is his mood of inner amusement. "This is the convention," he once said on opening day, "and there are those who love it." He described the Republican Convention as "an honest-to-goodness convention; last time it was a coronation," and said of Senator Everett Dirksen: "When he talks, the words come out distinctly like little rubber balloons filled with helium; they just float up to the ceiling."

Hundreds of television screens that do not carry the Brinkley program do carry imitations of the distinctive Brinkley style. Many newscasters have taken to clipping their words in Brinkley's decisive way and try to add a touch of wry humor to at least one item in each program. They usually fail because, as a man points out, "The secret of his success is his ability to be humorous in a few words. He writes very economically. Others try to match him. But they start from the 50-yard line, and by the time they get to the goal, their attempted humor is too labored. Brinkley can do it from inside the 20."

On Sundays at ABC, Brinkley is still the master over newer stars such as George Will and Sam Donaldson. Although Will and Donaldson are forceful commentators, they defer to Brinkley when he states the facts in his own tasty capsules.

---

one of many print journalists who do not quite grasp the power of pictures on television:

However paradoxical it may seem, the only immediate answer to most of the problems of television news lies not in pictures but in words. Given the powerful impact of pictures, the words covering them must supply the corrective. Most television reporting just describes pictures and, by doing so, reinforces them. But the object of words in television news should be to distract from the pictures, to say: "It was not quite so. This was not the whole story." Pictures simplify; the object of words should be to provide qualification and complication. Pictures involve; the object of words should be to detach the viewer, to remind him that he is not seeing an event, only an impression of one.

Nothing more quickly identifies a journalist devoted to print than such a profession of faith in the predominance of words. Powerful as they are, words cannot correct nor distract viewers' attention from pictures of news events. Attempts to contradict news pictures with words will merely irritate the audience. No one has decreed that the picture must dominate television news, but viewers' perceptions make pictures dominant. If television news-writers attempt to soften the impact of violent scenes by writing, "This is not a true picture of Detroit today; most of the city was peaceful," the power of their words to soften the reality of the scenes pictured approaches zero.

This fact worries responsible television journalists who are well aware that the camera can lie or at least distort the truth and who are aware that distortion grows inevitably from presenting a fragment of life in a way that suggests the viewer is seeing the whole. Broadcasters attempt to cope with this problem, often by trying to balance the elements of news programs so that violence, for instance, does not overshadow contrasting elements of the news. Sometimes the newscaster mentions *after* pictures have been shown that there have been other, more tranquil activities during the day. But television journalists do not try to counteract pictures of news events with words while the pictures are on the screen. The immediacy of the visual is the power of television. For the television journalist, words are only a limited partner in the enterprise: They must be geared to news pictures. This requirement has been recognized since the rudimentary beginnings of the medium.

The first "news spectacular" was telecast, in makeshift fashion, on the day Pearl Harbor was attacked in 1941. When the report of the bombing came by radio, CBS executives decided to go on the air with a sustained television news report. It was to be shown over WCBW, which had been developing news techniques during five months of experiments.

Those few who owned television sets at that time must have been at-tracted to the new medium by the novelty of that first telecast, but the presentation had little impact. Richard Hubbell pointed out on maps the locations of some other Pacific Islands that were liable to be targets of attacks. The vulnerability of Singapore and the Philippines was made clear, again on maps, and the last known positions of the ships of the United States Pacific Fleet were pointed out. Political and military analysts were put before the cameras. They, too, relied heavily on maps. What the handful of viewers saw, primarily, was an audiovisual program in the simplest sense: speakers using stock visual aids.

Immediate development of television was a by-product of World War II, and television's news function grew rapidly after the 1948 national po-litical conventions. As the CBS handbook *Television News Reporting* points out, however, "no matter how complex and varied is the arsenal of television news today, it has not discarded the basic techniques utilized on that Sunday in December, 1941."

Television writers must keep news pictures in mind as they fashion each sentence. As the authors of the CBS handbook emphasize:

Television news is a picture of the news; it is a factual, concise presentation of news which, in one way or another, has an effect upon the people who turn to your program for a picture of what is happening to their world. . . . A television program may reach back in time for some of its content; this development that has broken in the last hour. The television news show, because of its premium on time, does not lose any of the good newsman's habit of reporting all there is to report of the day's news. Limited though it is in time and space, television news must do more than ordinary justice to the major stories of the day. Because one of its chief concerns is to allow its viewer to *see* the news, television has freed itself from the obligation of the newspaper to make the news clear through printed words. . . . The television news writer does not have an easy task. Working against time, he has to produce scripts which are exactly clocked. In spite of limited show time, he must somehow manage to cram in all the pertinent facts, often dealing in twenty seconds with events which a newspaper covers in 12 column inches.

Despite the youth of the medium, general guidelines have developed, emerging gradually from the trial and error of early days. These guidelines enable television newswriters to cope with the complexities of work speedily.

Use many words for camera; few for film.   When the studio camera is focused on the newscaster, words dominate. Although newscasters should not orate, when they are on camera, pictures are subordinate to words. What is said dominates. There is nothing difficult about matching sight and sound during the straight newscast; the picture is simple, and viewers can give their full attention to words. But when the program features filmed scenes, the viewer must mesh words and pictures differently. The picture draws attention; words must be subordinated. Ideally, words become supplementary, explaining and blending with the mood of the film. Rich writing is almost certain to conflict with the drama of film, which demands the viewer's focused attention.

See the film before you write.   Ideally, writers should be on hand when news film is being edited, following the picture process through from the point at which a filmed scene is considered as a possible part of a news show. This approach enables them to help select the pictures they can use best to underscore significance. When time is too short to allow writers to participate in editing film, they must use spot sheets: detailed listings of the order, contents, and time of each scene—a word outline of the film. It is obviously to their advantage when the spot sheets are precise and complete. Otherwise, the writers are liable to have to write in a vacuum, guessing whether or not their words will fit each moment.

Let the picture describe.   Nothing is more likely to irritate viewers than hearing extravagantly detailed description of scenes they can see clearly.

Such descriptions bludgeon a point to death. Instead of duplicating filmed scenes in words, cue the scenes, sometimes in incomplete sentences: They should *identify* people and *explain* action, allowing both people and actions to speak for themselves. If writers must generalize to supply context for a scene, their generalizations should come before or after the film or against scenic shots; trying to make points that do not bear directly on the scene just when the action is at its height is confusing. Perhaps most important, television writers should not share the radio writer's fear of "dead air." Moments of silence are welcome on television, and overwriting is the mark of the novice. No competent professional will attempt to compete with dramatic frames of film.

Help viewers get ready to listen to the facts in televised news reports.

It is the disease of not listening, the malady of not marking, that I am troubled withal.   *William Shakespeare*, Henry IV

Borrowing from the techniques of radio writing, television writers learned long ago that viewers must be allowed a few seconds for orientation before they are prepared to absorb a series of hard facts. The strong force of pithy newspaper leads would be wasted on television viewers, and the complicated five "W"s of the standard newspaper lead would clearly be a disastrous beginning for televised news reports. The CBS handbook suggests:

> Give the meaning or significance of the story in the first sentence. Then the viewer has a reason for listening to the basic facts in the second sentence. For example:
> "Hopes for three new city schools suffered a jolt today. The city budget manager said . . ."
> "In Washington, still another hat in the political ring. Senator Blurt announced that he is available. . . ."
> "The French are at it again. For the twenty-second time since World War II, the French government has fallen. . . ."

Use whatever verb tense sounds most natural yet correct in the face-to-face encounter between television reporter and viewer.

To write well, one needs a natural facility and an acquired difficulty.
Joubert

The present tense of radio newswriting is apparent in television newswriting—but so is the past tense common in newspapers and the present perfect favored by the wire services. Beginning television writers are, understandably, confused. Should they write "says" (radio style), "said" (newspaper style), or "has said" (wire-service style)? There is no single answer. Television news uses each form (as radio, newspapers, and wire services do, at least on occasion), and it tries to recognize the peculiar values of each. According to the CBS handbook:

> Present tense carries an air of immediacy and is simple. Past tense is not only as justified on the ground that most actions are in the past; it also has the drama that goes with complete action.
>
> The present perfect shrouds the time of news events that cannot be described in the present, enabling the writer to avoid saying "yesterday" and to avoid monotonous repetitions of "today." (Like radio, television avoids mentioning "yesterday" wherever possible to preserve immediacy.)

You do not have carte-blanche to choose verbs randomly, selecting the one that suits your momentary fancy. Test each story, and decide which tense is the most natural for it.

National television news bureaus are fast-paced and competitive.

The open society, the unrestricted access to knowledge, the
unplanned and uninhibited association of men for its furtherance—
these are what they may make a vast, complex, ever growing, ever
changing, ever more specialized and expert technological world,
nevertheless a world of human community.   *J. Robert Oppenheimer*

The ABC network's Washington bureau demonstrates that television news decisions are the work of confused, anxious, and highly competitive committee members and that one minute of television news time may represent hundreds of hours of behind-the-scene effort by hundreds of diverse souls. The notion of political danger or even of political bias from this powerful medium seems an absurdity as seen from the perspective of the chaotic corridors of ABC-TV, Washington.

The sprawling ABC facility is perhaps a hundred feet long and half as wide, and the room is a jumble of humanity and machinery. At one end— the one nearest the door—are the desks of secretaries to the news executives. Behind them, in the slot, are the assignment editors and crew coordinators. Their desks are arranged like two giant U's, with the closed, base ends bumped up against one another. Along the base of one U sit the assignment editors, responsible for keeping track of what is happening and for deciding which reporters should be where and what needs attention first. Along the other U's base, across from each editor is a camera crew coordinator who must arrange for the Electronic News Gathering (ENG) equipment that will be used by the reporters. If a reporter has a hot story on Capitol Hill, the assignment editor can make arrangements for coverage with the crew coordinator without either of them leaving the desk.

Around the uprights of the U's are assistant editors, each with a typewriter and at least one ringing telephone; and beyond the editors, under the big clocks that show the time in New York, in California, in Moscow, all over the world, are another group of desks for the producers and newswriters. Behind these desks is an open area dominated by two big color television cameras and a profusion of hanging lights. The walls are heavily laden with ABC logos and big colored maps and art-deco stripings. This is where the Washington segment of "World News Tonight" is produced.

In the early morning, there's not much activity in the studio area. Most of the commotion centers on the editors' desks and on a small, glassed-in room adjoining the studio. Behind the glass, twenty of the new thermal-printing wire-service machines sputter quietly, making unfamiliar little hissing sounds as the matrix printer races back and forth across a roll of paper. There are the usual AP and UPI wires—several of which cover local, state, and national news—and there are the specialized services: Agence France Presse (AFP), Reuters, the *New York Times,* and the *Los Angeles Times–Washington Post.* Now and then, one of the editors slides back the glass, and the refined hiss of the machines swells over the room.

The outer walls of the big newsroom open into reporters' and executives' offices. At one end, near the entry corridor, are executive offices and a big conference room where everyone gathers each morning to decide on the news for the day. At the other end are the reporters' offices—some private, some shared, all cramped and modest at best.

By contrast, the offices of the executives—the vice president in charge of operations, the producer, and the chief news editor—are spacious and elegant, with big plush sofas, fine bookshelves, three television receivers, and walls peppered with pictures of former presidents and other celebrities.

By almost 10 A.M., some of the newsroom personnel begin to converge on the conference room near the executive offices. It is a daily ritual: Precisely at ten every morning, the corporate headquarters in New York telephones its bureaus and affiliates in order to plan the news agenda for the day. As the meeting time grows closer, the bureau executives rush into the room and the chief editors and correspondents reluctantly seat themselves around a long table with fifteen or twenty chairs.

In the center of the long table is a telephone and speakerphone that makes it possible to hear and be heard without having to bother with a receiver. One can hear the control switchboard setting up the conference call. This morning it involves Washington, New York, Dallas, Atlanta, Los Angeles, Chicago, and a special line to Camp David, where ABC has taken over a big part of the Cozy Motel in Thurmont, Maryland. The fidelity of the call is horrible. Screeching and rumbling erupt from the speakerphone: "Dallas on the line . . . SQUAWK, SCRRRRRRR, BLPPPP. . . ."

A secretary comes in and distributes a seven-page photocopy of the daily "troop movements." It tells where the ABC reporters are today, where they can be contacted, and what they're up to. There are five pages of stories that may qualify for "World News Tonight." Some of them are complete and "in the can," others are expected to be completed today, and still others are in the work-up stages, coming in within a day or so.

On the speakerphone, the New Yorkers are beginning to mutter among themselves. "I wonder what they *do* up there that takes them fifteen minutes to get going every morning?" someone in Washington asks softly, turning his head away from the speakerphone. Finally, one of the New Yorkers starts calling the roll. As each city is called, the answer comes back "Here." The men and women gathered at the table in Washington now settle into a resigned state of attention.

The Washington bureau has its turn first. Bob Zelnick, the director of news coverage, outlines what Washington will offer. He leans out over the table, craning his neck toward the speakerphone:

> Connally and his wife are testifying at the White House. Brit Hume and Vic Ratner are covering. William Miller is testifying before the Senate Finance Committee. Levinson is covering. We are covering with Levinson because we expect something on capital gains soon. New York already has a piece on this. Wordham will be monitoring the defense authorization veto. We think it's unlikely that there'll be a piece generated on this today. Dunsmore will cover the regular State Department briefing. Bergman is working Claybrook at NTHSA for a future spot. Bell will cover the 3:45 press conference. Gregory is working on a missing cafeteria at GSA.

After a short pause—and without any acknowledgment of the day's plans from Washington—the voice from New York says, "The other two networks were at Congressman Flood's. Did we know he was going to be indicted?" Both CBS and NBC had had camera crews at the Pennsylvania home of Congressman Daniel Flood, who had been indicted the previous day. ABC had scored a clean miss on this one, and the Washington bureau was being held responsible.

"No, sir," Zelnick says. His lips slam shut as if the word "sir" ended with a "p." "We had no information that he was going to be indicted yesterday."

"I thought we had some kind of word several days back on this," the squawking voice says.

"Well, I wasn't working. I'll check it out and find the slip," Zelnick responds, and the matter is ended—at least for the moment. The entire room has grown ever so slightly tense during the exchange. While Washington's role as a news-gathering center is surely uppermost, the shots are still called in New York. Washington missed one, and there is no hiding that from the people in New York.

The New York voice breaks the order of the round robin with another question for Camp David, which is coordinating its summit coverage with the Washington bureau. "Is there some way we can get information on where they're meeting? Anything we can get sketches from?"

"There'll be still pix of the inside, but that's all we can expect," says Camp David.

No answer from New York. Briskly, the voice in the box calls, "Chicago." Chicago reports it may have 330 people in jail in Marion, Ohio, where a teachers' strike is worsening. The Chicago editor suggests putting a crew on that story.

"Absolutely," says New York. Permission granted.

"And we'll get in some footage on the farmworkers. This is coming from our Columbus affiliate. They're a bit more reliable than Toledo."

Los Angeles now takes its turn. A researcher has discovered how to manufacture artificial insulin. The piece will be ready by 3 P.M., the California voice says. The time is important. The speaker meant 3 P.M. Eastern time—network news runs on Eastern time.

"Seattle integration will not happen today because our teachers are on strike," says Los Angeles. "We've also got an AP story on Howard Jarvis out of D.C. Three times before, he's raised cash for Senator Goldwater, Senator Hayakawa, and right-to-work, and every time the money was dispersed before it got where it was supposed to go."

New York asks about Seattle: If the integration story won't run, how about the teacher strike? "We'll have something by noon," replies Los Angeles.

Atlanta takes its turn with an odd assortment of offerings that arch eyebrows around the room. There is a small story on a runoff election, and a routine police story out of Memphis. Jim Bouton is coming to Atlanta from the minors. "Lake Fontina has an excellent feature for Steven Geer and his crew. There's a square dance festival of the world. Sounds like a fun-type piece."

New York asks about a Castro news conference. Miami will cover, says Atlanta, but it is going to happen too late for today.

The Atlanta voice rises and falls in a smooth, rounded Southern way, laconic in its presentation of its stories. Nothing is said from New York except: "Dallas."

"Dresser Industries is all we have," Dallas says.

Atlanta is back on the line to finish its budget. It wants to talk about a "tree-house story" that is destined to make it onto the air that evening as one of those oddities of human activity. "The crew will advise us if it's possibly competitive for tonight's show," Atlanta says. Plunging on to talk about the restive situation in Nicaragua, Atlanta says that nothing seems to be happening there. "If it doesn't, we can think about pulling out of there if it isn't too premature."

The sexual metaphor from the drawling Georgia editor is too much for his many listeners. Everyone around the table in Washington finds this exceedingly funny. Laughter briefly punctuates the static chattering through the telephone lines from Los Angeles and New York.

Atlanta is still not finished. It wants to talk about the lobster war. "I had copies of the *Miami Herald* sent up overnight. It might be a good story and apparently hasn't gotten much play yet."

Suddenly, the telephone is overcome by bursts of clatter and an intermittent shrill tone. New York's turn has come, and it will not be put off. The editor shouts over the noise. The Russians are trying another dissident. There's another Indian flood. ABC is buying videotape of the disaster from UPI's television syndicate, and ABC will add its own announcer's audio at its London studios. Then there are the French and British airshows, which will make good frames for other stories if nothing else. Coverage of the Pope is being shipped to London from Rome.

New York pauses. Everyone pauses.

"Anybody else?" New York asks. The words do not seem to mean what they are meant to say. Everyone bolts, the line goes dead, and the meeting is at an end. ABC's news agenda for the day is set. Unless something really shattering happens, the news will be generated from these possible stories.

As the people file out of the conference room into the noisy chamber of the main newsroom, somebody from the "Good Morning America" staff hails one of the evening news producers. The "Good Morning America" people have secured footage on Congressman Flood. "Screwed up again, huh?" the crewman jeers. "Once again, the morning news saves the collective ass of World News Tonight."

Nobody laughs. New York's mere reference to the missed story was plenty of retribution for everyone. This is national television, where stars will rise and fall on mistakes like that one.

Reporters who work for local television stations are nearly always generalistic and must air very short reports.

... the most universal quality is diversity.   *Montaigne*

Because almost any television station has only a limited number of reporters and camera operators—twelve of each on any one day would be unusually many—and perhaps as much as three hours of local news programs must be filled, reporters are assigned to two, three, and even more stories a day. In-house personnel like writers and producers commonly oversee tape editing and write lead-ins, voice-overs, and follows, so that reporters can cover additional stories breaking before airtime.

The limited number of reporters means that all are generalists and many find themselves covering stories that are not interesting for them or, worse yet, are on subjects or events about which they are poorly informed.

The demands of breaking news stories often mangle preplanned schedules for interviews or the coverage of scheduled events. A camera operator can be in only one place at a time, and a television reporter without camera coverage can do practically nothing.

Sometimes the construction of the news program, which is the program producer's area of authority, will dictate that a reporter not appear on camera for a story the reporter did. This may happen to avoid giving the audience the impression that the reporter has been running from story to story that day. At other times, the anchorperson may deliver the story to increase its impact or enhance his or her image with the audience.

And, finally, the most vexing constraint on local reporters is that fast-paced newscasts limit reporter film/sound or videotape/sound to one minute thirty seconds or even one minute fifteen seconds unless it shows Jesus' second coming.

An experience described by Rollin Post illustrates the time problem. Post, the highly respected political reporter who is one of the very few specialists on local television for KRON in San Francisco, remembers, "During the early days of Senator Ted Kennedy's 1980 Presidential campaign, he was severely criticized for moderating his traditionally liberal positions and lacking enthusiasm for his mission. President Jimmy Carter was dominating the news because of the Iranian hostages. While all Presidential candidates had agreed not to comment on the Iranian situation, the Iranians had American hostages because of security," Post emphasized.

"On a Sunday night, at the end of Kennedy's three-day campaign swing through California, I interviewed him in a hotel room. It was the same day the Shah of Iran had been moved from a New York hospital to Lackland Air Force Base. I asked Kennedy to comment on Ronald Reagan and Henry Kissinger's contention that refusal to grant asylum to the Shah was a betrayal of a loyal ally and it would hurt this country's image throughout the world."

Kennedy, for the first time, ripped into the Shah and condemned any American policy that supported him. Furiously, Kennedy said, "The Shah had the reins of power, and ran one of the most violent regimes in the history of mankind, in the form of terrorism, and of the basic and fundamental violations of human rights under the most cruel circumstances to his own people. How do we justify that in the United States: On the one hand, accepting that individual because he would like to come here and stay here with his umpteem billion dollars that he'd stolen from Iran, and at the same time say to the Hispanics who are here legally that they have to wait for nine years to bring their wives and children to this country? Or someone who comes across the border from Mexico whose only desire is to work and provide for his family that we may even put him in jail?"

Of course, that answer was worth broadcasting. Post also asked Kennedy another question: "But you don't think that these years, though, he wasn't a loyal ally of the United States?"

Kennedy responded with, "I think he was looking out after one person, himself. I think that was the number one interest of the Shah: to look out after himself." Kennedy went on and on in that vein.

Post came into the station with only an hour and a half left before the eleven o'clock news and asked to provide both of Kennedy's answers. Using both of Kennedy's comments would have taken two minutes and fifteen seconds, but the producer said he had time to use only less than a minute. So Post went on the air with Kennedy's answer to the second question.

"This was sad," Post says, "because it was one of those rare instances when a local television reporter broke a story of international importance."

Signals for coordinating the elements of televised reports are included in news scripts.

Dispatch is the soul of business.   *Philip Dormer Stanhope*

The following excerpts are from a student-produced television news program. Two newscasters are seated behind a long table, faced by three cameras. Camera 1, at the far left, centers on the person on the far right. Camera 2, in the middle, focuses on both people. Camera 3, at the far right, centers on the person at the left. The initials at the left coordinate images and sound and are explained in parenthetical notes. Some newscasters prefer to have their scripts typed entirely in uppercase letters. An ellipsis (. . .) indicates that the speaker should pause.

LIVE

        GOOD EVENING. I'M LIZ
EGAN AND THIS IS DAVID FISHER.
        COMING UP NEXT ON THE
CAMPUS REPORT--
        THE SYMBOL AGAINST
APARTHEID--A SHANTYTOWN BUILT
BY STUDENTS--IS DESTROYED.
        AND WE'LL HAVE THE LATEST
ON THE TOXIC WATERS.
        AND A FRESHMAN SKATES TO
THE TOP OF THE WORLD . . . ON ICE.
        THOSE STORIES, PLUS
EXPANDED SPORTS AND A SPECIAL
TOPIC FOR POINT-COUNTERPOINT

. . . ALL NEXT ON THE CAMPUS REPORT.
THE UNIVERSITY'S BLACK STUDENT
UNION EXPRESSED OUTRAGE AT THE
DESTRUCTION OF A CARDBOARD AND
WOODEN STRUCTURE CALLED
SHANTYTOWN.

VTR/VO (Video Tape Recorded/ THE STRUCTURE STOOD IN WHITE
        Voice Over) PLAZA AND SOUGHT TO SYMBOLIZE
THE PLIGHT OF BLACK SOUTH
TRT: 0:18 (Total AFRICANS . . .
      Running Time) MEMBERS OF A STUDENT GROUP
CALLED OUT OF SOUTH AFRICA
HAVE ANNOUNCED PLANS TO REBUILD
AND MAINTAIN THE STRUCTURE.
POLICE BELIEVE THAT THE
CONSTRUCTION WAS VANDALIZED
EARLY SUNDAY MORNING . . .
THE UNIVERSITY PRESIDENT
COMMENTED YESTERDAY THAT THE
VANDALISM UNDERMINES EFFORTS
TO EDUCATE STUDENTS ABOUT
RACISM.
OTHERS SUCH AS SOPHOMORE STUDENT
CHRIS CORR CALLED THE INCIDENT
MORE THOUGHTLESS THAN RACIALLY
MOTIVATED. CORR EXPLAINED:
"SOME GUYS PROBABLY GOT DRUNK
AND KICKED IT OVER."

VTR/VO A SENATOR FROM OAKLAND IS
PROPOSING A STATEWIDE BILL THAT
TRT: 0:25 WOULD PREVENT STATE UNIVERSITY
STUDENTS FROM HANDLING TOXIC
MATERIALS. SENATOR NICOLAS
PETROS OUTLINED THE TWO POINT
BILL THAT WOULD REQUIRE STUDENTS
TO TELL SCHOOL OFFICIALS OF ALL
TOXIC MATERIALS HANDLED.
ALL THIS SINCE UNIVERSITY OF
CALIFORNIA STUDENT SPOKESMAN
JESSE SHAW REPORTED THAT TOXIC

O/C

```
WASTE WAS BEING DUMPED IN
TRASHCANS.
LABS LIKE THIS CHEMISTRY
FACILITY AT THE UNIVERSITY WILL
BE AFFECTED SHOULD THE SACRAMENTO
LEGISLATION PASS . . .
PETROS IS PLANNING TO MOVE
RESTRICTIONS INTO PRIVATE
UNIVERSITIES AS WELL.
FRESHMAN DEBI THOMAS BECAME
A CELEBRITY THIS WEEK . . .
SHE WON THE NATIONAL FIGURE
SKATING CHAMPIONSHIPS,
BECOMING THE U.S.' TOP
FEMALE SKATER. SHE'S THE
FIRST BLACK WOMAN TO DO SO.
HER CLOSEST COMPETITORS WERE
CARYN KADAVY AND TIFFANY
CHIN, WHO WAS LAST YEAR'S
CHAMP. IT WAS CLOSE ALL THE
WAY TO THE END . . .
SATURDAY'S LONG PROGRAM
COMPETITION DETERMINED WHICH
OF THE THREE WOULD WIN, AND
THOMAS EMERGED WITH A NARROW
BUT CLEAR VICTORY.
```

Here is a professional script. At left, words in parentheses identify initials the first time they are used:

```
JOHN HAMBRICK              The Federal Energy Administra-
(ON CAMERA)                tion has begun a round of
                           hearings to get the views of
                           John Q. Public on solving
                           energy problems. One of those
                           meetings was held in New York
                           today.


JOHN HAMBRICK (SI VT/VO)    Those at the New York meeting
(Means "Silent Videotape    sounded familiar themes--hopes
 with Voice Over.")         for solar energy, fears about
```

nuclear energy--above all, though, suspicion regarding the oil companies.

UNIDENTIFIED SPEAKER (SOVT) (Means "Sound on Videotape")

I'd like to see a breakup of the oil companies where they don't completely dominate the energy field and that they own the oil companies, integrated . . . there is no distribution of oil other than theirs . . . where they own the coal mines, and where they own the production of nuclear energy. There is no competition in the energy field.

JOHN HAMBRICK (SI VT/VO)

One young man just looked around and found something valid to complain about.

UNIDENTIFIED YOUNG MAN (SOVT)

And I can't see why this room here, all these curtains are closed. On a sunny day we have all these lights on-- at an energy hearing, mind you. All right? I mean, it starts. You know, this is . . . this is stuff like this. You open those curtains, you'll have sunlight. You won't need all these lights.

JOHN HAMBRICK (ON CAMERA)

(reacts with a furrowed forehead, and says nothing about the young man's observation.)

Here's a second professional story that shows other initials used to guide broadcasts:

JONES

VTR: 27 SOT UNDER
(Means "Videotape Recording,"
which runs for 27 seconds,
and the SOT means "Sound on
Tape" is to be heard
softly under the
narration.)

SUPER: HOLLYWOOD
(Means the word "Hollywood"
is to be superimposed on
the picture at the bottom
of the screen.)

WIPE TO VTR
(Means the writer chose
to go directly to a
videotape of another
story of rain in the area.
To the viewer, a "wipe"
gives the impression that
the second picture pushes
the first one off the
screen.)

Rainwater on the Hollywood
Freeway tonight caused
northbound traffic to back
up all the way from the
downtown area to the Vermont
Overpass in Hollywood. More
than two feet of water
collected on the freeway
before work crews were able
to drain it off.
Some of the lanes were open . . .
but heavy Saturday night
traffic still made driving,
from downtown to Hollywood
difficult through the evening.
At this hour, all northbound
lanes are officially open but
traffic is still congested.

RADIO

Radio, unlike television, relies on words alone; unlike newspapers, it relies on the spoken word. Writers need to learn which style works best on radio.

Radio reporting is much like reporting for newspapers, but radio reports are much simpler and more immediate.

Let thy speech be short, comprehending much in few words.
Ecclesiastes 32:8

Many broadcast journalists have argued that radio is a better medium than television for presenting news. The picture, according to some who support this argument, is the most powerful means of reporting some events, but pictures are often used only because television is a visual medium, rather than because they are essential.

Henry Fairlie, who was quoted at the beginning of this chapter, has pointed out one limitation of television news, contrasting it with newspaper reporting:

> For a good story, both newspapers and television prefer covering a major strike to covering negotiations which prevent a strike. But a newspaper reporter can make negotiations almost as exciting a story as a strike itself; by word of mouth he can collect a picture of the comings and goings which are the essence of negotiation and, by his words in print, vividly describe them. But what can television do with negotiations? It can only show pictures of people arriving at a building and people leaving it. However colorful they may be—and the modern business executive is not normally colorful—these shots do not show exciting news.

Because radio, too, is a "word" medium; it can cover strike negotiations and many other "nonvisual" events without sacrificing its essential strength. In this respect, radio news is like newspaper news. Many newspaper reporters move into radio news and perform well with little coaching, which suggests the similarities in writing for newspapers and for radio. Some of National Public Radio's news programs, such as "Morning Edition" and "All Things Considered" are excellent examples of how well radio can cover nonvisual events.

Newspaper reporters who assume there are no differences, however, are certain to stumble—and some have. Basically, the newspaper reporter and the radio news reporter share most attitudes, techniques, and purposes. Both search out the most important aspects of any event, and both try to capture the attention of a mass audience by reporting a story's most interesting and salient elements first. Moreover, as anyone who reads a newspaper carefully and listens closely to radio news can attest, newspaper reporters and editors, as well as radio reporters and editors, often apply the same tests of newsworthiness. But one consideration dictates a difference in their writing: Radio news is to be heard, not read.

What this difference means for the news story is suggested by this item from a radio news script:

> Federal investigators are now trying to determine the cause of this weekend's midair helicopter collision.
>
> One person was killed and ten others injured when the two helicopters returning passengers from Catalina Island collided as they approached their landing pad in San Pedro.

Investigators say they don't have any clues about the cause of the crash yet, but they're still sifting through the rubble.

That is all: three sentences that emphasize the present ("are now trying:", "say," "still sifting,"—not "have tried," "said," "have sifted.") The writer made no effort to crowd the five "W"s into the first sentence. As for the details that flesh out news, the writer ignored them. This kind of skeletal story is customary in radio newswriting, especially when the item is considered of only secondary importance.

The contrast with newspaper reporting should be obvious. The first sentence of a newspaper account of the same story ran more than three times as long as the radio lead. Moreover, the newspaper reporter went on for eight additional paragraphs, naming the investigator, quoting three sentences from an official, and supplying many other details.

Clearly, the standard radio news program makes no real effort to compete with the news columns of a newspaper. Rather, radio news emphasizes its great advantage, speed, by making immediacy its hallmark. A radio newswriter can't always use the present tense, but note how the writer of these items used the present tense at every reasonable opportunity, offering only the highlights of a news report:

```
A PAIR OF HOLDUP MEN, DRESSED IN SLACKS,

SPORTCOATS, TIES AND TAN GLOVES, ROBBED THE

SHERATON-PALACE HOTEL OF $2000 YESTERDAY. . . . THE

CASHIER, ROBERT SATTERLEE, SAID ONE OF THE MEN

HELD A GUN, AND THE OTHER MAN ORDERED HIM TO FILL

A CIGAR BOX WITH THE RECEIPTS. . . . BOTH MEN ESCAPED

THRU THE LOBBY, CROWDED WITH PEOPLE UNAWARE OF

THE HOLDUP. . . . POLICE SAY THERE IS NO CONNECTION

BETWEEN THE PALACE HOTEL ROBBERY AND ONE AT THE

FAIRMONT HOTEL TWO WEEKS AGO IN WHICH THE HOLDUP

MAN ESCAPED WITH $1500. . . .

ALSO MISSING THIS MORNING IS A 125-POUND

SCULPTURED HEAD, STOLEN FROM THE FRONT YARD OF SAN

FRANCISCO SCULPTOR EMIL JANEL. . . . THE ART-LOVING

THIEVES HOISTED THE FIVE-FOOT OBJECT OVER A 4-1/2

FOOT FENCE, TOPPED BY STEEL SPIKES. . . .
```

The script form for radio news depends largely on the preferences of the newscaster. The one who read these stories prefers all capital letters and paragraphing only between items. But the major rules obtain whatever the form of typing the script: short sentences, simple words, few details, the present tense whenever possible.

Consider this radio news script:

```
5:30 P.M.                    7 SEC FANFARE

                             HERE IS ED ARNOW


    A strike against Lockheed has been called to

start one minute after midnight, a week from this

coming Wednesday. The November 28th strike call

would affect all of the company's farflung

aerospace system, from Hawaii to Cape

Canaveral . . . including the Lockheed installation at

Sunnyvale.

    There is the firm indication that the federal

government will attempt to ward off the walkout.

But just what action it could take was not clear.

The International Association of Machinists and

Lockheed are deadlocked over the issue of a union

shop. The union demands that the employees have

the opportunity to vote on this. The company

refuses.

    In one other report on the aerospace

industry, 14-million dollars has been allocated to

the National Space Agency's Ames Research Center

at Moffett Field.

    More news after this message. . . .


    ONCE AGAIN . . . Ed Arnow . . .
```

On the New York Market today, stocks moved
irregularly lower on normal trading. What was
described as a backing and filling action was
attributed to a technical adjustment. All told,
sales totaled three-million, 410-thousand. The
Dow Jones Closing Averages showed industrials down
4-point-88 . . . rails up to point-47 . . . utilities up
point-13 . . . and 65 stocks were down point-71.

On the Pacific Coast exchange . . . stocks moved
lower also, with Lockheed one of the sharpest
losers . . . dropping a point and a half. All told,
101 issues declined and 76 were higher.

Now, here's the weather forecast. It'll be
fair thru tomorrow night except for occasional
drizzle or light rain on the coast from Eureka
northward. And there will be light variable
cloudiness over northern sections. Also, it'll be
slightly warmer. This region will be fair thru
tomorrow with a low tonight of 45 to 55. The high
tomorrow, 65 to 73. And there'll be westerly
winds up to 15-miles an hour in the afternoon.
This is Ed Arnow.

CLOSE: THIS HAS BEEN YOUR REPORTER, BROUGHT TO
         YOU TWICE DAILY AT 7:30 EACH MORNING AND
         AGAIN AT 5:30 IN THE EVENING. FANFARE
         TO 5:35 P.M.

An analysis of this newscast reveals several techniques fairly common
in radio news reporting. (Few of these points have the force of rules; differences, especially in the preferences of on-the-air reporters, make it impossible to establish rules, in the strictest sense, for radio.)

1. The stories are clustered. Clustering similar stories enables the listener to focus his or her attention.

2. Each story is short. The local newspaper and many other papers devoted twenty times more words to stories that paralleled the reports making up this radio news program. Although all the radio stories were short, however, Arnow devoted different amounts of time to different stories. Varying story length not only relieves monotony within a newscast, but it also grades the news. (Generally speaking, the longer the story, the greater its importance.)

3. Each sentence is short. Most sentences are in the ten-to-twenty-word range, but the sentences are not *exactly* the same length. The variety of sentences in conversation marks this collection of items, keeping it from sounding relentlessly staccato. A staccato quality is valuable in a bulletin message that interrupts a regular program; it demands attention. But few listeners will be pleased with five minutes of unvarying bulletins.

4. The words are not only somewhat shorter and simpler than those in newspaper stories on the same subjects, but some are also more relaxed, giving the newscast a shirtsleeve tone. Note especially "It'll be fair," "Now, here's the weather forecast."

5. Consider, too, the typographic devices that make for easy reading: (. . .), "thru," "point-13," and the like. For most announcers, these devices are essential.

6. Finally, note the introductory phrases: "On the New York Market today," "on the Pacific Coast exchange," and so on. Such phrases would be wasted words in print, but they are valuable in radio newswriting. They move the newscast from one topic to another, but they are not merely transitional devices. Actually, they serve as informative pauses: breaks in the flow of items that allow listeners time to orient themselves. Without the introductions, listeners would be caught in a waterfall of words and subjects.

All-news radio provides abbreviated stories, aired repeatedly.

The times change and we change with them.   *Lothair I*

All-news radio stations serve their constituencies admirably, provided radio news is the *beginning* of the listener's information. Unfortunately, for some people, the radio is becoming their sole news source. People who listen to all-news radio and perhaps also watch television news hear the headlines and a bit more, and some of these people barely look at newspapers. Newspaper circulation is failing to keep pace with the growing United States population.

KCBS, the first of San Francisco's all-news radio stations, announced nearly twenty years ago that the station was becoming an all-news operation. At a meeting of Sigma Delta Chi, the journalistic society, the general manager of KCBS announced half-jokingly to the newspaper journalists, "We are going to bury you." It sounded like a real challenge. When they heard the news on KCBS, however, the newspaper people relaxed. KCBS was nothing more than a headline service, with its stories repeated again and again. Today listeners seem satisfied with the news broadcast on their radio and television sets. How can they understand the news when it is treated so superficially?

For example, consider the way in which a radio journalist reports the day's news:

Here's a collection of stories on Washington.

The Labor Secretary and most of the president's Labor Management Advisory Committee have gone on record in favor of a 10-billion dollar tax cut.

A presidential committee on equal-employment-opportunity says blacks are winning a bigger share of federal government jobs. In the last fiscal year one of every six new federal jobs was filled by a black.

The Commerce Department reports that personal income tax has climbed more than two million dollars in October. That's the largest gain since April and represents a 5 percent hike over last year.

In another report on the aerospace industry, 14 million dollars has been allocated to the National Space Agency's Research Center at Moffett Field. The money is to construct four new research facilities there, including one facility that will simulate space flight to the moon and the planets.

In contrast, it might well take you over an hour to read all the details about these stories in the *New York Times*. The subject of the tax cut, for instance, might be covered in four different stories.

To cover fast-breaking news, radio news editors may help to report the news as they organize coverage.

Harmony in discord.   *Horace*

It is sometimes essential to report a fast-breaking even just before a regular news program goes on the air. In these circumstances, a news editor at a station with a relatively small staff must both organize coverage and help to report the news. Here is how Jeff Skov of KSFO organized and helped to report a crisis at San Francisco International Airport.

Rick Wagstaff of KSFO News was closest to the phone when it rang one afternoon at about 3:30. An excited voice said breathlessly, "Hello, this is Bill Stevens, and I'm working here at San Francisco International Airport, and I wondered if you guys knew anything about the 747 that had trouble getting off the runway."

"No sir," replied Wagstaff. "We haven't heard anything about it. When did this happen?"

"Just now. I saw it."

"You're at San Francisco International?"

"That's right."

"And what was it you saw, Mr. Stevens?—is that right?" Wagstaff asked.

"Right. Well, I'm working here at the shops unloading, and planes are taking off all the time, but just a few minutes ago, this big 747—I think it was a Pan Am—sort of staggered, you know, almost as if it hit the water or something."

Wagstaff called the airport, Pan American Airlines, and the fire department while Skov sent Aaron Edwards and Lloyd Edwards, two KSFO reporters, to San Francisco International. Fifteen minutes later, Aaron Edwards was talking to Skov over the shortwave.

"Okay, this is 458 to news. I'm just pulling into the airport, Jeff. I'll get back to you by telephone as soon as I can get a good overview location and as soon as I can learn anything."

The "overview location" Edwards had in mind was the tower, but, meanwhile, Skov was running from the newsroom to the studio, where disc jockey Carter B. Smith was doing his afternoon show. The strains of a Burt Bacharach melody floated placidly from the speaker. The microphone was off.

Skov opened the door. "Hey, C. B., I've got something I've got to put on right away."

"Do you want me to wait until the end of the record, or do you want me to dump it right now?" Smith asked.

"No, I think we ought to go right away."

"Okay, stand by."

Fading out the record, Smith gave Skov an introduction. Skov came on and told 100,000 listeners:

> This is KSFO news. Details on this story at this point are very sketchy, but we'll tell them to you as we know them. A Pan American Airlines plane—a 747—has apparently skimmed part of the water at the end of one of the runways at San Francisco International, and in so doing, has lost part of its landing gear. They don't know how much; the plane is in the air, and for now the plane is okay.

The Coast Guard is sending a helicopter and an airplane over the water to try to determine just how much of the landing gear was lost. After that determination has been made, it is presumed, and again, this is only preliminary information from the San Francisco Fire Department and from officials at the airport, the plane is apparently heading out to sea to dump some fuel and then will attempt a landing at San Francisco International Airport.

Aaron Edwards is at the airport . . . and the moment there is anything new, we will let you know. Unfortunately, we do not have the identification of the flight . . . we'll keep you posted the moment we have any further information. This is KSFO news.

The news secretary then called Warren Bogges, KSFO traffic reporter, and his helicopter was in the air within minutes.

While Bogges was winging toward San Francisco and Smith was assuring listeners that KSFO would keep them informed about the situation at the airport, Skov was talking once again to Lloyd Edwards over the shortwave.

"Eight-five-six-oh-seven; Lloyd, Aaron is going to go to the inside of the airport so he can watch this thing from the tower and see the landing. I'd like for you to get out on the runway with the emergency vehicles so you can be there when it touches down, over."

"Ten-four, that's going to be a hard one, Jeff. They've been turning vehicles away ever since this thing came up, and the security, as you can imagine, is tight, but I've got an idea I can get over through one of the buildings—one of the hangars here, so I can give it a try. . . ."

The brassy sound of "What's New?" flashed over the air, trumpets, drums, and horns heralding the news Skov was about to bring to an anxious audience at 4:00 P.M.

This is KSFO news. A Pan American Airlines 747 jetliner is in trouble . . . it is Pan Am flight 845 which took off from San Francisco International Airport around 3:15 this afternoon, and somehow damaged its landing gear, apparently hitting some sort of a light at the end of the runway. Just how badly the gear is damaged isn't known at this point, but, as a precaution, the jet has been dumping fuel into the Pacific in preparation for an emergency landing at San Francisco International Airport, probably within the half-hour. . . .

The jet screamed in, bouncing on the runway with its badly damaged landing gear, which had been jammed through the fuselage when the plane nicked the runway light tower. Lloyd Edwards was, of course, on the runway, and he gave eyewitness accounts of the tense landing.

WRITING AND EDITING CONVENTIONS FOR BROADCAST MEDIA

News writers and news editors for radio and television need to follow certain conventions, to make what is written more effective as spoken copy. When a story is breaking, there is not much time for rewriting or for editing—so the writer should always keep basic principles in mind.

1. Write more informally for broadcast than for print, remembering always that the words are to be spoken. Read the copy aloud so that you can get a feel for the way it sounds.

2. Be very careful in using pronouns, making certain that "he" or "she" actually refers to the person intended. The problem is considerably more serious for broadcast writing than it is for print because the audience has only one chance to get the meaning of a statement.

3. Simplify and round off figures whenever you can. Delete numbers not essential to the story. Put all numbers in easy-to-grasp form. For example, instead of "66 point 7 percent," write "two-thirds" or "two out of three." Never write "a million"; it will sound like "8 million."

4. Make qualifying statements at the *beginning* of a sentence, not the end. You must make certain that the listener actually hears the qualifier.

5. Although newspaper and magazine writers often use transitional words in the middle of a sentence (using "however" after an introductory clause, rather than at the beginning of the sentence, is usually smoother in print), broadcast writing calls for using transitions at the beginning. The listener should always be aware of the direction of a statement—whether it is following in the line of the preceding sentence or taking a new course.

6. Cut all but the most essential details. Print is well adapted to providing details; broadcasting is not.

7. The immediacy of broadcasting demands that it carry the *latest* news up to the time of the broadcast. Broadcasters cannot compete with newspapers for details and full-fleshed stories.

8. The voice of the broadcaster makes radio news more "emotional," from the standpoint of the listener, than print does. Writers must be sparing with gruesome details of crimes and accidents. Be sure all pictures are in good taste. Even some common sights—for instance, a person receiving a hypodermic injection or having blood drawn for a blood drive—can upset many viewers. Extreme care is essential in handling stories that might create panic.

9. Read all copy aloud for awkward sounds. Be sparing in the use of "s," "th," and "ing" sounds. Avoid words like "thrusts," "wrists," and

"frisked," all of which are difficult to pronounce aloud. Word combinations like "quartz wrist watch" can also prove troublesome.

10. The clever writing signified by alliteration, puns, and tongue-twisters tend to confuse many newscasters and may cause listeners to focus so strongly on the sound that the sense escapes them. Simplicity is vital.

11. Avoid lists, especially of names or numbers. Local names are good to use, as are names of famous people. All other names can usually be deleted and the person's job or role in the story substituted for the name. Remember, what the person does is usually more important than the person's name. This rule is particularly handy when the name is a difficult one to pronounce. For example, it is simpler for all concerned if you write "the head of the British delegation" instead of "Wladislav Brznewski."

12. Use only widely known abbreviations—YMCA, PTA, and the like— or make sure that names of organizations are used in full before any abbreviated form is introduced.

13. Make certain that pronunciation guides are provided for any words that may prove difficult. Even fairly simple words can sometimes cause problems, so provide a pronunciation guide if there is the slightest possibility that the word may be mispronounced. Pencil in needed guides above the difficult words, using uppercase letters for accented syllables and lowercase letters for unaccented syllables.

14. Cut long stories down as much as possible. The audience has a short attention span. You will do better to strive for a news program with many brief stories than one with a few long ones. Try to keep radio stories under forty seconds and television stories under one minute. Of course, there will be times when this isn't possible, but never let a long story pass without giving it an extra look to see if more cannot be cut.

In the broadcast media, you should also attribute at the beginning of any sentence containing a direct quotation to be read by the newscaster. (A direct quotation is the exact wording used by a source, and direct quotations always appear within quotation marks.)

Whenever you can, you should directly quote sources by showing or playing a tape of the source saying whatever is significant. Having a newscaster read a direct quotation on the air can confuse your audience, which— unable to see quotation marks—can't be sure where direct quotations begin and end.

Newscasters should read direct quotations only when the audience needs to know the exact words a source used and only when the source cannot be filmed or taped presenting the information. When newscasters do read direct quotations, attribution must always be supplied *before* the quotation begins to let the audience know that the words it is about to hear aren't the newscasters. You should also precede the direct quotation with a phrase like "in her words," "the exact words she used were," or "quoting now" and follow the quotation with some clear signal the quotation has ended, like beginning the first sentence after the direct quotation with the source's name. Newscasters once said "quote" before they read a direct quotation and "end quote" afterward; today's writers for the electronic media rely on signals that are just as clear as "quote" and "end quote" and that also sound more natural.

Keep direct quotations that must be read on the air short. When a long direct quotation absolutely must be read by a newscaster, break it up into pieces with paraphrasing or summary in between sentences of direct quotation, or use phrases like "and still quoting" to remind your audience that what they're hearing is still a direct quotation.

EXERCISES

1. Make notes to yourself while performing the following experiment. To test the power of television pictures, turn on the set without the power of words, and watch it for an hour. Then turn up the sound, and watch for another hour. Finally, type your notes on the relative power of pictures and words and turn them in at the next class meeting.

2. With three other students, plan a campus television news program of five minutes. One of you will be the reporter, the second the writer, the third the director, and the fourth is the newscaster. When the reporter comes in with news, he or she and the writer and the director should work together in producing the program. Although a professional newscaster seldom does much more than read the script, on this experimental program, it is better to have the announcer participate with the others in planning the program. The program should be shown to the entire class.

3. With another student, plan a five-minute campus news radio program. One of you will be a reporter-writer, the other the announcer. When the reporter has the required amount of news, he or she should work with the announcer to shape the program, which will be read aloud or taped for the entire class.

The essential American strategy: publicity.
Richard Rovere

I don't care what is written about me so long as it isn't true.
Katharine Hepburn

Planned public relations is usually a stepchild of conflict.
Kinsey M. Robinson

The purpose of public relations in its best sense is to inform and to keep minds open; the purpose of propaganda in the bad sense is to misinform and to keep minds closed.
John W. Hill

If you write one book and then go on to another, readers pay half attention to the book and half attention to the publicity.
Harold Brodkey

A writer is always admired most, not by those who have read him, but by those who have merely heard about him.
H. L. Mencken

It took me fifteen years to discover I had no talent for writing, but I couldn't give it up because by that time I was too famous.
Robert Benchley

CHAPTER 8

Writing Public Relations Stories

Public relations may be the most misunderstood of the writing careers we discuss. Just about everyone knows that advertising is supposed to sell; but what does public relations do? Does it help gloss over a company's deficiencies? Does it exaggerate an institution's good points? Defining what public relations is and how it relates to journalism is the basis for this chapter. We want you to understand how a public relations story is written and distributed.

WHAT IS PUBLIC RELATIONS?

Much of what the information media present as news originates in public relations firms.

Man's mind is indeed a factory busy with making idols.   *Martin Luther*

In *PR: How the Public Relations Industry Writes the News,* Jeff and Marie Blyskal tell how public-relations practitioner Robert Wiener publicized Coleco's Cabbage Patch dolls. In an interview with the Blyskals, Wiener said, "When Bryant Gumbel or Jane Pauley . . . says 'Here's the season's hottest item,' it means more to consumers than if Coleco says the same thing. The credibility that achieves far outweighs an advertisement."

The authors outline the skill Wiener used in staging attention-getting events such as a mass adoption of the dolls by a group of Boston schoolgirls. Having achieved some coverage, Wiener could expand it easily. Using local newspaper clippings about shop-floor skirmishes over the Cabbage Patch dolls, Wiener convinced NBC that the story was worth covering. He also gave the pregnant Jane Pauley her own doll. These actions led to NBC's

191

"Today" program devoting five and one-half minutes to the story, opening the gates to national publicity.

Wiener's ability is duplicated by so many public-relations firms that the Blyskals estimated 40 to 50 percent of all news stories originate there. The Blyskals concluded that "whole sections of the news are virtually owned by PR."

Public relations is the pursuit through the information media of public confidence and consent.

With public opinion on its side, nothing can fail.   *Abraham Lincoln*

Like advertising, which we discuss in the next chapter, public relations (PR) differs from but is closely connected to journalism. Both journalists and the general public need to understand how PR works. Much of reporters' work requires that they assess the work of public-relations specialists. Reporters also need to recognize that "public relations" and "publicity" are not synonymous.

When Paul Garrett went to Detroit to work for General Motors in 1931, he was the only public-relations employee on the company payroll. When he retired as a vice president twenty-five years later, General Motors was spending more than $1 million each year on a public-relations program that involved more than two hundred employees.

Such growth is one small measure of the rapid expansion of public relations in the American economy. General Motors has not been alone in recognizing the value of the craft, which one of the most thoughtful of the early public-relations specialists, Edward L. Bernays, called "the engineering of consent."

Garrett's early experiences with General Motors are typical in one respect. When he arrived, he was asked, "How do you make a million dollars look small?" The management then was acutely sensitive about the company's size. Garrett said that he not only had no answer to the question, but that he also did not consider it his task to provide one. Public relations is the practice of winning confidence, he insisted, not of putting on an act. As a consequence of his ideas, General Motors is now engaged in an extensive permanent public-relations program with many facets: plant, city, and field relations; educational relations; a speakers' bureau; and institutional advertising. The primary effort is to convince everyone that General Motors, though huge, is a desirable company.

Many other public-relations practitioners who might once have been expected to perform magic tricks with public opinion or simply to get some positive publicity have been able to convince their employers that a continuing program of good relations is the proper task of public relations.

"Space-grabbing," as many journalists call publicity efforts, is still the prime mission of a few public-relations workers, notably press agents in the entertainment world. The Public Relations Society of America (PRSA), whose membership includes many leading practitioners, plays down this aspect of the craft. PRSA members and a good many others tend to define their work broadly. Spokespersons for leading public-relations firms responded to a survey with varying definitions of public relations. These two were typical:

> Public relations is the skilled communication of ideas to the various publics with the object of producing a desired result.

> Public relations is finding out what people like about you and doing more of it; finding out what they don't like about you and doing less of it.

One of the best definitions was adopted in 1978 at Mexico City during the First World Assembly of Public Relations Associates and the First World Forum of Public Relations:

> Public relations practice is the art and science of analyzing trends, predicting their consequences, counseling organization leaders, and implementing planned programs of action which will serve both the organization's and the public interest.

To the extent that this broad definition fits the work of a public-relations firm or division of a business, public relations involves a great deal more than "publicity." In fact, many public-relations practitioners see publicity as only one of many tools they use. A news story, a speech, a film, a photograph—each is the tool of public relations.

To make these tools work, public-relations workers need access to the media. The media are vital to public-relations practitioners; without them, PR people face a virtually impossible task in conveying their companies' positions to the public.

WRITING PUBLIC RELATIONS STORIES

Because they are usually intended for the media, public-relations stories are written like news stories.

Don't do or say or write anything you wouldn't want to see on the front page of the *New York Times.*   *Kerryn King*

A PR professional may be thought of as an organization's in-house journalist. PR specialists chronicle the activities of the company, university, or government agency for which they work and then disseminate that news to the outside world. The job differs from that of reporters, however, in that management nearly always has the right to approve, edit, or kill the PR story. Furthermore, the PR person usually deals only with news that benefits the organization; except when it will come out anyway, bad news is rarely offered for public consumption.

The PR person's job does resemble a reporter's, however, in many ways. He or she gathers news from around the organization, interviews executives and technical people for stories, and covers the organization's area of interest just like a reporter covers a beat. In most large corporations, which involve themselves in diverse activities and industries, PR people cover divisions of the company in the same way that reporters cover city hall, the school board, and the fire department.

Public-relations writing comes in two forms—external and internal. External public relations consists of dealing with members of the public and the outside media. Internal public relations, increasingly important to all large organizations, consists of dealing with employees within the company, government agency, university, and so on. For the writer, internal public relations can involve many types of publications: newsletters, quarterly magazines, posters, brochures, memos—even audiovisual programs and slickly produced videos that include original music and professional narration. The field of in-house "corporate communications" represents a growing career opportunity for graduates of journalism and public-relations programs.

Because the PR person is essentially the organization's journalist, PR writing is journalistic in form. Many articles in the better company magazines resemble pieces found in *Forbes, Fortune,* or *Business Week.* Especially in producing news releases, the PR person uses the technique of straight newswriting to present the story to the press, radio, and television.

The reasons are twofold. First, the straight-news format grew out of the need to communicate information clearly and quickly, with the most important items at the top where they could be read first. The reporters who are the PR person's audience appreciate that efficient style of communication as much as the public does. Second, the well-composed news release can be published in the newspaper almost verbatim, so long as it is written in newspaper style. Smaller newspapers and many trade magazines, both of which are typically shorthanded, often use good releases with a minimum of rewriting. (One California PR man once went so far as to make up an imaginary new electronic product and mail out a bogus news release, just to see what would happen. Around a dozen computer magazines ran the release without even calling to check on the story.) Large metropolitan newspapers almost never run news releases as they are sent; if the story is interesting, the editor assigns a reporter to cover it.

A few conventions of format are routine in all news releases. At the top left of each news release, above the headline, is the *release date*—the date before which the media are asked not to publish the information. Almost always, the item is slugged with the line, "For immediate release," because reporters usually don't feel compelled to hold onto news once it's in their hands. If the public-relations agency or department has an advance agreement with reporters not to run certain sensitive stories before a particular date, the release date typically reads, "Please do not release before December 14, 1986," and so on. Such advance releases are often used for major product introductions, when public-relations people want to brief reporters and editors beforehand, to whet their appetites and provide time for an in-depth story. Using such a strategy, however, depends on a relationship of trust and cooperation between PR people and reporters, and a firm understanding that the news will not be leaked before the company's announcement date.

Also at the top are names and telephone numbers of *contacts* within the company, whom reporters can call to follow up the story. Listing contacts is vital to getting coverage; many editors are unwilling to run a news release without talking for themselves with someone in the organization. Generally speaking, the higher up the contact, the more likely reporters will be interested in conducting an interview. Usually, executives at the vice-presidential level are empowered to speak for the company; many lower-level managers have that authority, also. As a routine matter, the public-relations director is also listed as a contact and may be the first person called by a reporter. However, reporters generally prefer to speak to "someone in charge" rather than the usual "company spokesperson." If an executive or key technical person can be made available to speak to the media, coverage usually increases.

Here is an example of a news release written in the conventional format:

For immediate release   Contact: Steven R. Pierce,
                                                             President

                                         Laura D. Hanley,
                                         Communications Manager

ZANE-MACGREGOR & COMPANY ANNOUNCES THIRD-QUARTER EARNINGS RISE

MENLO PARK, CALIFORNIA, September 7, 1986—Third-quarter earnings rose 17 percent over 1985 levels for Zane-MacGregor & Company, the Northern California-based developer and corporate real-estate services firm, Z-M president Steven R. Pierce reported today.

Net receipts for the quarter, ended August 31, totaled $2.3 million on revenues of $8.7 million. Comparable figures a year ago were a net of $1.96 million on revenues of $8.1 million.

"Despite the current glut in commercial real-estate in the Bay Area, we have continued to grow because of our custom site-location services, which are currently very much in demand," Pierce said.

Pierce also attributed the improved earnings to the full leasing of two Z-M office developments in the Pacific Northwest, River Park Place in Portland and Market Square Business Center in Seattle. Both projects were completed in 1985.

Zane-MacGregor & Company is a diversified real-estate firm specializing in developing office and industrial sites and in assisting corporate clients in finding new locations for long-term growth.

# # #

Note that the writer of the release put the news in context, not only reporting the company's earnings but also showing that the quarter's results represented a dramatic increase over those of the same quarter the year before. For the reporter, that is where the news really exists—not in the simple fact that the company earned $2.3 million in the quarter. Many companies do that; the real news is that the company is doing better at a time when many companies in the industry are faring worse.

The quote from the company president highlights that fact, and, just as important, provides the "why" and the "how" of the release: The company is faring well because one of its lines of business is helping it prosper even while the industry as a whole is hurting. Finally, this news release, like many, includes a closing paragraph that summarizes what the organization does, for reporters who may not be familiar with the company and its business.

It's important to quote sources in news releases for the same reason it's important in news stories: Quotations add authenticity and life to the article. Also, as we have discussed, a statement from the president, vice president, or other senior executive will give the story more weight because it represents a willingness for top management to go on record and take responsibility for the organization's performance.

To increase your chances of placing a news release, get straight to the point.

The most hazardous undertaking of man is the transmitting of an idea from one mind to another.   *Frank McGee*

In the example that we just saw, the writer might easily have started the story like this:

MENLO PARK, CALIFORNIA, September 7, 1986—Driving along the Bayshore Freeway, one of the main arterials of Northern California's Silicon Valley, you can't help but notice all of the shiny new office buildings that line the roadway. As one wag on the local real-estate scene recently observed, it seems the construction crane has become the Bay Area's new official bird.

There's something else you can't help but notice about all those shiny new developments. The parking lots are empty. For now, at least, the Bay Area commercial real-estate market is becoming seriously overbuilt, creating hard times for developers and realtors.

But Steve Pierce doesn't look worried. Despite the bad times pervading the industry, Pierce's firm, Zane-MacGregor & Company, has just posted net earnings of $2.3 million for the third quarter, up 17 percent over a year ago. . . .

This feature-type lead is attractive—similar, in fact, to the leads in most front-page stories in the *Wall Street Journal*. It also provides much more background and color than the original news release. Why, then, did the writer play it straight?

News people are busy and tend to skim over news releases when they read them at all. A feature-style lead takes time to develop, and most reporters and editors simply will not take the time. They'll typically decide in the first paragraph whether they want to use the story. For this reason, it's important to write leads that get the facts out right away. Let the reporter write the fancy lead for his or her story; the job of the PR person is to interest the reporter in the first place, and the reporter won't be interested if he or she can't find the point of the story quickly.

The following press release was prepared by a student when a noted graduate of the university was soon to appear on campus. The comments beside the press release are designed to explain why a public relations practitioner should write as a professional reporter.

COMMENTS	STORY
The subject of this release was famous only in a small circle, so the writer wisely chose not to include his name in this lead.	A Stanford graduate, who is co-executive producer and head writer of "The Cosby Show," will speak and show film clips of the Cosby program at 1:15 Thursday, February 26, in Room 2, History Building.
The writer uses a bit of history in this paragraph that is primarily on Markus's appearance.	John Markus, who graduated in 1978 with a degree in English literature, will show film clips and explain how he wrote and produced them. "The Cosby Show" is still No. 1 in ratings.
Here, the writer focuses on Markus's awards.	Markus has received an Emmy for his work on the Cosby show. Recently, he won his second Humanitas Prize, awarded annually to the television script that best promotes human values.
This is an advance story, so the writer does not focus on this aspect. In a later story, after Markus's performance,	After graduating, Markus went to Hollywood. For three years—and much to his parents' concern—he found only spasmodic work as a television writer. A writing assignment on the "Taxi" series,

he makes these facts and other facts a feature lead.

Knowing that Markus had graduated nine years earlier, he placed these facts last. Why? All undergraduate students had been in grade school when Markus had graduated.

however, led to a job as a staff writer on "The Cosby Show." During the show's first season, Markus wrote nine episodes and was promoted to his present position.

While Markus was a Stanford undergraduate, he concentrated on his weekly radio program on KZSU, his opinion column in *The Daily,* and was a saxophonist in the Jazz Ensemble.

The most successful PR stories avoid an abundance of hyperbole. Certainly the PR writer wants to present company news in a favorable light, but excessive hype is almost always cut immediately and may cause the story to end up in the editor's wastebasket instead of the newspaper.

With complex stories—the formation of a new company, a new-product introduction, a medical or scientific breakthrough—the main news release is often accompanied by a wealth of supporting material. Additional items might include technical papers, one-page biographies of key people, relevant news clippings, photographs, and a question-and-answer sheet of quotes ("An Interview with the President") that reporters can use in creating their own stories.

Write PR releases for broadcast media in a broadcast style.

Our life is frittered away by detail. Simplify. Simplify.
Henry David Thoreau

Radio and television reporters are far more receptive to news releases written in a broadcast style than they are to releases that were obviously intended primarily for the print media. The reasons are simple and obvious.

First, anything composed in a print style, with longer sentences in uppercase and lowercase letters, must be rewritten for broadcast. At a minimum, it must be retyped all in uppercase so that the announcer can see the copy easily to read it on the air. The sentences must typically also be made shorter—and that should be the job of the public-relations writer, not the broadcast news editor.

The second reason has more to do with courtesy than journalism. If a broadcast reporter receives a newspaper-style news release, the reporter will automatically think that the PR person considers the station less important than the newspapers; after all, the newspaper reporters aren't asked to make do with a news release written for broadcast. Because the PR practitioner's job is to create the best possible relations with all media, such an unintended gaffe is to be avoided.

PR people can also win points—and increase coverage—by providing short taped interviews along with the story. The interviews are typically with a company executive or an important technical person who can speak knowledgeably about the subject at hand. Some PR firms now specialize in creating entire news videos—the broadcast version of a press release—which they deliver ready for broadcast to television stations.

ACCESS AND ETHICS

How do you get your news releases recognized by the right people? Good writing is just the beginning. As we'll see, public-relations practitioners rely on an old-fashioned method (personal contact) and a very modern one (computer databases).

To gain access to the print media, seek out the publications whose audiences have an interest in your client, make your contact with the media as personal as possible, and provide only information that is genuine news.

Depend not on fortune, but on conduct.   *Publilius Syrus*

In February 1984, the Learning Periodicals Group, a California magazine publisher, launched a new magazine called *Family Learning*. As part of the effort, the company developed a public-relations campaign to create interest in the magazine among potential advertisers. A principal goal was to generate exposure in New York, where the magazine's advertising salespeople would be calling daily on the nation's major ad agencies.

For Scott Dailey, the magazine group's promotion manager, the first task was to identify the publications whose readers would be interested. Using the *Editor & Publisher Yearbook*, Dailey created a computerized file of the business editors of every daily newspaper in every metropolitan area of more than 50,000 population in the nation. He also assembled a list of managing editors of the advertising and publishing trade press (such magazines as *Advertising Age, Adweek,* and *Folio*). The list ultimately included more than 700 names.

Next, the company devised both a short-term and a long-term strategy, deciding what kinds of messages it wanted to send and whom it wanted to receive them. The initial news release announcing the magazine would be mailed to all of the editors on the master list. But subsequent stories would, it was hoped, chronicle steady increases in circulation and advertising pages—information of interest mainly to people in ad agencies. Thus, the second

Scott Dailey

Scott Dailey was sixteen years old when he took his first public-relations job—for no pay.

"It was the summer of 1971, and I had just lost the student-body election at my high school to one of my best friends," says Dailey, who now runs his own advertising and public-relations firm in the San Francisco Bay area. "As the new student-body president, my friend had some political spoils jobs to give away. He gave me my pick, and I chose the job of student publicity director.

"As it turned out, losing that election was one of the best things I ever did, because I got an introduction to PR and newspapers, and also got my first reporting job as a direct result. It probably also helped me to get into college, because my grades were usually good, but never great. Having that responsibility probably made up for a less-than-spectacular academic record."

Dailey's job was to publicize student activities, and when he began making his rounds in his suburban Bay Area hometown of Livermore, California, a local newspaper offered him a job as a stringer at 10 cents per column inch.

"In retrospect, it was a PR person's dream," says Dailey. "Whenever we had an event to publicize, all I had to do was write it up and hand it to the editor, and he'd usually find a place for it. I didn't find out until much later how difficult it really can be to get the media's attention."

Later came college at Stanford, where Dailey, a skinny high-school track athlete, lifted weights to bring himself up to 150 pounds and discovered that he had to lift open a few books to keep himself in school.

"How I didn't flunk out in my freshman year, I'll never know. I came to college with no study habits, no discipline. Fortunately, I could get credit for learning to write, and, at least during that first year, that's probably what saved me."

Dailey covered sports, drama, and campus news for the Stanford *Daily,* an alternative, magazine-style publication called *Live Oak,* and KZSU, the college radio station. Graduating with a major in English and almost a full second major in communication, he held jobs as a reporter, a technical writer, and a college instructor before signing on in 1983 as promotion manager for the Learning Periodicals Group, one of the nation's largest publishers of magazines for teachers.

It was at Learning that Dailey—bearded, balding, approaching 30—began in earnest to practice the art of public relations. "The first thing I found out was that it takes more than writing a snappy news release to get noticed by the news media. You've got to get out there and talk to people—get to know people, pitch the story, get the reporter interested.

"That's why the smart PR people join the local press clubs, as well as the public-relations societies. If you get to know the news people who cover your industry, rather than just mail stories to them all the time, you're probably going to get a lot more press, and you're probably going to be a lot more credible, just because people know you."

When Dailey worked for Learning, the company's most satisfying PR successes came through contacts with reporters. In early 1984, the company introduced a new magazine called *Family Learning,* aimed at parents of elementary-school-aged children. The PR campaign included news releases mailed to hundreds of newspapers across the country, but also emphasized contacts with major papers such as the *New York Times* and *USA Today.* Not coincidentally, two of the most glowing reviews of the magazine came from those two publications.

"Why is personal contact so important?" asks Dailey. "Look at it from the reporter's point of view. Let's say it's ten o'clock Wednesday morning, and the reporter's kind of aimlessly going through the mail, looking for something to write about. If you're the sort of PR person who just ships out news releases, your story's going to be read for maybe the first paragraph, and then probably tossed. And then you're dead in the water.

"But let's say you've met this reporter two or three times at the press club, you've found out that she likes jazz, gardening, and the Chicago Cubs, and on this Wednesday morning you call her up. You say, 'Hey, how 'bout those Cubbies, there's a big flower show in town next week, and, by the way, I have a story here that might interest you.'

"If you do that, you're a lot more likely to get a story placed, and if you're smart, you'll do a little probing to find out what other stories she might be interested in, and then see if you can't develop some of those as well.

"You've got to remember that a reporter gets a ton of mail every day, and a lot of it is blatantly self-serving. When I was at *Learning,* we used to get news releases from some company that did market research in the education field. One time they sent us a story that started out, 'As the XYZ Research Company predicted to its subscribers last month, sales in the textbook market rose 10 percent in the first quarter of this year.' One of my sarcastic colleagues underlined that sentence and wrote next to it, 'Aren't they wonderful?'

"Now, that's the reaction of someone who's in the PR business. Imagine how a reporter is going to react.

"I once asked Charles Kuralt of CBS what he thought constituted news. He said, 'News is whatever interests reporters.' So the moral is, if you're going to place a story, you've got to get the reporter's interest up. You've got to know a little bit about sales, because what you're really doing is selling that story to the reporter."

(continued)

Scott Dailey *(continued)*

Like many writers, Dailey has wide interests, from fly-fishing to history, music, drama, politics, and sports. That, too, is important, he says, to the success of the PR professional. "One of the most effective PR people I know is a guy who's interested in absolutely everything. He can hold his own in a conversation on just about any subject I can think of, from physics to the Grateful Dead. And that's one reason why I think he's so successful. He can talk to people about whatever they're interested in.

"If you don't like talking to people, you probably shouldn't be in PR. In fact, you probably shouldn't be in journalism. Because from the journalistic side, you need to be able to talk to people to write about them, or to write about issues that concern them.

"On the PR side, you not only need the journalistic skills, you typically have to field questions from reporters, which can be a difficult, adversarial process. Plus, you have to convince them of the importance of your story, which is often competing for space with a lot of other stories. That means you have to know how to talk to people, and, most important, how to be persuasive."

At first meeting Dailey, he seems the epitome of the confident, polished professional. But the gap-toothed grin, the easy laugh, the quick one-liners represent a victory in a long battle with shyness and self-doubt.

"In my senior year in college, I got an interview for a television news job in Medford, Oregon. They flew me up from California, and I bombed. I just couldn't come across. They sent me back a letter that said, 'You're an excellent writer, but our present need is for a strong on-air personality.' Now, that's the kind of letter that'll do wonders for your ego.

"I didn't really get over being shy until I opened my own business in 1985. I knew I was going to have to get clients, and I wasn't going to win anybody's confidence by sitting around doing my imitation of a dumbwaiter. So I forced myself to start being a little more outgoing, and the more I did it, the easier it got.

"Now, I'm pretty comfortable meeting people, and in selling myself to them. So I guess my message is, if you're shy, you need to get over it to succeed in this business—but you can work on it and eventually you can get over it."

Today, Dailey's business serves clients primarily in the high-tech corridor between San Francisco and San Jose. As a flourishing one-man operation, his firm's main stock in trade is brochures for companies ranging from a major stock brokerage to electronics manufacturers, a testing laboratory, a real-estate developer, a magazine publisher, a large savings-and-loan, and other clients in California's "Silicon Valley."

Staying afloat means devoting at least half of his time to business development. A couple of clients keep him busy with monthly projects, but, as he puts it, he's always out "pressing the flesh" to keep business coming in.

"I get all of my business from personal contacts," he says. "Really, they're vital in this business. If I had one piece of advice to give, it would be, 'learn how to make contacts.' For success in PR, I can't think of anything that's more important."

---

wave of news releases would be mailed only to the core of publications that served the magazine industry and the advertising business.

Blue-penciled and redrafted, the initial news release was ready to be mailed on the second day of January 1984.

For immediate release   Contact:

Morton Malkofsky, Publisher

Cathy Souza, Marketing Manager

LEARNING PERIODICALS GROUP ANNOUNCES LAUNCH OF FAMILY LEARNING

BELMONT, California—The nationwide alarm over the quality of education delivered by America's public schools is propelling the launch of *Family Learning,* the Learning Periodicals Group's first entry into the field of consumer magazines.

Produced by the publishers of *Learning,* the respected professional teaching journal, *Family Learning* will advocate a partnership between parents and educators and offer creative strategies for helping kids learn both at school and at home.

The new, bimonthly magazine, due out in February, is aimed at the parents of America's 31 million elementary and junior high school children, who represent nearly 14.5 million households across the country.

An initial audience of 150,000 upscale readers is guaranteed for the first year of publication.

"With all of the various reports and commissions over the past year, the entire nation has become aware that education is in urgent need of help—and that help has to come from the home of each individual child," said Morton Malkofsky, publisher of *Family Learning* and head of the Learning Periodicals Group.

"Moreover, in the 11 years that we've published *Learning*, we've found more and more that teachers and principals are eager for parental support that goes beyond the bake-sale, fund-raising variety. A home environment that fosters learning is of critical importance. Our goal is to help parents establish such an environment.

"Beyond that, our intent is to demystify the black box called school. Parents must know what they can expect from teachers and how to make those expectations clear. *Family Learning* will serve as the guide to these parents."

According to Malkofsky, parental involvement in education already has risen along several fronts.

PTA membership, he noted, increased nationally in 1983 for the first time in nearly 30 years. Other instances have come from such diverse locales as Los Altos, California, where parents in the Bay Area have started a foundation for public schools, to Newark, New Jersey, where parents have joined together to operate the Ironbound Community School.

Accompanying the renewed concern for education is strong evidence that parents are searching for home products to buy that promise educational benefits to their children. The computer and educational game booms are only one of many indications.

These encouraging trends, said Malkofsky, suggest outstanding growth potential in *Family Learning*'s primary market—young families, often with considerable discretionary income.

Family Learning's start-up circulation of 150,000 contains impressive numbers. Average household income, for example, exceeds $34,000 per year, with 70 percent of fathers and 33 percent of mothers employed in professional and managerial fields.

Nearly two-thirds of all initial readers are college graduates, and 92 percent own homes.

Charter advertisers who appear in early issues of the magazine are currently being offered six ads for the price of four, with combined frequency discounts available for the other Learning Periodicals publications—*Learning, Classroom Computer Learning, Curriculum Product Review,* and *Educational Dealer.*

"The initial response to *Family Learning*—from parents, teachers, and the business community—has been very encouraging," said Malkofsky. "We're coming out with a magazine that has important things to say, at a time when people want to listen. It's a nice position to be in."

# # #

Local responses came quickly. The *Peninsula Times-Tribune,* in nearby Palo Alto, sent a reporter and photographer the next day to interview Malkofsky. The neighboring *San Mateo Times* ran a story on January 4.

The metropolitan San Francisco and San Jose newspapers were silent, but as the weeks went on, the company was about to get a big break where it needed it most—New York. The president of the company, David Lake, mailed a package consisting of the magazine, the news release, and the magazine's advertising sales kit to Philip Dougherty, who writes a widely read column on advertising in the *New York Times*. Two days later, Lake was on the telephone to Dougherty, and a couple of days after that, *Family Learning* was the lead item, complete with a picture of the magazine cover, in Dougherty's column. Wrote Dougherty, "The magazine is *Family Learning* and it is subtitled, 'For Parents Who Want To Help Their Children Learn.' Who is going to say no to that?"

Personal contact was paying off at another big paper, *USA Today*. Rebecca Turner, a writer in the editorial department, knew someone who was a friend of *USA Today* columnist Charles Truehart. A copy of the magazine went out, and a praise-filled review came back in Truehart's column.

Next, *Family Weekly*, the nationwide Sunday supplement, picked up the news release written by Dailey's colleague, Liz Sloan, who was handling editorial publicity. Mentions in the *Chicago Tribune* and the *Atlanta Journal* followed.

On the surface, *Family Learning*'s campaign would seem successful. But, observes Dailey, "In retrospect, I'd say we were lucky to get as widespread exposure as we did. True, we had a timely product—a magazine about learning when the nation was up in arms over the state of education. But with our resources spread thin, we had almost no time to follow news releases with phone calls, and no time to cultivate relationships with reporters. And personal contact and relationships are vital—remember that two of our best notices, in the *New York Times* and *USA Today*, came as a result of personal contacts."

Kathleen Pender, a business reporter for the *San Francisco Chronicle*, stresses how crucial personal contact can be.

"Getting rapport with a reporter is really important. I probably don't open even half my mail. But if I have good rapport with somebody, I'll open a letter from that person.

"There's a guy in the forest products industry, which is one industry I cover. Every once in a while, he just sends me interesting letters or articles about what the industry is doing. They're not even always about his company. It's just good information that I can file away and use when I need it. That sort of thing just engenders good relations."

If you're looking for coverage, Pender says, use a personal approach— and make sure you have something important to say. "I think a personalized letter is the most effective way to pitch a story. When I worked on the *Fort Worth Star-Telegram*, I used to write a lot about personal finance. One PR agency that represented a financial firm used to send me letters with all kinds of story suggestions about personal finance—and I used a few of them.

"We really are looking for story ideas all the time. But it has to be a real news story. People call us up with junk all the time. And that's a bad strategy for the PR person, because it gets a little like the boy who cried 'wolf.' If you always send in a bunch of junk, we'll ignore you when you have something important to say.

"One way to give your story news value is to peg it to something that's going on right now. For example, I cover international trade, and San Francisco gets a lot of traveling executives coming through the city. So I'll get a note telling me that the trade minister of some country is coming to town, and would I like to interview him. Well, I may not know much about the trade situation in that country, so I might not be very interested. But if that note says the trade minister will be prepared to talk about the rise of the dollar and its effect on American trade with his country, then that's something I might be able to use.

"Trend stories are also good when you want to get your company in the news. Newspapers—especially big-city newspapers—are reluctant to do single-company stories, particularly if it's a small company. But if it's a company that's on the cutting edge of a trend, or, say, your company is one of a half-dozen leading companies that do whatever it is they do, then you stand a lot better chance of getting your story in if you pitch a trend in the whole industry."

How do you keep track of contacts—old ones, potential ones, specialized ones?

Ellen Rony, long a public-relations practitioner, now is considered a database expert. She was born in Hollywood, California—which she says is "smoggy and noisy"—and lives in Northern California at Tiburon. She learned how to use databases while writing instruction manuals for IBM personal computers and other microcomputers.

Here are Rony's words about how she became a public relations manager.

In February of 1983, I was hired by Stoneware, Inc., of San Rafael, California, to assist with the documentation of a complex business software program for the IBM-PC. . . .

I was one of four writers working on the project. We were in the best position to demonstrate the program because other than the two men who designed it, we were the only ones who worked with it daily. As such, I was taken to COMDEX (for Computer Dealers' Exposition), the major computer convention held semi-annually in Atlanta and Las Vegas.

These conventions draw all the cognoscenti of the industry: hardware vendors, dealers, media folk, software developers. The particular shows are used as a staging ground for new product introductions and to generate dealer interest in existing products. They also serve to prove the financial health of a company.

In the past two years the shows have typically drawn 65,000–80,000 attendees during the course of five days, with 1,200 to maybe 1,450 vendors. And all day long we stand in our booth and demonstrate our products.

Demonstrating a software program day after day is a tiring affair. The rewards for a successful show are usually delayed, showing up weeks later in dealer orders and magazine reviews. . . .

Each show has itinerant press people. They review products for industry magazines. They highlight personalities, products and companies. They come up with some reason to be considered "PRESS" so that they can get into the convention free, use the press lounge and attend press parties. They are identified by the green "PRESS" ribbons below their show badges.

[One year] there were more than 150 high tech magazines, with new publications announced at each show. It seemed to me that if I was going to demonstrate the product, I would do so for a member of the press. My journalism training made indelible to me the power of the press, and of all the people associated with my newly chosen industry, I felt most closely connected to its media component. Since I had written for several major computer magazines, I already knew some editors. Hence, when I attended a show, I would always try to snare press people into the booth for a demonstration. I recognized the longer term value of selling the product to the press rather than to a dealer or two. A good review would be read by thousands of dealers and sell the product long after energy and enthusiasm generated by the show was gone.

. . . The product manager noticed that I always had these people with green press ribbons at my work station. When he became president the following year, he decided that I would have more value to the company working as its public relations manager, a task I began in February of 1984.

Prior to my shift into that position, public relations was not even included on the organizational chart. Only three press releases had been issued about the company and its products during the prior year. No press release list existed; no press kits had been designed. Although nothing in my training directly addressed itself to public relations, I intuitively knew the value of maintaining visibility. Immediately I issued news about the change of management and began sending out a press release each week. Other tasks I added to my domain included sending review copies of the product to editors, soliciting reviews for magazines, and finding customers to profile for articles. . . .

All marketing activities (except the public relations now) were being handled by a well known, very expensive high tech advertising agency located 60 miles away. I was very verbal in my disappointment with their work. The first brochures were expensive, incorrect, and hard to read. They didn't carry out our color theme, using instead a purple/orange file folder design that looked like high tech pizza. The typeface with which the agency was enamored was hard to read. I expressed enough concern about Stoneware's overall image that the president (who doubled as director of marketing) began giving me marketing tasks. At first I was just writing short sales pieces, but soon he had me redesigning the brochures. The agency was told its services were no longer needed. When I complained that my public relations work was shoved down to the last 15 percent of my available time, he solved the problem in a way I hadn't expected: by giving me a new title, marketing communications manager. And public relations continued to get the last 15 percent of my time throughout my term at Stoneware.

Balance the need to promote your client's interests with concern for accuracy and fairness.

Who can be . . . loyal and neutral, in a moment? No man.
William Shakespeare, Macbeth

A public-relations practitioner's success with the media depends on one aspect more than any other: a reputation for accuracy, truthfulness, and fairness. In essence, the PR professional serves two masters—the organization and the news media, and, by extension, the public.

The words of an investment banker in describing his relationship with clients apply equally to public relations: "Lie once in this business and you're through." Neither the media nor the public necessarily has the right to know everything that happens in a private company, but they do deserve—and expect—to be told the truth. By lying, PR people suffer instant and irreparable damage to their credibility, and credibility is the most important quality they have to offer in presenting the case for their organization. In public agencies, which also often employ large public-relations staffs, the public indeed has a right to know what is going on most or all of the time, because the public is paying the bill. Even more than those in private industry, PR people in public agencies have a special obligation to be forthcoming in their statements to the press and to the public.

Occasionally, PR people will offer exclusives to reporters—or, increasingly, reporters will demand exclusives as a condition of covering the story. This practice puts PR practitioners in an uncomfortable position, because the reporters who get left out will usually be angry about being scooped by their competition.

Naturally, friendship does affect source-reporter relationships. Observes Matthew Cooney, who runs the Office of Communication for the U.S. Department of Commerce, "If a cabinet officer knows a particular correspondent and has had a relationship with that person in the past, he would want to make sure that the correspondent gets in on a story. If that's currying favor, I don't know how you'd avoid it."

Cooney insists, however, that his staff gives every reporter the same access to information. Playing favorites is no way to run an effective public information office.

Public relations has the potential to serve the public interest.

The fate of the country . . . does not depend on what kind of paper
you drop into the ballot box once a year, but on what kind of man
you drop from your chamber into the street every morning.
Henry David Thoreau

As a summary, the best definition of the use of public relations has been composed by Robert L. Heilbroner, who wrote an article for *Harper's* magazine called, "Public Relations: The Invisible Sell." He ended his compelling article with these words:

> . . . by an unexpected twist, public relations has become a weapon whose recoil is greater than its muzzle blast. Good public relations has come to be something very much like the corporate conscience—a commercial conscience, no doubt, but a conscience none the less. If the public relations profession can bolster this role, if it can become the corporate conscience openly, fearlessly, and wisely, speaking not only *for* business but *to* business, then it will have more than redeemed its name.

EXERCISES

1. In the first few pages of this chapter, we presented three different definitions of public relations. Although many PR people think the last definition is the best of the three, choose the one that you consider the best definition. Be prepared to defend your choice.

2. Combine at least two of the definitions (or all three) in what you consider a better definition. Hand in your combined single definition.

3. Using elements of each definition of public relations, or ignoring all three, make up your own definition.

4. Perhaps you noticed while reading Kathleen Pender's words that this journalist said, "People call us up with junk all the time. And that's a bad strategy for the PR person. . . ." Other journalists are also critical of public relations practitioners, not only because some PR people do call with junk, but also because some of them seem not to know exactly what a news story is. Keeping these facts in mind, list other reasons why many PR practitioners

arouse suspicion in some journalists' minds. Turn in your list and be prepared to explain in class why your list is accurate.

5. Imagine that your college or university has a football, baseball, or basketball team that is having a year of losing twice as many games as it wins. Although the team has neither the size nor talent to win all or many games, it has players who work at their play as though it is the most important game anywhere. As if addressing the athletic director of your school, explain how he can use the spirit of the team to good advantage, even though it may continue to lose.

It is advertising that has been the death of words. The word "personal" now on an envelope means "impersonal"; "important," "unimportant." "The finest, the best, the purest"—what do they mean now? Something somebody wants to sell. We are a nation of word killers: "hero," "veteran," "tragedy"— watch the great words go down.
Edna St. Vincent Millay

Advertising is the art of making whole lies out of half truths.
Edgar A. Shoaff

If advertising encourages people to live beyond their means, so does matrimony.
Bruce Barton

Let advertisers spend the same amount of money improving their product that they do on advertising and they wouldn't have to advertise it.
Will Rogers

I do not read advertisements—I would spend all my time wanting things.
Archbishop of Canterbury

Nothing's so apt to undermine your confidence in a product as knowing that the commercial that is selling it has been approved by the company that makes it.
Franklin P. Jones

9

C   H   A   P   T   E   R

Writing Advertising Copy

The codfish lays ten thousand eggs,
The homely hen lays one.
The codfish never cackles
To tell what she has done,
And so we scorn the codfish
While the humble hen we prize,
Which only goes to show you
That it pays to advertise.   *Anonymous*

David Ogilvy, for years head of one of the largest advertising agencies in America, once asked an indifferent copywriter what books he had read about advertising. "He told me that he had not read any; he preferred to rely on his own intuition. 'Suppose,' I asked, 'your gall bladder has to be removed this evening. Will you choose a surgeon who has read some books on anatomy and knows where to find your gall bladder, or a surgeon who relies on his intuition? Why should our clients be expected to bet millions of dollars on your intuition?' "

WHAT IS ADVERTISING?

Here is the first rule of ad writing: Keep it simple. Except when they're specifically shopping for something, few people seek out advertisements. In fact, many people go out of their way to avoid them. The simply written, direct ad is far more likely to compel a reader's attention than is a complex litany of prose.

213

David M. Ogilvy

Born in England in 1911 and educated at Oxford, David Ogilvy wrote *Ogilvy on Advertising*, which was published in 1983; it became *the* book among advertising people. Here is how he began:

> I do not regard advertising as entertainment or an art form, but as a medium of information. When I write an advertisement, I don't want you to tell me that you find it "creative." I want you to find it so interesting that you *buy the product*. When Aeschines spoke, they said, "How well he speaks." But when Demosthenes spoke, they said, "Let us march against Philip."
>
> In *My Confessions of an Advertising Man,* published in 1963, I told the story of how Ogilvy & Mather came into existence, and set forth the principles on which our early success had been based. What was then little more than a creative boutique in New York has since become one of the four biggest advertising agencies in the world, with 140 offices in 40 countries. Our principles seem to work.

Ogilvy's system does work. It is based on research and drumming research into the heads of his employees: Research shows that commercials with celebrities are below average. Also: Research suggests that if you set the copy in black type on a white background, more people will read it than if you set it in white type on a black background.

But there is much more to advertising than research, as Ogilvy agrees. John Caples, perhaps the best of copywriters, said, "I have seen one advertisement actually sell not twice as much, not three times as much, but 19½ times as much as another. Both advertisements occupied the same space. Both were run in the same publication. Both had photographic illustrations. Both had carefully written copy. The difference was that one used the right appeal and the other used the wrong appeal."

Using the right appeal and other basic techniques are the subjects of *Ogilvy on Advertising*. This book also describes how to get a job in advertising, how to create advertising that makes the cash register ring, twelve kinds of TV commercials that sell and four that don't, how to write successful copy and get people to read it, sex in advertising (good and bad), eighteen miracles of research, six giants who made modern advertising, and what the future holds in store for advertising.

Ogilvy did not start out to be an advertising executive. He has also been a chef in Paris, a stove salesman in Scotland, a director of the Gallup Research Institute, a secretary in the British Embassy to Washington, and a farmer in the Amish county. Ogilvy has left advertising and lives in France in retirement on a palatial estate.

Think of the advertising slogans that you remember. Most are probably short and to the point: "Coke is it." "Pepsi—the choice of a new generation." "This Bud's for you." "Dodge trucks are ram-tough." "Pontiac—We build excitement." "Like a good neighbor, State Farm is there."

An advertising slogan generally has to be short for two reasons: It has to be noticed and it has to be remembered. If it's too long or too complicated, it will fail—and so will the product that it is attempting to sell.

Journalism informs; advertising persuades.

The careful reader of a few good newspapers can learn more in a
year than most scholars do in their libraries.   *F. B. Sanborn*

Doing business without advertising is like winking at a girl in the
dark. You know what you're doing, but nobody else does.   *Luther Feck*

Writing advertising has much in common with writing news pieces. In both, the headline is paramount in grabbing attention and communicating the main message. In both, pictures are often vital. And when both are at their best, a compelling story unfolds.

Where advertising differs from journalistic writing, however, is in its basic mission. Whereas the main intent of journalism is to inform, the only goal of advertising is—or should be—to sell.

What advertising people do is fairly easy to describe in a general way. They plan, compose, and disseminate sales messages designed to identify or persuade. The field of advertising is too complex to be easily described, but advertisements themselves can be classified broadly as consumer, industrial (or business-to-business), and institutional.

Consumer advertising is direct and usually calculated to sell consumer products or services to the public. The great majority of ads in general-interest publications and on television and radio are consumer ads. In *industrial,* or *business-to-business* advertising, companies sell to one another. Many smaller ad agencies succeed by creating ads for businesses selling products that most consumers will never hear of. *Institutional advertising* talks generally about a company. It may lead directly to the sale of goods and services, but its primary aim is to promote a favorable image of an entire corporation, rather than sell a single product.

Advertising uses diverse avenues of appeal.

Business? It's quite simple. It's other people's money.
Alexandre Dumas

Dumas' aphorism probably holds better in advertising than in just about any other business. That is because, in advertising, clients often pay millions to advertising agencies to create campaigns that may bring fabulous fortune—or absolute disaster. In either event, advertising relies on four major avenues of appeal, which have been described by Albert Frey:

Primary—those aimed at inducing the purchase of one *type* of product.

Selective—those aimed at inducing the purchase of a particular *brand*.

Emotional (sometimes termed *short-circuit* and *human-interest* appeals)—those aimed at the emotions rather than the intellect.

Rational (sometimes termed *long-circuit* and *reason-why* appeals)—those directed at the intellect.

Advertising messages are delivered by a variety of media, including television, radio, newspapers, magazines, billboards, and direct mail. As we shall discuss, writing for each medium presents its own set of challenges.

Leading figures in advertising have some highly individual notions about how merchandising should be carried out. One prominent success is the frenetic Rosser Reeves, whose chief contribution to advertising theory is known as "USP":

We can't sell a product unless it's a good product, and even then we can't sell it unless we can find the Unique Selling Proposition. There are three rules for a USP. First, you need a definite proposition: buy this product and you get this specific benefit. Pick up any textbook on advertising and that's on page one—but everybody ignores it. Then, second, it must offer a unique proposition, one which the opposition *cannot* or *does not* offer. Third, the proposition must sell. Colgate was advertising "ribbon dental cream . . . it comes out like a ribbon and lies flat on your brush." Well, that was a proposition and it was unique, but it didn't sell. Bates [the Ted Bates advertising agency] gave them "cleans your breath while it cleans your teeth." Now every dentifrice cleans your breath while it cleans your teeth—*but nobody had ever put a breath claim on a toothpaste before.*

David Ogilvy, founder of Ogilvy & Mather, a leader in brand-image advertising, specializes in building an aura of sophistication. Ogilvy has written, "It pays to give your brand a *first-class* ticket through life. People don't like to be seen consuming products which their friends regard as third-class."

Ogilvy is noted for choosing models who exude elegance. He hired Baron George Wrangell, a Russian nobleman, to pose, black eye-patch prominently shown, as "the man in the Hathaway shirt." In a speech at a meeting of the American Association of Advertising Agencies, Ogilvy pronounced his major theme: "Let us remember that it is almost always the total *personality* of a brand rather than any *trivial product difference* which decides its ultimate position in the market."

Ogilvy is known for his methodical, scientific approach to advertising, an attitude born of his early experience as an opinion poller and analyst in the George Gallup surveying organization. By contrast, Ogilvy's contemporary, William Bernbach, simply hired the most creative copywriters and artists he could find and threw them together at his agency, Doyle Dane Bernbach. Bernbach held that advertising is not a science, but an art. Speaking to other advertising specialists, he said:

> Why should anyone look at your ad? The reader doesn't buy his magazine or tune in his radio and TV to see and hear what you have to say. . . . What is the use of saying all the right things in the world if nobody is going to read them? And, believe me, nobody is going to read them if they are not said with freshness, originality, and imagination.

WRITING ADVERTISEMENTS

Basic writing principles—be clear, be simple, make your most important points in an effective manner—apply equally to newswriting, feature writing, public relations, *and* advertising.

Different media require different writing styles.

I make my advertising men so good that I can't keep them.
Albert Lasker

Just as journalists write differently for different media, so do advertising copywriters. A newspaper ad presents problems entirely different from those of a television or radio commercial.

A full discussion of various writing techniques could easily fill a textbook. Following, however, are some basic rules of thumb for writing in the different advertising media.

Newspapers. Remember that the purpose of a newspaper is to communicate *news*—stories that carry information about current events. Whenever it makes sense, newspaper ads should be newsy, as in "TWA Announces New Fares to London," or "Here's How You Can Save on Your Next Purchase of Kellogg's Corn Flakes." Newspaper ads should carry big headlines, just as news stories do. Ads that look like editorial layouts are often effective, even when the newspaper's management inserts the disclaimer, "advertisement," over each column.

Magazines. Magazine ads often rely on graphics as much or more than copy, because of the excellent reproduction quality available in this medium.

Because magazines are usually feature-oriented, ads need not be newsy to be in context. Copy can be short or long; magazine ads often offer the opportunity to tell a lengthy, well-illustrated story about a product.

Radio.   As with newswriting in radio, write short, declarative sentences. It's often an effective strategy to lead with a question whose answer is undeniably, "Yes"—such as, "Want a way to save on your income tax?" Radio takes away the visual medium of newspapers and magazines, but in its stead offers sound, which can be just as effective in inviting the listener to visualize a scene. When appropriate, sound effects should be used to add authenticity and to make the commercial come alive. Music can also be used to punctuate key lines in the copy or, in the case of a product jingle, actually to deliver vital selling points and help the listener remember the brand name.

Television.   Television is the most lifelike of all advertising media, and allows the use of visual and auditory signals that reinforce each other. As in all advertising, repetition is vital in television. When crafting a television commercial, remember these points offered by David Ogilvy:

1. Identify brands. Use the name of the brand in the first eight to ten seconds. Later in the commercial, repeat the name of the brand at least three times.

2. Show the package. Always show the package, especially at the end of the commercial.

3. Use close-ups. Show the package in close-ups.

4. Avoid voice-overs. It is better to have an actor on camera speak than to use his or her voice off camera.

5. When you do use voice-overs, superimpose print that says precisely what the soundtrack says.

Direct mail.   Direct mail is the fastest-growing segment of advertising in the United States. In direct mail, as in all advertising, be conversational. Even though your words may be read by millions, you're still talking to one person at a time. Speak to that person as though he or she were your closest friend, someone to whom you wished to impart some particularly useful advice. Here again, the "yessable" question is an effective opener; it arouses interest and gets the reader agreeing with you from the outset. Always include a "teaser" (one or two provocative lines of copy) on *both* sides of the envelope or postcard—you never know which side will land face up in the mailbox. Studies show response to direct mail is increased by including a headline at the top of the letter, by highlighting key points with under-lining, indention, or use of a second color, and by repeating the offer several times, both in the letter and in other pieces in the package. Always include a business reply postcard; headline it with a positive statement, such as,

"Yes! I want to win a trip to Hawaii *today*! Sign me up for a subscription and enter my name in your free travel sweepstakes."

To write effective advertisements, you must usually put objectivity aside, focusing on benefits rather than facts.

My wants are many, and, if told,
Would muster many a score;
And were each wish a mint of gold,
I still should long for more.
John Quincy Adams

"People who go looking for a quarter-inch drill bit aren't really all that interested in the drill bit. What they really want is a quarter-inch hole."

So wrote an influential practitioner in *Advertising Age*, the leading trade publication in advertising. This point is important because one mistake common among beginning ad writers—especially those who have been journalists—lies in merely describing product features instead of promoting benefits to buyers.

Think of the reasons that you buy products. Do you choose a pair of shoes simply because the leather is double-stitched, or because the double-stitching will give the shoes longer life? Do you buy a brand of perfume or after-shave because of its specific chemical makeup, or because it makes you feel attractive? The purpose of advertising is to communicate to you how much money you'll save with longer-lasting shoes, and how much sexier you'll feel wearing that particular scent—and then to motivate you to buy that product.

Speak in terms of your audience's interests.

The way we sell is to get read first.   *Raymond Rubicam*

As in any kind of writing, it's easy to assume in advertising that your experience mirrors that of your audience. And, as elsewhere, it's a trap to avoid. You may buy clothes for warmth and durability, but your roommate may buy them for style. Whenever you're writing an ad, concentrate on what your audience wants, not what you want. After all, you're not the one who needs to be convinced.

Successful copywriting begins with research.

You have to throw yourself away when you write.   *Maxwell Perkins*

What's the best way to find out what your audience wants? Generally, it's through research. Companies spend millions each year to find out what customers are thinking, and firms have grown large specializing in consumer research. Research is important because it keeps everyone, from the copywriter to the marketing manager, from making false assumptions about the needs and wants of the customer. Research provides the candlepower to illuminate an ad; without it, the writer might as well be working in the dark.

In 1985, AT&T Technologies opened a design center for complex electronic circuits in the heart of California's Silicon Valley. For a hefty consulting fee, AT&T was offering its engineers and equipment to help electronics companies in the area create new products. In introducing the new center, AT&T's marketing people originally thought they should stress the company's tremendous size and success in electronics. A simple survey of their potential customers, however, showed that local executives were largely unimpressed with bigness; some, who had started their own small companies, actually resented big firms, whom they associated with their competitors.

With this knowledge, AT&T's advertising agency developed a campaign that emphasized a partnership between the company and its customers. The campaign, so successful that it was later extended to AT&T's European operations, portrayed the company as a friendly and experienced innovator that would work hand-in-hand with local firms to help them succeed. The campaign worked for many reasons, but chief among them were these: (1) it was grounded in research, (2) it spoke to the interests of the audience, and (3) it offered specific benefits to the customer.

THE PSYCHOLOGY OF ADVERTISING

Perhaps even more than in other kinds of writing, advertising writers need to know their audience—how it thinks and how it feels. Advertising makes much use of methods that let it understand people.

Advertising is based on psychology.

A man alone in a room with the English language, trying to get
human feelings right must call for advice from psychologists.
Anonymous

Finding out what appeals to people and what moves them to act is the province of the social scientist. Because advertising's twin goals are persuasion and motivation, it's not surprising that successful advertising people look for guidance in the findings of psychologists and sociologists.

An Account
Executive's Job

When Mary Anne Rothberg was an undergraduate at Stanford University, she performed so well that she was chosen to graduate with distinction. When she was twenty-four years old she became an account executive at the largest advertising agency in the world, J. Walter Thompson. After two years as an account executive, she went to the Harvard Business School and graduated in 1987. Here is her account.

Advertising. To industry outsiders this conjures up the exciting world of Madison Avenue, the casting couch, and the three-martini lunch. Tell a fan of 1960s television that you're in advertising, and his mind immediately will turn to thoughts of Darren Stevens and Larry Tate wining and dining clients.

I was in advertising for three years, two of which were spent at J. Walter Thompson in New York. No! JWT isn't on Madison Avenue. Few advertising agencies are on Madison due to high rents. And no. I didn't spend my afternoons playing golf with clients. The job I had was quite different from the one glamorized on TV. I was an account executive (AE). And this is my account of a day/week/month in the life of a real AE.

The Account Management group—the group of which I was a part—is at the center of the organization. As an account executive, I performed a variety of functions. To a certain extent, I was the PR man for the agency, responsible for the day-to-day running of the account and maintenance of the agency/client relationship. I coordinated the work of the various support groups and presented this work to the client. My job was to make sure that the various agency support groups were following the same strategy. Death to the AE who permits the Creative Department to produce an MTV-like commercial for an advertising spot purchased by the Media Group on the Lawrence Welk Hour!

I was also responsible for generating ideas concerning the marketing of various products. The extent to which the AE needs to be a marketing "expert" varies from account to account. In general, the packaged goods accounts are more marketing oriented; the service accounts (e.g., fast food) are more executional.

But the most difficult part of the AE's job is managing people over whom he has no direct authority. Egos frequently get in the way and in the advertising business, there are some pretty large egos. Thus the AE must be a skilled manipulator and politician. The AE must persuade the support groups to meet deadlines without being able to impose

(continued)

An Account
Executive's Job *(continued)*

sanctions. The AE must never act like a pest. He or she must win the respect of co-workers or he or she will fail.

Each account executive is assigned to one account for the period of one to two years during which time he or she lives, eats, and breathes his or her assigned product. At J. Walter I was assigned to a variety of packaged goods accounts including Impulse Body Spray, Chewels gum, and Sticklets gum.

My agency had a knack for assigning the wrong people to the wrong accounts. The woman in the next office, for example, had written her college senior thesis on the abuses of the Nestle company in the third world. You guessed it. She was assigned to the Nestle account. I used to imagine that somewhere in the executive offices someone was getting a good laugh at the employees' expense.

I was assigned to oversee the Warner Lambert gum products. But everyone in the agency knew I didn't chew gum. In fact, they knew that I was completely repulsed by gum. And yet my job every day for over one year was to spend a minimum of eight hours per day thinking about gum. Daily I pondered the deep dark secrets of the world of gum: Why do people chew gum? How does the personality of the person who prefers peppermint differ from that of the spearmint chewer? How large is the ideal wad?

Of course, the agency has a variety of support groups who are assigned the task of finding answers to these and other penetrating questions. The key groups include the following:

Media. The media group unfairly is considered to be the lowest group on the agency totem pole most likely due to the tedious nature of the job. The department is divided into media planning and media buying functions although many large clients do their own buying in-house. The planners are responsible for determining the best way to allocate the client's advertising dollars so that the advertising will reach the desired target audience. The buyers negotiate with the TV networks, magazines, radio stations, and newspapers for time or space and they execute the buys.

Research. The researchers are the scholars of the agency. They look at long-term consumer and media trends (e.g., the impact of fifteen vs. thirty-second commercials) and implications for the agency, as a whole. And they focus on the day-to-day client research needs, writing questionnaires and setting up research studies. The work of the Research Department is the key to determining the way a product should be positioned.

Creative. Creative service is the most important agency function. After all, it generally is the reason why the agency has been hired. The creative group is divided into copy writers and art directors. Each account is assigned one copy writer and one art director who work as a team to develop the advertising concept from strategies which have been outlined by the account executives in conjunction with the client. They write the copy and lyrics and sketch the storyboard—frame-by-frame mock ups of the commercial. They also work with producers and directors who will shoot the commercial. (All filming and taping is contracted out.) True to their titles, the Creatives dress creatively. It is not unusual to spot one en route to a client meeting attired in leather and chains.

There is tension among all the groups for power. But the biggest agency rift is between the account executive and the creative. Each sees himself as the key player at the agency. The truth of the matter is that having both a strong account team and a strong creative team is essential to providing good client service.

At JWT, the balance was tipped slightly in favor of the creatives as the agency was attempting to rebuild its reputation as a creative powerhouse.

What is a typical day in advertising? I usually arrived at the office by 8 A.M. to have one hour to collect my thoughts, plan the day's activities, and work on assignments before the 9 A.M. rush of telephone calls. The telephone plays a major role in the life of an account executive, serving as a vehicle for coordinating activities among the departments.

A typical day was spent responding to client crises. The wrong ad had been aired the previous night and the client had been watching TV. The right ad had been aired last night at the wrong time (e.g., the fast-food ad had been shown during the Richard Simmons Show). Or the client's ad budget had been cut in half and the media plan would have to be revised. This would often result in a flurry of phone calls to the various support groups followed by a rash of meetings to determine what caused the problem and potential solutions.

Meetings came in a variety of types and sizes. We had client meetings several times a week to present and sell creative material, media plans, or research findings. To prepare for a client meeting required at least two in-house meetings. The Brand Review meeting was held for new team members, both client and in-house, to acquaint them with the history of the brand and past advertising challenges. And brainstorming sessions were held once or twice per year to work on pressing brand issues.

Between meetings, I generated a lot of reports. Every two months, I sent out a sales analysis compiled from Nielsen reports which showed

(continued)

**An Account
Executive's Job** *(continued)*

product share by size, district, color, etc., as well as shares of competitive products and implications for our brand. Much time also was spent drafting agency points of view reports for clients. A typical report contained suggestions for new promotions or ways to improve sales in depressed areas. And every month I prepared a project report outlining the status of all the other reports and projects with estimated completion dates.

Between noon and two o'clock the office emptied for lunch. Lunch could be as casual as grabbing a sandwich from the company cafeteria and eating at my desk. Or it could be as formal as a meal with clients or agency personnel at a posh New York restaurant to discuss client issues or to forge good relationships.

The best days were spent at commercial shoots. It is standard procedure for the AE to cover the shoot. Yet my supervisors frequently expressed renewed and profound interest in my product when the shoot occurred in California or overseas. When I attended the shoots, my job was to make sure everything the client wanted filmed was filmed or recorded. I covered the agency's behind for fear that the client would view the advertisement and refuse to pay for it. Despite the gravity of the task, all of the important decisions had been made in advance at the creative meetings. So I simply walked about the set and observed.

The day ended at 6 P.M. After work, the AE's congregated in the JWT bar to discuss client problems and agency gossip. Occasionally I would join them. Or I entertained clients who had just been promoted and who couldn't celebrate at lunch time. Approximately once per month, the agency threw a party to celebrate the winning of a new multi-million dollar account, the loss of a pain-in-the-neck account, Secretary's week, or Thank God It's Tuesday. The idea behind the parties and the bar was to give the employees a chance to get to know each other informally to facilitate formal communication.

From the standpoint of the psychologist, copywriters are concerned with creating opinions. Fortunately for copywriters, the process by which people make up their minds has been extensively studied.

In 1968, the social scientist Robert P. Abelson postulated an "opinion molecule," which he believed was made up of three components: (1) a belief, (2) an attitude, and (3) a perception of support for that attitude. Or, as Abelson put it, the "three F's" that constitute an opinion: a fact, a feeling, and a following.

Psychologist Daryl Bem, in his book, *Beliefs, Attitudes and Human Affairs*, illustrates the opinion molecule like this: "It's a fact that when my Uncle Charlie had back trouble, he was cured by a chiropractor (*fact*). You know, I feel that chiropractors have been sneered at too much (*feeling*), and I'm not ashamed to say so because I know a lot of people who feel the same way (*following*)."

Consider how the opinion molecule underlies the following print ad, which promotes foreign industrial development in Austria:

Headline: THE BEAUTY OF AUSTRIA (As seen by GM.)

Picture: A complex interlocking set of mechanical gears

Copy:

Behind the dazzling scenery and Viennese waltzes beats the highly industrialized heart of Europe: Austria. Second only to Japan in growth of GNP, productivity and export sales.

GM recently completed a new $500 million manufacturing facility on the outskirts of Vienna, where 2,500 skilled workers are building high quality engines and transmissions at the rate of 70 per hour.

GM's not alone. In the past few years, more than a thousand foreign manufacturing firms have found a second home here. For obvious reasons.

Austria offers German quality and efficiency at 30 percent less than Germany's production costs. Skilled labor with virtually no strikes. A centralized location affording duty-free access to all European markets. All adding up to Europe's most promising return on investment opportunity.

Plus a wide range of incentives ranking among the best in Europe.

Austria's dynamic economy, stable currency and unmatched quality of life are still other beautiful inducements.

Write or phone for a complete picture on the beauty of business in Austria.

Tagline: AUSTRIA

Come see the sites.

This is a solid ad for several reasons, but for now, let's examine the way it touches every element in the opinion molecule.

First, there are facts—lots of them. Austria is second only to Japan in growth of GNP, productivity, and export sales. Austria's labor costs are 30 percent less than Germany's. Strikes are rare. The country is centrally located within Europe and offers duty-free access to other European countries.

The facts add up to a feeling: Austria is a beautiful place in which to locate a manufacturing plant—not because of the Alps and the lakes, but because of the excellent business environment there.

And, if more convincing is necessary, consider that Austria has attracted General Motors and more than a thousand other foreign companies. If you're an executive looking for a plant site, you won't be alone in deciding on Austria.

Emotional benefits have strong appeal.

His heart runs away with his head.   *George Colman*

Of the three points in the opinion molecule, two concern the emotions. The second element—the attitude—is, after all, the way we *feel* about something. The third element—the perception of support—also hinges on an emotion—namely, reassurance.

Most people agree that emotion is a more powerful motivator than is rational thought. With our minds we assess the facts and attempt to conclude a logical course of action. But our hearts tell us what is right and what we must do as a consequence of our beliefs. Knute Rockne, the legendary football coach, could have told his Notre Dame team that the day's opponent had many weaknesses that the Fighting Irish could exploit for a victory. But instead, he gathered the team around him in the locker room and reminded them of George Gipp, a great teammate who had died not long before. Rockne's emotional plea, "Win one for the Gipper," propelled the team onto the field ready to destroy the opposition and has since become one of America's most famous rallying cries.

Given its power, it's easy to see why emotion forms the basis for many of the most effective ads. Browsing through a magazine or watching an hour of television will yield advertisements that appeal to an entire spectrum of emotions: love, fear, pride, anger, happiness, self-esteem, ambition, patriotism, and so on.

Earlier, when we spoke of emphasizing benefits, we talked about practical, tangible benefits—getting a quarter-inch hole from a quarter-inch drill bit. But even more powerful are intangible, *emotional* benefits—the ways in which a product promises to increase our self-esteem, help us find love, advance our careers, or protect us from something we fear.

A TV commercial for Lipton Cup-a-Soup, for example, shows a mother serving soup to her young children, who smile at her and make her feel appreciated. With the line, "Cup-a-Soup puts a smile on your face," the commercial touches many emotions, most prominently a mother's love and sense of responsibility for her children. That has far more powerful appeal than simply saying, "Lipton Soup makes a nourishing, good-tasting meal for your family on a cold winter afternoon."

Products need a personality to differentiate them from each other.

Eventually knowing a new product is learning what you didn't even know you didn't know.   *Anonymous*

Most products, in and of themselves, are not exciting. Moreover, many products are essentially similar. Toothpaste, scouring powder, laundry soap, shaving cream—many such "parity products" are distinguished only by minute differences in actual makeup. The differences that we perceive in the products are often created largely by advertising—and particularly by giving the product a personality.

As we mentioned, David Ogilvy is a master at creating a personality for a product. When Ogilvy & Mather landed the Hathaway account, the client was a relatively obscure shirtmaker. Moreover, there wasn't much to say about a shirt that hadn't been said thousands of times already; the styles don't change much, and just about all dress shirts are comfortable and well-made.

Instead of concentrating on the shirt, Ogilvy zeroed in on *the man who wears the shirt.* "The man in the Hathaway shirt" was in real life a Russian nobleman whose distinguished carriage and black eyepatch gave the product a classy, confident, individualistic image. Hathaway's sales soared.

Likewise, Ogilvy used Commander Whitehead to create a personality for Schweppes club soda and tonic water—two parity products that bore virtually no distinction from their competitors, except in their very clever advertising. Here again, the image was high-tone; the Commander was seen constantly serving Schweppes mixers on his yacht, at lavish parties, and other luminous social occasions. The public quickly came to perceive Schweppes as the high-class mixers—even though they were not substantially different from any others on the market.

Personality can also enliven a mundane product. For years, Owens-Corning has used the Pink Panther cartoon character as a symbol for its building insulation. Rather than drone on about the advantages of Owens-Corning insulation, the ads show the Pink Panther busily laying down rolls of insulation, then enjoying cool summers and warm winters. Like the panther, Owens-Corning fiberglass is pink, and the tagline to the commercials for years has been, "Put your house in the pink."

The Pink Panther is clever and whimsical, Commander Whitehead and Baron Wrangell downright aristocratic. The personality traits that they bring to their products are the traits that we see in ourselves—or at least wish we did. That is what makes personality work in advertising. Beyond differentiating products, personality attempts to make products extensions of ourselves, or to indicate that they will bring to ourselves qualities that we wish we had. When we buy Calvin Klein jeans, we hope a little of Brooke

Shields's sex appeal will rub off. When we buy Delco auto parts, we're certain, at least subconsciously, that we, too, will be imbued with "the right stuff" of their spokesman, General Chuck Yeager, the man who "never waits for trouble."

ATTRACTING THE AUDIENCE

What is the most effective way to get your point across? It varies, depending on the product and the medium, of course, but good ad writing calls upon the same elements that draw us to read anything: a good story, drama, mystery, and so on.

Writing a good ad is like writing a good story.

I often wonder whether others do the same—if a thing has really come off, it seems to me there mustn't be one single word out of place, or one word that could be taken out.   *Katherine Mansfield*

What makes a good story? Conflict, suspense, beautiful narration, continual surprise. It's only natural that the same elements make up an effective advertisement, because an ad is itself a story—the story of a product and how it will enhance the life of the customer.

In print advertising—ads for newspapers, magazines, and, in a broad sense, billboards—the headline and the picture should sum up the whole story. That is because most readers—and all drivers—are only casual viewers of advertising messages. Therefore, the message must hit them quickly and evocatively, so that even if they don't stop to read the copy, an impression will have been made.

Many of the most compelling ads carry tension between the picture and the headline. In these ads, the headline seems almost to collide with the picture to create an irony or a double meaning. The result is a combined message far stronger than the headline or the picture could have conveyed alone.

Consider the "Beauty of Austria" ad. Reading the headline, we would normally imagine the snow-tipped Alps, deep blue lakes, and rolling green valleys. But instead, the picture shows us a finely tooled set of transmission gears. The ad works because it takes a common—even stereotypic—idea and pulls from it a second meaning: Austria offers a kind of beauty that you may not have considered before. The tagline—"Come see the sites" (that is, the industrial sites)—completes the play on a traditional sightseeing ad.

Ads such as this one work because they are surprising; like a good play or story, they set up one set of expectations and then deliver something entirely unexpected. Billboards, especially, make use of this strategy, because by nature they must often consist only of a picture and a headline. One memorable billboard for Alaska Airlines proclaimed "The best fare to Seattle," accompanied not by a ticket price but by a tempting platter of the food served on the airplane.

Other ads, equally effective, also rely on a basic storytelling technique: a resolution of conflict. Consider this ad, which relies on words alone to tell its story:

Headline: NIGHTS, HE'S LOADED.

MORNINGS, HE'S SORRY.

I HATE NIGHTS AND MORNINGS.

People dependent on alcohol and drugs spend much of their life filled with remorse. But, addiction is a disease and remorse cannot cure it. If this sounds like someone you love, call The Phoenix Program at a hospital near you. We are trained to help you, and them, gain control of life again. Call one of our 24-hour Helplines. Do it now. Nights and mornings *can* be some of the best times of your whole day.

Tagline: Phoenix Recovery Programs

Alcohol and drugs pull families apart. We bring them together.

There's nothing fancy or particularly clever about this ad. Yet it is tremendously effective, because the people it is trying to reach—addicts' families—will immediately recognize their lives and their emotions in the headline and the body copy. For someone whose family is being pulled apart by alcohol and drugs, the promise of being brought back together is probably worth the telephone call.

Note that these two ads make a specific request of the reader, namely to get in touch with the advertiser. In sales, this is called "asking for the order," and it is a key element in the success of an advertisement. Always make sure that the reader knows what he or she is expected to do—"call us," "come in for a test drive today," "don't miss this movie," and so forth. Otherwise, the reader will feel less compelled to take action—and an otherwise strong ad will have less of a result.

Mystery and drama make advertisements— especially television commercials— effective.

Suspense in news is torture. *John Milton*

Time magazine once called David Ogilvy "the most sought-after wizard in the advertising business." Not long after *Time*'s praise, Ogilvy wrote that showing the effects of television commercials in the pages of a book was impossible. Nonetheless, Ogilvy attempted to show why some television commercials work, in the pages of his book, *Ogilvy on Advertising*.

We will try to do much the same here, showing how two television commercials lured their audience.

Mystery. "Do you know me?" These words are said first by celebrities as they are featured in commercials for American Express. Of the dozens of celebrities, one whose face is least widely known is James Michener, author of many best-selling novels. Here is the way this Michener commercial appears:

James Michener is pictured landing from a small boat in Hawaii, arriving on a beach. He is not identified by name.

Michener: "Do you know me?"

The next picture shows Michener with only water and a reef behind him.

Michener: "I've written many books about faraway places."

The picture then shows him a little farther up the beach.

Michener: "But even after five million words, my face often draws a blank."

In the next picture, Hawaiian men and women appear well behind Michener.

Michener: "That's why I got the American Express Card."

Next, he is shown with a few additional people behind him.

Michener: "Now I can get a reception like a page . . ."

As he says these words, he is kissed on the cheek by a Hawaiian girl.

" . . . out of *Hawaii*."

The following picture shows an American Express Card with "James A. Michener" being printed on the card.

Voice-over: "To apply for a card . . ."

The next picture shows two American Express Cards mounted on a large poster. The cards are surrounded by pineapples.

" . . . look for this display wherever the card is welcome."

The last picture shows Michener seated by an elderly Hawaiian woman with other Hawaiians behind them.

Michener: "The American Express Card. Don't leave home without it."

Many advertising specialists say that testimonials by celebrities are seldom good advertisements. American Express, however, has used this kind of commercial since 1975. Why? The difference between this commercial and all the other attempts by other advertisers are captured in the suspense created by the first words, "Do you know me?"

Drama.   Almost all advertising agency people dislike "talking heads." There is, however, one talker who produces results for the advertiser. John Houseman, an aged actor who has been performing for more than fifty years, has a facility for emphasizing the proper words in a powerful way. Houseman says in his commercial for a brokerage house, "Smith Barney makes money the *old-fashioned* way. They *earn* it." As in the film, "The Paper Chase," in which he starred as the daunting Professor Kingsfield, Houseman in this commercial portrays a commanding figure whose words are forceful and dramatic—and doubted at one's likely regret.

Another kind of drama is represented by an advertisement in which a problem is surmounted with the help of a client's product or service. On television, these thirty- and sixty-second vignettes have become commonplace, but continue to be effective. An eight-year-old boy bursts through the door, covered with mud; his mother tosses the soiled clothes into the washer with her favorite laundry detergent, and, *voila*! Once again, whites are whiter and brights are brighter.

These ads, amazingly simple and predictable, remain effective because they *demonstrate* the product at work and show someone being pleased by the outcome. Viewers can see for themselves how good the product is and can imagine feeling as good as the actor or actress when the problem is resolved. Here again, a basic rule of writing is in operation: Rather than just telling about the product, the ad is *showing* how it works and how people benefit.

Short copy attracts readers; long copy increases sales.

It is quality rather than quantity that matters.   *Seneca*

George L. Dyer, advertising manager of the clothing company Hart, Schaffner & Marx, often wrote long, word-packed advertisements. Max Hart, his employer, argued that short, punchy ads with large pictures were more impressive. Dyer told him, "I bet you ten dollars I can write a newspaper ad of solid type and you'll read every word of it." Hart laughed at him. Dyer responded, "I don't have to write a line of the ad to prove my point. I'll tell you the headline: "This Page Is All About Max Hart." Hart paid the bet.

Considerable research has been done to answer the question, "Which works better—long copy or short?" The answer, generally speaking, is this: Short copy attracts more readers, but long copy makes more sales. David Ogilvy, for one, has always been particularly fond of long copy and is one of its most artful practitioners.

Both forms are difficult, for opposite reasons. Short copy must summarize the sales proposition in a headline and anywhere from one to five or six crisp sentences. Long copy, on the other hand, must unfold a story that will captivate the reader until, completely convinced, he or she reaches the company logo at the bottom of the ad.

With short copy, pictures are truly worth a thousand free words. In a full-page magazine ad for Martell cognac, an alluring woman sits poised to hand the reader a snifter, accompanied by the single line, "I assume you drink Martell." With only five words, this copy speaks volumes. Here, a basic tenet of the short story applies: Rather than tell, imply. The reader will have no trouble filling in the blanks, often more vividly than the writer could have expressed in words.

Use sex to sell only products related to sex appeals, and guard against tastelessness and exploitation.

She (Aphrodite) spoke and loosened from her bosom the embroidered girdle of many colors into which all her allurements were fashioned. In it was love and in it desire and in it blandishing persuasion which steals the mind even of the wise.   *Homer*, The Iliad

There is no question about it; sex sells. Thus, we are treated to color pictures of bikini-clad women clenching a lug wrench in each hand. Titillating photographs promote blue jeans, perfume and automobiles, liquor and cigarettes. The comedian George Carlin once summed it up neatly: "The commercial shows a couple standing on the train. The announcer says, 'Should a gentleman offer a lady a Tiparillo?' And then they cut to the train going into the tunnel. Now, you don't have to be Fellini to figure *that* out."

Sex appears in so many ads because it is a basic human desire, and successful advertising connects products to fundamental human needs. The effort to gain sex appeal motivates many purchases we make, from toothpaste to clothing to cars. It is natural that sex should be part of the sales message for many products.

But sex can be troublesome, and even downright silly, when it's used for products with which it has no real connection. A picture of a sexy woman astride a new tractor may be alluring, but it doesn't have much to do with why a farmer should buy that tractor. Consequently, the ad may not figure much in his purchasing decision.

Aside from often being incongruous, sex can backfire in at least two other ways. The more obvious way is that many people find sex in the media offensive and therefore resist the sales message. Less obvious is this fact uncovered by research: The audience, far from being offended, may be so attracted to the sexual nature of the ad that the sales message is forgotten or altogether ignored.

One of the chief problems in using sex is that people's tastes and moral standards vary wildly. A sexy commercial that clicks in Hollywood may bomb in conservative Orange County, only an hour's drive away. In all cases, good and sensitive taste should guide an advertisement's writer, artist, and producer. And one fast rule is increasingly pervasive: Sexual scenes that overtly exploit women are a mistake.

What constitutes exploitation is an open question, but ads that show persons of either sex in submissive poses can easily be classified as exploitive. One ad for a shopping mall showed a sultry woman in a clinging black dress, head arched back, face pouting, handcuffs shackling her wrists in front of her. A real-life sheriff stood by in the shadows. The headline read, "Crimes of Fashion," with the caption, "Her only crime was looking good."

This advertising, created by a woman, was intended to spoof the fashion-conscious detective show, "Miami Vice." Instead, it prompted immediate picketing by outraged women's groups and was cancelled on the morning it appeared.

EXERCISES

1.   In this chapter, we say "Short copy attracts readers; long copy increases sales." Explanations are presented, but to test the above words, clip, only from magazines, two examples of short copy ads and two examples of long copy ads. Read all four ads carefully, then explain at least one other reason, in addition to the arguments in this book, why long copy ads increase sales.

2.   In this chapter, you found five simple rules for crafting a television commercial. Station yourself before a television set and find at least two commercials that do *not* observe these rules. Write a paper that identifies each commercial and explain which rules each commercial did not observe. (Hint: Local rather than network commercials are more likely not to observe the rules.)

3.   Think of any product you like, then create a mystery beginning for a television ad for the product—the kind of beginning the American Express commercial uses: "Do you know me?" Think of a different question that creates a mystery, then write an ad.

Along with responsible newspapers we must have
responsible readers.
Arthur Hays Sulzberger

The only authors whom I acknowledge as American
are the journalists. They, indeed, are not great
writers, but they speak the language of their
countrymen, and make themselves heard by them.
Alexis de Tocqueville

If a newspaper prints a sex crime, it's smut, but
when *The New York Times* prints it, it's a sociological
study.
Adolph S. Ochs

The price of greatness is responsibility.
Winston Churchill

Few things help an individual more than place
responsibility upon him and to let him know that
you trust him.
Booker T. Washington

News is the first rough draft of history.
Ben Bradlee

If you sat down all the political reporters in a room
and told them only those who had never given
advice to a politician should stand up, hardly a soul
would dare rise.
Mary McGrory

10

C   H   A   P   T   E   R

Reporters'
Rights and
Responsibilities

A professor we know writes:

> I had to run to catch the bus. Just as I was mounting the first step, I dropped something. What? I couldn't think at all. Just as I got to the top step and handed the driver my transfer, it happened: I could hear an enormous bell clanging. I was looking at a woman sitting near the front of the bus; she seemed not to hear the bell.
>
> My right arm began to feel odd, then numb. I looked at it, confused. I thrust it into my pocket and stood there, weaving a bit, and then felt weak. After one step forward I turned awkwardly and sat down. During the next twenty minutes, which seemed to go on forever, every thought that I began to have faded immediately. I didn't try to speak; I just tried to think. Over and over, my thoughts ended in confusion.
>
> . . . I tried to get up and discovered my right leg wouldn't support me. I still didn't try to speak but tapped the driver on the shoulder, slipped, and hung onto the back of his seat.
>
> "Here, I'll help you," the driver said. He took my arm over his shoulder, and, with another passenger, pulled me into a small store. The driver said something to the store's owner, but I couldn't understand what he or the owner said. Feeling unbelievably tired, I tried to thank the driver. Nothing would come out.
>
> The store owner patted me on the shoulder and called an ambulance. After that he didn't return. I sat there with my head half-bowed. I could open my mouth and, perhaps, adjust my tongue, but still nothing came out. The only thought I had wasn't in words, yet told me somehow that I couldn't speak. It was as though I were watching myself. Over and over I opened my mouth. No sound.
>
> When the ambulance came, I was loaded in the back and driven to the hospital. At the hospital an orderly asked for my watch. I took it

235

off my wrist, gave it to him, and never saw it again. Another orderly asked for my wallet. Using my left hand, I took out my wallet, which held $26, and gave it to him. When I received my wallet back from the hospital, it held $1. A few hours later, my right arm and leg started working again. After six months, I could think and speak clearly.

A fellow who had earned his Ph.D. in my department told me what he had heard from other graduates who knew me. They said I had been walking down a street in the city, had had a stroke, and had fallen to the pavement. Then, they said, four young men had found me; stripped all my clothes off; taken my watch, money, and rings (I've never worn rings); and left me in the gutter.

WHAT ARE THE RESPONSIBILITIES OF THE PRESS?

You, the graduates who told others what they had heard about the professor's stroke, and everyone else who speaks or writes act as reporters every day. Professional reporters do formally and for a large audience what everyone does habitually: They tell people what they have heard, seen, and read.

Everyone reports events and ideas to others; professional reporters, though, must be more careful than amateurs not to distort the truth.

A writer's problem does not change. He himself changes and the world he lives in changes, but his problem remains the same. It is always how to write truly and, having found out what is true, to project it in such a way that it becomes part of the experience of the person who reads it.   *Ernest Hemingway*

In addition to sharing the actual reporting of events, professionals *present* news much as amateurs do. When we tell others about an event we consider important—a friend's car accident, an athletic victory, a celebrity's death—all of us are likely to give the results first and then fill in the details. Professionals follow the same pattern in a standard news story: results first and then details. You also resemble a professional reporter because you describe events differently to different listeners. You give all, some, or practically none of the details, depending on how interested you think a particular listener is in what you have to say.

Your everyday actions even resemble the work of the professional editor. When you listen to someone you know describe an experience you also took part in, you're likely to correct—or try to correct—any errors your companion makes in telling what happened.

You can see from the professor's account of his stroke and from what people who knew him said about it, though, how amateur reporting can radically distort information. One quality that sets the competent professional apart from the amateur reporter is an overriding regard for the truth.

The importance of truthfulness in reporting today stems from both the successes and the failures of American journalists during the past two centuries. (Throughout this text we use "journalists" to refer to those who write and edit stories for the electronic as well as the printed media and "the press" to refer to television and radio as well as newspapers and magazines.) Because reporters have given American citizens the information they have needed to protect their own interests and to function effectively as citizens, our nation has endured to become the oldest democracy in the world. But because of (1) conflict between advocates of strong government and the press that has existed since our Constitution was written, (2) pressure on the news media since the nineteenth century to entertain mass audiences, and (3) technology that has made news instant and pervasive during this century, today's reporters face challenges that only an understanding of history can equip them to understand and successfully meet.

A free, vigorous, and responsible press is the lifeblood of democracy.

If a nation expects to be ignorant and free, in a state of civilization, it expects what never was and never will be.   *Thomas Jefferson*

Every American citizen has the power to affect what our government does about nuclear and space weapons; decay in traditional industries and growth in technological and service occupations; abortion, genetic engineering, and euthanasia; and a vast array of other pressing and complicated issues. We also have the purchasing power to influence private enterprise. Most of us, however, learn practically nothing about public issues from personal experience. In a huge and complex society, we find the days too short for much beyond our work and our families and friends. We see for ourselves very little even of what happens in our own communities, and even public officials and businesspeople know from experience about only a tiny segment of the web of government and commerce. Our knowledge of public affairs, then, and our ability to make wise decisions about everything from whether we should buy a particular frozen dinner to who is the best candidate for president depend largely on what the information media tell us.

We do catch an occasional glimpse of a candidate for public office or do business with a government agency once in a while, and our circle of relatives, friends, and acquaintances may include a few who know or work with public officials, work with certain types of products like cars or hair dyes, or conduct research themselves. For the most part, though, the information media are the conduit and filter through which we become familiar with our government and society. Even if we don't read newspapers or magazines or listen to broadcast news, we learn from those who do. We can find out about and influence our city councils and school systems; the White House, the Pentagon, and Congress; and private business and can even decide what products are the best buys and how to change our habits to avoid illness only to the extent that the media seek out and provide a truthful picture of reality for us to judge and act on.

The architects of our nation, recognizing that information empowers the people who make up a democracy, gave journalists immense power by making the press the only privately owned business institution guaranteed its freedom by the Constitution. To the extent that reporters work at giving their audiences the information they need, freedom of the press serves the American people. Journalists who live up to the power they enjoy by seeking out and reporting significant truths give the members of their audience the power to make wise choices for themselves and society; in turn, the citizenry served well by the information media has an interest in preserving and guarding press freedom.

The press has set the agenda for public discussion and decision, then, since the 1700s; but the press has changed from the earliest newspapers, which served as competing political advocates, to a ubiquitous amalgam of magazines, newspapers, and radio and television stations striving, for the most part, to speak objectively.

RIGHTS VERSUS RESPONSIBILITIES

Because a free press plays a part in restraining government, reporters sometimes come into conflict with public officials.

The government has not only the right but sometimes the obligation
to lie.   *Jody Powell*

A thread woven throughout the fabric of American journalism is conflict between the press and public officials. Since Alexander Hamilton argued against absolute press freedom and George Washington protested the attacks on him published in anti-Federalist newspapers, American public officials and journalists have played roles that make them at least occasional adversaries.

Most public officials provide some information freely; but because they function as advocates, they often attempt to withhold information that doesn't suit their purposes. Tension between reporters and public officials usually remains far beneath the surface, but an absence of tension usually shows that a journalist isn't doing the job. Public officials nearly always try to create an image; the degree to which they succeed depends on how carefully journalists examine what officials say. Public officials themselves and the voters who have the power to influence those officials can act wisely only if they are truthfully informed by the news media.

As our democracy has matured, our presidents have had less and less opportunity to control the press. As the number of newspapers that were mouthpieces for political parties declined, presidents began to give interviews and press conferences. Although some presidents now avoid press conferences, none can escape them entirely. Even infrequent press conferences provide public examination of the president on difficult issues. And presidential press conferences serve another purpose, too: The private briefings that precede them keep our presidents informed about even the most potentially damaging comments and actions of their administrations.

Although the 1967 Freedom of Information Act and similar state and local laws have given journalists unprecedented access to government documents, however, public officials still succeed, through procedures like closed meetings and declarations of executive privilege, in withholding information from the press and public. Consider these strategies, cited by Walter Karp in the November 1985 issue of *Harper's* magazine and all employed by the administration headed by Ronald Reagan:

1981: A State Department spokesman says "no comment" and "I can't say" more than thirty times during one forty-five-minute press briefing.

1982: Reagan shows Congress the final draft of an executive order that allows reclassification of government documents. The order would permit government officials to reconceal information that has already been released to the public. Ed Meese blames the draft order on "overzealous bureaucrats" at a March National Newspaper Association meeting and the President then signs it. Pentagon officials call a technical journal in April, ordering it to shred a manuscript about Army weapons systems.

1982: The Department of Health and Human Services suggests that changes in rules affecting the poor, the disabled, children, and the elderly be carried out without public notice. The department has concluded that the "delay" resulting from public participation in rule-making "outweighs the benefits of receiving public comment." As of late 1985, no final regulation has been published and this proposal remains on the department's agenda.

1983: The Budget Office suggests a change in its Circular A-122, "Cost Principles for Nonprofit Organizations" that would require organizations speaking out on public affairs to give up federal funding. Reagan then signs an executive order that excludes "any organization that seeks to influence . . . the determination of public policy" from participating in the federal government's workplace.

1983: The United States invades the island of Grenada, and for the first time in the nation's history, reporters are barred at gunpoint from observing military action. Restricted to a nearby island, journalists receive official statements to transmit to the audiences they serve.

1984: The Central Intelligence Agency files a complaint with the FCC that may lead to ABC's loss of its broadcast licenses after it has aired and then retracted a false charge against the CIA. (The FCC eventually rules against the CIA.)

1984: After the military purpose of the Discovery space shuttle flight scheduled for January 1985 has been publicly available for months, the Defense Department asks the news media to suppress stories about the shuttle's mission. The *Washington Post* publishes a story on the shuttle flight anyway, and the Secretary of Defense uses the Constitution's definition of treason, to "give aid and comfort to the enemy," to denounce the *Post*.

The public doesn't know how frequently the press reports what public officials want it to; columnist Richard Reeves has estimated that the White House is the source of twenty percent of national news. Journalists have an obligation to dig out the information beneath the surface of official reports, finding and relaying to the American people any information that helps them protect their interests and function as effective citizens.

When a public official's statements disagree with your own conclusions, challenge what he or she has said. Challenge the conclusions of closed meetings and the withholding of information that your audience may need to know. But grant respect to those officials with whom you disagree; assume that they honestly believe they are serving the public through their actions. And be especially wary of those official statements that agree with your own preconceptions.

Freedom of the press is a product of law, and laws can be changed.

Injustice anywhere is a threat to justice everywhere.
Martin Luther King, Jr.

Americans' increasing willingness to restrict the freedom enjoyed by the news media shows in the contrast between the ethical codes drawn up by the American Society of Newspaper Editors in 1922 and the codes composed later for broadcast journalists. The newspaper code, "The Canons of Journalism," refers in general terms to journalists' responsibility to be truthful. The broadcast codes are much more explicit and contain many more prohibitions, reflecting fear among leaders in the electronic media that their freedom will be reduced.

Although newspaper reporters tend to doubt the credibility of broadcast reports, the public continues to trust television more than it does its news-

Martin Luther King, Jr.

Martin Luther King, Jr., was born in 1929 in Atlanta, Georgia, and was assassinated in 1968 in Memphis, Tennessee, when he was only thirty-nine years old. Such a short life.

But this was the black man who said these words: "I still have a dream. It is a dream deeply rooted in the American dream. I have a dream that one day this nation will rise up and live out the true meaning of its creed: 'We hold these truths to be self-evident that all men are created equal.' "

These famous words are those that most Americans will remember years later when the memory of what King looked like will have faded. Nonetheless, King titled his speeches provocatively. Here are three:

I Shall Die, but That Is All I Shall Do for Death

A Knock at Midnight

Remaining Awake Through a Great Revolution

King's books were also provocatively titled:

The Strength to Love

Where Do We Go from Here: Chaos or Community?

A Drum Major for Justice

Letter from Birmingham Jail

Beyond Vietnam

The Trumpet of Conscience

Why We Can't Wait

A reviewer of *Why We Can't Wait* wrote: "The book's logic and eloquence strike hard at the jugular veins of two American dogmas—racial discrimination, and that even more insidious doctrine which nourished it, gradualism."

A reviewer for the *Virginia Quarterly Review*, commenting on *The Trumpet of Conscience*, wrote: "King saw clearly, four months before he died, that the white man's hatred and the rich man's dollar remain the West's most powerful forces, despite the preaching and example of his movement and the many moral outcries preceding him."

King told a *Playboy* interviewer that three important things came about as a result of his *Letter from Birmingham Jail*, which was written during one of the terms he served for civil disobedience, in reply to eight clergymen who had been critical of his work in Birmingham. "It helped to focus greater international attention upon what was happen-

(continued)

Martin Luther King, Jr.
(continued)

ing in Birmingham. Without Birmingham, the march on Washington would not have been called. It was also the image of Birmingham which helped to bring the Civil Rights Bill into being in 1963." King knew the power of free speech, and he used it in conjunction with civil disobedience to let the world know about injustice and discrimination.

Ironically, King grew up in a middle-income home in Atlanta and was fourteen before he himself experienced racial prejudice. With a teacher, King was returning home from Dublin, Georgia. He told an interviewer: "Mrs. Bradley and I were on a bus returning to Atlanta, and at a small town along the way, some white passengers boarded the bus, and the white driver ordered us to get up and give the whites our seats. We didn't move quickly enough, so he began cursing us. I intended to stay right in that seat, but Mrs. Bradley finally urged me up, saying we had to obey the law. And so we stood up in the aisle for the ninety miles to Atlanta. It was the angriest I have ever been in my life."

In 1987, a junior at Stanford who spends much of her free time transcribing King's speeches and letters into a computer has dismissed her earlier image of King as an omnipotent, unreachable figure: "He was human and I feel like I'm working very close with him."

---

papers. In a 1985 poll of over 1,000 reporters and editors working for daily papers—carried out by MORI Research, Inc., of Minneapolis—nearly all the journalists surveyed said that they would rely on newspapers rather than television if reports from the two media conflicted. Only 36 percent of a sample of the general public questioned during an earlier study by the same organization said they would rely first on newspapers, though, and half of the public sample said they would trust the information they heard on television and question what was printed if broadcast and print accounts of a single occurrence disagreed.

A quarter of the public sample gave the newspapers they read low ratings for credibility, and only 32 percent rated their papers as highly believable; Harris polls in 1966 and 1972 showed the public ranking the information media near the bottom, surpassing only organized labor and advertising, in a survey of public confidence in all social institutions.

A public that lacks faith in journalists has no reason to support press freedom; and incomplete, slanted, or false reporting destroys public confidence in the news media and justifies secrecy on the part of public officials. Many newspapers have established local press councils to evaluate press performance and have appointed ombudsmen to assist those who object to the way newspapers have treated them, but the surest way for reporters working in both the print and the electronic media to protect their Constitutional rights is daily rededication to the ideal of truthful reporting.

EXERCISES

1. Air Force investigators approach one of your professors an hour before she is to deliver a paper on arms control verification to an audience of colleagues. They warn the professor that if she delivers the paper she may be prosecuted under the 1917 Espionage Act. Nonetheless, the professor delivers her paper. Write a paper of at least 300 words that tells what you think of the professor's action.

2. Read again the anecdote at the beginning of this chapter about the professor whose actions were distorted by several graduate students in his department. Think of something you have done, then discovered that others have learned wrong information about your actions. Write a paper of at least 150 words to explain the truth and the distortions.

What is moral is what you feel good after.
Ernest Hemingway

Two things fill the mind with ever new and
increasing wonder and awe—the starry heavens
above me, and the moral law within me.
Immanuel Kant

The attributes of a great lady may still be found in
the rule of the four S's: Sincerity, Simplicity,
Sympathy, and Serenity.
Emily Post

An ethical man is a Christian holding four aces.
Mark Twain

The more corrupt the state, the more numerous
the laws.
Tacitus

I don't want a lawyer to tell me what I cannot do; I
hire him to tell me how to do what I want to do.
J. Pierpoint Morgan

Laws are spider webs through which the big flies
pass and the little ones get caught.
Honoré de Balzac

A verbal contract isn't worth the paper it's
written on.
Samuel Goldwyn

Ethics
and the
Law

ETHICS

When we discuss the ethics of journalism, we should keep in mind that they are inextricably tied to the responsibility of journalism: to report the truth as completely as possible.

In judging journalists' ethics, consider your own biases and the diversity of the information media and their audiences.

There is an inevitable divergence, attributable to the imperfections of
the human mind, between the world as it is and the world as men
perceive it.   *James William Fulbright*

Considering "the public" as one great mass is a favorite folly of journalists. The world, a nation, a city, a small town—each by the fact of its existence represents a single community of interest, but each also embraces an overwhelming multitude of varying interests and concerns. The smallest township is actually a patchwork of groups that may be considered "publics." There are as many publics as there are groups with varying levels of income, education, taste, and civic awareness, as many publics as there are groups with different political allegiances, different religious loyalties, and so on. What concerns or convinces one public may be trivia to another.

Moreover, the definition of each public is never static; it changes as the issues change. For example, when Florida is voting for a governor, a Gainesville college student is a member of a large and diverse public that includes a Miami stevedore and excludes a college professor at the University of

245

Maine. But when higher education in the United States is at issue, the college student is a member of a public that includes the professor and excludes the stevedore—except that the stevedore's working partner may have a daughter who attends the University of Idaho . . . and so on into bewildering variety.

Taking this concept of the many publics too far, chopping and dicing and refining, leads to absurdity. As A. Lawrence Lowell pointed out in *Public Opinion and Popular Government,* "If two highwaymen meet a belated traveler on a dark road and propose to relieve him of his watch and wallet, it would clearly be an abuse of terms to say that in the assemblage on that lonely spot there was public opinion in favor of redistribution of property." Endlessly subdividing leads to semantic confusion.

Remember nonetheless that there *are* many publics, for much discontent with the information media springs from the impossibility of pleasing everyone in a heterogeneous society. Cultivating public opinion is further complicated by the fact that the media attempt not only to inform, but also to guide and entertain. How does one simultaneously inform, guide, and entertain a bank president and the janitor who keeps the bank clean, a Pulitzer Prize winner and his cousin who was content with a tenth-grade education, a novelist and a worker for the city sanitation department, a wealthy member of the Junior League and a poverty-stricken mother of five, a convinced Republican and a devout Democrat, a Catholic and a Baptist? The answer, of course, is that the mass media must inevitably fail in their ultimate purpose of reaching everyone. And discontent with the media is just as inevitable.

Not all negative criticism of the mass media arises because critics fail to take account of the differences among people (although certainly some do). Instead, many of the criticisms should be tempered with this understanding.

Perhaps more important, even the most erudite critics must recognize that they are sometimes as subject to bias—especially through selective perception—as the most uneducated reader. Thus a scholarly professor used the discussion period following an address by a freelance journalist to berate a newspaper that had long been the object of his scorn. The professor had read an Associated Press report of a news conference and found it quite different from the one that appeared in the paper he disliked. "They took that Associated Press story, changed the headlines, changed the words, then published the whole biased business," he said. The journalist replied that one part of the charge could not be true because the Associated Press does not send the headlines with its dispatches. It was enough to cause him to check up on the complaint. He found that the paper had not used the Associated Press report at all but had printed a story from its correspondent—and clearly labeled it with a by-line. Even though the professor had been schooled in the dispassionate methods of scholarly criticism, he had allowed his disdain for the paper to color his perception of its report.

Such incidents suggest the validity of the judgment of a political analyst who says, "Most of the voters I talk with are far more biased in their political views than the newspapers they read. Whatever the newspapers do, most voters will continue to shut their eyes and ears to all except what they agree with."

But even though the thrust of this statement indicts readers, the analyst also indicts the press: "more biased than the newspapers" certainly indicates some measure of press bias. Many thoughtful journalists will admit, even as they maintain against acid and sometimes uninformed criticism that most of the organs of the mass media are as objective as human will can make them, that at least a few are biased.

Only from this foundation can criticisms of the mass media be meaningfully assessed. One must begin by recognizing that not all fault lies on one side or the other. Without the understanding that critic and journalist alike have human failings, both criticism and defense degenerate into a shouting contest.

Some journalists defend their profession on the somewhat complacent ground that all human enterprises are subject to human failings. An executive of *Time* said, "All writers slant what they write no matter how hard they try. All readers slant what they read." As far as it goes, this statement is true. But it does not go far enough, especially to explain *Time* magazine. T. S. Matthews, who worked for *Time* for more than twenty years and eventually became its editor, wrote in his autobiography, *Name and Address:* "I said that I thought the presidential campaign of 1940 was the last one that *Time* even tried to report fairly. . . . In 1952, when it sniffed victory in the air at last, there was no holding *Time*. The distortions, suppressions and slanting of its political 'news' seemed to me to pass the bounds of politics and to commit an offense against the ethics of journalism."

Although this chapter is concerned with all the mass media, it is important to consider whether an indictment of one publication says anything about any other. *Time*, for example, does not claim to report the news objectively. Indeed, its founders declared that, since absolute, machinelike objectivity is obviously impossible, *Time* would not even attempt to present an objective report. Instead, in judging a controversial issue, the editors would indicate which side "has the greater merit." But newspapers—and many magazines and the electronics media—have an entirely different orientation. They are committed to report as objectively as is humanly possible in their news columns and broadcasts. The extent of the failure of any one to accomplish this aim cannot be judged according to the standards of *Time*, or even by the failings of most other media, but must be judged individually.

Similarly, one must discriminate in criticizing the mass media for publishing and broadcasting entertainment rather than information. Critics tend to view the information media—newspapers, magazines, radio, and television—as a single entity and to make scalding judgments about the trivia that seems to pervade the mass media generally. The basic orientation of each medium is different. Radio and television are primarily instruments of entertainment; most newspapers and magazines are given largely to disseminating information and only partly to entertaining in the customary sense of that abused word. The point is that one cannot tar all the media with one broad brush.

College newspapers must sometimes confront ethical dilemmas.

It is doubtful that any act is right in itself. Every act is a link in a chain of causes and effects.   *William Temple*

Nine Stanford students were arrested for sitting in at a university administration building, the Old Union, one Wednesday in 1985. None of the students gave their names to reporters, but from previous stories on anti-apartheid protests and from social ties, the editors of the college daily knew some of their names. The students chose not to give their names to the police, hoping to stay in jail long enough to go on a hunger strike to demonstrate their opposition to the university's investments in South Africa.

The question for the editors was whether they should print the names they knew. They discussed the question for four hours before deciding. Here are their arguments:

1. The editors did not have all the names. By printing time, they knew four of the nine. The editors said it wouldn't be fair to the first four to publish their names, while not publishing the others.

2. By printing names, the editors would be "creating the story," in that if they printed the students' names, the police could probably have matched names to faces and released the protestors on their own recognizance. A newspaper should not predetermine the outcome of the news in this way.

3. College journalists should support progressive political movements. Editors should be professional, but they should be "human" too.

4. Readers would want to know the names, so the editors should publish the names they had. Professional newspapers publish partial news often.

5. Police were, obviously, not releasing the names because they didn't know the students. Attribution is necessary in a story about a case as serious as this one, so the names should be published to make attribution possible.

The editor-in-chief, Tim Grieve, said this:

At the beginning of the night, I was dead-sure that we should publish the names. By the end of the night, I wasn't sure either way. I felt uncomfortable in that we would only be able to identify four, and because I was undecided what we should do at press time, I decided to wait on publishing the names. It wasn't that I was sure I was doing the right thing, but I knew if I published the names I couldn't change my mind later and take them all back. By not publishing them, I left my options open.

In deciding not to publish, I told our news editors to do their damnedest to find out all nine names, thinking I would be more comfortable if we could run them all, and not just some. By Thursday night, two of the protestors had given up and given their names, and we had figured out the names of five others. That gave us seven. We were fairly sure that we would have all nine by the end of the weekend, when we next published, and at that point, I think we would have run them. On Friday, however, the others all gave up on their protest and solved our problem for us.

Professor Marion Lewenstein consulted professionals from three newspapers. James Risser, two-time Pulitzer Prize reporter when he worked for the *Des Moines Register Tribune,* said his first inclination is to publish whatever he knows. But in the end, he decided that he wouldn't have been sure and probably would have waited for at least another day. The editor of the *San Jose Mercury News* said he definitely would have run the names, while two managing editors from the *Los Angeles Times* said they would have waited.

(The authors are grateful to Tim Grieve, former editor-in-chief of the *Stanford Daily,* for writing about college newspapers.)

Ethics also must be considered when a television station must take quick action.

Journalism, by its nature, rushes about shouting. The country, by its nature, moves slowly and talks softly.   *Charles Kuralt*

A young man, Joe Graham, who lives in Los Angeles, went out to jog late one afternoon wearing his usual clothes. As Graham jogged past many stores, he was passed by two men, running away from a liquor store they had just robbed. Graham heard a police siren, and in seconds his hands were grasped by a policeman, then handcuffed. Another policeman caught the robbers and handcuffed them.

When Graham was being taken to the police car, a television truck arrived and the cameraman recorded Graham and the two robbers handcuffed. The cameraman hurried to his truck and returned to the station. That night's news program showed all three supposed robbers.

Two hours after arriving at the police station, Graham had satisfied the police that he wasn't one of the robbers and was released.

James V. Risser

When a reporter becomes an investigative reporter, according to Howard Simons, former managing editor of the *Washington Post,* "The singular most important trait is the uncanny knack of linking A to Z to F and Y by reading Yiddish footnotes or eye movements." Simons added that they also "write in turbid fashion."

James Risser, however, cannot read Yiddish footnotes or eye movements, yet he has won two Pulitzer Prizes for investigative stories. Moreover, reading a few paragraphs by Risser makes it evident that he does not write in "turbid fashion." Here are three of his leads on the 1978 stories about the impact of modern farm practices on the environment. These stories and others won Risser his almost unprecedented second Pulitzer Prize.

NEVADA, IA—Driving down the back roads of Story County after a rain, even a casual visitor with a minimal knowledge of farming and soils can see that something is wrong.

In the middle of one field of healthy soybeans is a 50-foot-wide swath of mud, resembling a small black glacier that has moved down the gently sloping field, ripping out soybeans, covering others, and piling up several feet thick at the roadside.

The scene is repeated, in varying degrees, on farm after farm—precious topsoil eroding from the land, uprooting crops, filling farm ponds with silt, carrying pesticides and fertilizer into the creeks and streams that make up the Skunk River watershed.

WASHINGTON, D.C.—Chiseled in the stone high above the entrance to Union Station is a collection of noble sentiments praising American commerce and industry. One reads:

"The Farm—best home of the family, main source of national wealth, foundation of civilized society, the natural providence."

To which a cynic might add: "The Farm—destroyer of the soil, fouler of the nation's waters, threat to the public health, the great polluter."

WASHINGTON, D.C.—Agricultural chemicals have become the lifeblood of America's intensive farm production over the past 30 years, but they also have turned into one of the country's most vexing environmental problems.

Powerful insecticides, herbicides and chemical fertilizers continue to be applied to farm fields in ever increasing amounts, and, in the case of insecticides, despite mounting evidence that some bugs are growing resistant to the chemical killers.

His combinations of words are clear and provocative. Risser, who had become the Washington bureau chief of the *Des Moines Register* in 1976, reached that post through an unlikely career.

Risser was born in Lincoln, Nebraska. Although he had worked on the student newspaper in high school, he majored in psychology at the University of Nebraska. He decided while in college to become a lawyer. Risser said, "I don't really know why." Nonetheless, after graduating from law school, he practiced law for two years—and wanted to be a reporter. Working part-time, Risser took all undergraduate journalism courses required for a degree. He joined the *Des Moines Register,* and for five years he covered city and state government, then became a Washington reporter for the *Register.*

Risser won his first Pulitzer Prize in 1976, and the way he found his story should be a lesson for all reporters. He remembers the beginning of his first Pulitzer:

> On March 31, 1975, I found in the Agriculture Department package (of releases) a short and blandly worded release that led me to the most interesting story I've worked on in my 11 years in journalism.
>
> The release announced the suspension of five grain inspectors in Houston, Texas, because of their having been indicted by a federal grand jury for accepting bribes to certify that ocean-going ships were clean and acceptable for loading with grain to be shipped overseas. What struck me about the release was the fact that the inspectors, although federally licensed, were employees of a private inspection agency called the Houston Merchants Exchange. Judging by its name, it seemed likely to me that the exchange was some sort of business group and might be made up of people in the grain and shipping businesses. If that were the case, the regulators and the regulated might, in effect, be the same people—a serious conflict-of-interest situation.

Risser studied the grain inspection law and regulations. He also interviewed Agriculture Department grain division officials at their headquarters in a remote shopping center. As Risser said, "I think it was the first time a news reporter had come to their offices in years."

He learned that the Houston indictments were part of an investigation in New Orleans. Several other inspectors had been indicted the previous August. Perhaps Risser was the only reporter anywhere who knew of both the Houston and New Orleans indictments.

Risser went to New Orleans and Houston, studied all the court records that were available, and interviewed federal investigators, grain division personnel, grain-trade, and inspection officials. His first story about corruption in the grain export trade appeared in the *Register* on May 4, 1975. Here are the first two paragraphs of his story:

> NEW ORLEANS, LA.—Federal agents here and in other port cities have uncovered what appears to be widespread corruption in the grading and shipping of U.S. export grains.

(continued)

James V. Risser *(continued)*

Seven federally licensed grain inspectors in New Orleans and another five in Houston, Texas, already have been indicted on charges of accepting bribes in exchange for certifying that ships were clean and acceptable for loading with grain.

As usual, Risser wrote these sentences clearly and on target.

Between May and December 1975, Risser wrote 67 other stories about this corruption. *Register* editors chose ten stories to represent Risser's work before the Pulitzer jury. Of course, he won, as he did again in the 1979 competition for the Pulitzer.

Will Risser win another Pulitzer for reporting? No, he is no longer a reporter. He is now Director of the John S. Knight Fellowships for Professional Journalists program at Stanford. Perhaps he can enter the Pulitzer competition for history with the story of Joseph Pulitzer, John S. Knight, or. . . .

The following day, the station's early-morning editor reached the station at 5:30 and began preparing that morning's news program. Although the editor had opportunities to read that morning's newspaper—which carried nothing about Graham, only the two robbers—the editor didn't read the newspaper. When the morning news program was shown, there was Graham again, apparently guilty of robbery. The editor had simply shown last night's pictures of the police action after the robbery.

Graham, enraged by the television's actions, sued the television station. After hearing all testimony, the judge said the television workers had not had enough time before the night's news program to determine that Graham was not a robber. The station, however, was to blame for showing Graham again in handcuffs the following morning.

Several similar cases like this one exist, and many other articles and books would discuss such cases under their consideration of law. We list Graham's case as an ethics case because the editor at the television station failed to meet his responsibilities when he did not read the morning newspaper before presenting his news program. It does not matter that the editor worked for a television station; he, like all other journalists, must find the truth wherever he can. Shirking that duty is like giving up.

The Society of Professional Journalists, Sigma Delta Chi, *begins* its Code of Ethics with these words: " . . . the duty of journalists is to serve the truth." As if the framers of the Code of Ethics were attempting to make this point even clearer, the section "Accuracy and Objectivity" begins: "Truth is our ultimate goal." Like many ethics cases, the Graham case is much wider than law. The truth transcends any other principle.

THE LAW

When conflicts between the press and the government or the press and public figures are major items in the news, we seem to think that the First Amendment is being attacked in a way it never has been before. In fact, such conflicts have always been part of our history.

The First Amendment confers absolute press freedom, but other laws limit journalists' rights.

The theory of a free press is that truth will emerge from free
reporting and free discussion, not that it will be presented perfectly
and instantly in any one account.   *Walter Lippmann*

During the three decades when they served together on the U.S. Supreme Court, Hugo Black and William Douglas argued that the First Amendment to the Constitution means *literally* what it says. Justice Black said in *Ginzburg v. United States,* "I believe that the Federal Government is without power whatever under the Constitution to put any type of burden on speech and expression of ideas of any kind." In his book *The Right of the People,* Justice Douglas wrote:

> The First Amendment does not say that there is freedom of expres-
> sion provided the talk is not "dangerous." It does not say that there is
> freedom of expression provided the utterance has no tendency to sub-
> vert. . . . All notions of regulation or restraint by government are absent
> from the First Amendment. For it says in words that are unambiguous,
> "Congress shall make no law. . . . "

In practical effect, Justices Black and Douglas were arguing that a journalist (or anyone else) has a right to print and broadcast accusations that anyone is a murderer, thief, embezzler, adulterer—anything, without fear of successful libel action. The other members of the Supreme Court have not interpreted the Constitution that literally. The journalist who assumes the words of the First Amendment actually are unambiguous is asking for trouble.

Superficially, the range of freedom seems quite wide. Consider newspaper and magazine publishers. Within certain limits that we'll describe later, publishers can do what they like with their publication (there are much stricter limits for broadcasters). If they oppose the Democratic candidate for mayor, that candidate's name can be eliminated from their publications. If they hate golf, they can instruct their sports editors to forget that the game exists. If they visualize thousands of little circles of family readers being offended by photos revealing the sex of naked animals, they can have their art department use airbrushes to render the animals sexless. The Democrats, the golfers, and the artists on their staffs may rebel; readers may protest; a rival newspaper or magazine may compete more successfully as a result; but the publishers' power in such cases is unmistakable.

This freedom springs from the libertarian philosophy on which this country was founded: that everyone should be free to speak and write his or her own thoughts. The clash of conflicting ideas, the Founding Fathers believed, was the system most likely to produce truth.

But this interpretation reflects the lofty *philosophy* of freedom. However ringingly a nation's constitution states a belief in individual rights, in practice every society restricts free expression. The basic controls in most countries take the form of laws designed to protect individuals against defamation, copyright laws to protect authors and publishers, statutes to preserve community standards of decency and morality, and statutes to protect the states against treasonable and seditious utterances. In the United States, laws against invasion of privacy also affect journalists.

Journalists must become familiar with laws regarding defamation.

We, like the eagles, were born to be free. Yet we are obliged, in order to live at all, to make a cage of laws for ourselves.   *William Bolitho*

On June 7, 1971, the Supreme Court ruled that a Philadelphia radio station, WIP, had not been guilty of libel when it referred to a local magazine shop owner as a "smut distributor." The shop owner, George Rosenbloom, had been arrested on charges of criminal obscenity but was acquitted. At the libel trial, he was awarded $25,000 in compensatory damages—he said that the broadcasts had put him out of business—and $725,000 (later reduced to $250,000) in punitive damages. Had the Supreme Court upheld the libel judgment, WIP would have had to pay Rosenbloom a total of $275,000. But the Court ruled that WIP had not broken the law.

This decision was a pivotal one for American journalism, the climax of seven years of Supreme Court decisions that had eroded libel laws to a point where, as the *New York Times* stated, "It is now close to impossible for anyone to collect substantial damages for a libelous remark printed in a newspaper or magazine or book or broadcast on radio or television." The phrases "close to impossible" and "substantial damages" are important qualifications; the laws of libel have not been repealed. Journalists must understand the definition of "libel."

A person's reputation is a valuable possession. A ruined reputation can mean the end of a thriving business, the loss of a job, the end of friendships, and the loss of community respect. The law protects people against undeserved harm to their reputations.

"Defamation" means unjustly exposing someone to hatred, contempt, or ridicule, or causing someone to be shunned or avoided or to suffer injury to his or her business. Almost any expression that tends to make others think worse of someone without just cause is defamation. As the media frequently publish material that is unflattering, critical, and even derogatory, they need to be concerned with the complicated law of defamation.

People can be libeled in PR releases and in advertisements. One state had a recent libel suit because an ad agency used a generic accident photo as part of an anti-drunk-driving campaign. The problem was that the woman in an old accident photo was identifiable and was not drunk.

Slander is spoken defamation. Libel is usually written and is considered more harmful than slander, although now that spoken words can reach across a continent and around the world, the courts have reconsidered whether libel is necessarily more damaging than slander just because libel is written. If broadcast defamation has been written or prepared (as in a script), it is treated as libel. If it is spontaneous (as a comment during a talk show might be), it is considered slander.

The modern journalist is faced with fifty-one varieties of libel law—a particular problem for journalists whose work reaches beyond the border of a single state. While some states have codified their libel law—that is, written it down in statutes—many states have no such statutes, relying instead on centuries of decisions made by judges.

Among the defenses against libel that have been recognized by state laws are truth, qualified privilege, the privilege of fair comment and criticism, and absence of malice.

Truth.   Should a person be paid for the ruin of an undeservedly good reputation? Some states say no and protect a truthful libel. Some say that no one should suffer damage to his or her reputation unless the libeler published with good motives and justifiable ends.

Libel cases often concern information that is correct in its essential facts. Journalists must always be prepared to prove the truth of their statements and may also need to defend their motives for publishing even damaging statements that are true.

Qualified privilege.   The law also protects statements made in certain types of situations from being taken as libelous. Those in official government proceedings or those fulfilling official government responsibilities have an absolute privilege to say what they think necessary without fear of losing a libel suit. Prosecuting attorneys could not do their job without this protection. If prosecutors were not protected, every time they failed to convince a jury beyond a reasonable doubt that a defendant had committed the crime charged, they would be courting a libel suit.

256 ETHICS AND THE LAW

Because the public must be informed about the content of government and court proceedings, the media are extended a qualified protection. Reports must constitute a fair and accurate representation of what has happened and what has been said. Journalists lose their protection from prosecution for libel if their reports fail to meet this standard.

Fair comment and criticism. Because a jury cannot possibly judge whether *opinion* is true or false, courts developed the privilege of fair comment and criticism for the media. This privilege protects the media from libel cases based on journalists' criticism of public acts by public persons and institutions and of work offered for public judgment.

This review of the Cherry Sisters' vaudeville act was held protected by the defense of fair comment and criticism in 1901:

> Effie is an old jade of 50 summers, Jessie a frisky filly of 40, and Addie, the flower of the family, a capering monstrosity of 35. Their long skinny arms, equipped with talons at the extremities, swung mechanically, and anon waved frantically at the suffering audience. The mouths of their rancid features opened like caverns, and sounds like the wailings of damned souls issue therefrom. They pranced around the stage with a motion that suggested a cross between the *danse du ventre* and fox trot—strange creatures with painted faces and hideous mime. Effie is spavined. Addie is stringhalt, and Jessie, the only one who showed her stockings, has legs with calves as classic in their outlines as the curves of a broom handle.

The decision protected the review's writer because the criticism was directed at a public act. The law would have been less generous if the reviewer had criticized the private lives of the Cherry Sisters with the same enthusiasm.

Absence of malice. After the Civil War, the United States adopted the Fourteenth Amendment to the Constitution to more closely regulate states' authority over the fundamental rights of their citizens. Section one of the Fourteenth Amendment includes these words:

> No State shall make or enforce any law which shall abridge the privilege or immunities of citizens of the United States; nor shall any State deprive any person of life, liberty, or property, without due process of law. . . .

The Supreme Court ruled in 1931 that the First Amendment was incorporated in the Fourteenth and that the states could not deprive their citizens of the rights guaranteed by the First Amendment without due process of law. Then, in 1942, the Supreme Court stated that libel did not have the protection, as free expression, of the First Amendment, only to reverse that decision in 1964 in *New York Times Co. v. Sullivan.*

The *Sullivan* case involved an advertisement placed in 1960 in the *New York Times.* The ad described events at Alabama State College during a civil rights demonstration. It also appealed for funds for the student movement, for voting rights, and for the legal defense of Martin Luther King, Jr. The ad carried the signatures of sixty-four prominent Americans and sixteen Southern clergymen.

There were errors in the advertising. One Montgomery police commissioner, L. B. Sullivan, alleged that his reputation had been damaged by the errors, even though he had not been named in the ad. He sued the *New York Times* and four black clergymen and was awarded $500,000 in damages. The Alabama Supreme Court upheld the award, and the *New York Times* took the case to the U.S. Supreme Court.

In reversing the judgment, the Supreme Court set down a constitutional rule:

> The Constitution prohibits a public official from recovering damages for a defamatory falsehood relating to his official conduct unless he proves that the statement was made with "actual malice"—that is, with knowledge that it was false or with reckless disregard of whether it was false or not.

The Court also stated the principle that "debate on public issues should be uninhibited, robust, and wide-open, and it may well include vehement, caustic and sometimes unpleasantly sharp attacks on government and public officials."

The Court protected not just the truth, but some falsehood as well: "Erroneous statement is inevitable in free debate, and . . . it must be protected, if the freedoms of expression are to have the breathing space that they need to survive." If honestly presented statements are not protected, the Court held, the news media will hold back from the scrutiny and spirited criticism of government and government officials that the First Amendment was intended to protect.

The law guards against invasion of privacy that fails to serve the public interest.

When a man assumes a public trust, he should consider himself as public property.   *Thomas Jefferson*

By the standards of law, which develop over centuries, the right of privacy is quite young. The intellectual framework for it is usually dated to 1890, when Samuel Warren and Louis Brandeis wrote in the *Harvard Law Review:*

The press is overstepping in every direction the obvious bounds of propriety and decency. Gossip is no longer the resource of the idle and vicious, but has become a trade, which is pursued with industry as well as effrontery. To satisfy a prurient taste, the details of sexual relations are spread broadcast in the columns of the daily papers. To occupy the indolent, column upon column is filled with idle gossip, which can only be procured by intrusion upon the domestic circle. The intensity and complexity of life, attendant upon advancing civilizations, have rendered necessary some retreat from the world, and man, under the refining influence of culture, has become more sensitive to publicity, so that solitude and privacy have become more essential to the individual; but modern enterprises and invention have, through invasions on his privacy, subjected him to mental pain and distress, far greater than could be inflicted by mere bodily injury.

From this beginning has developed a doctrine protecting privacy, generally defined as "the right to be let alone, the right of a person to be free from unwarranted publicity."

When the law of privacy was taking root in the early twentieth century, the courts ruled in favor of many of those who brought suit against journalists, holding that people did have a right to be let alone. The courts tended to draw a line between public persons and private citizens, with celebrities and officials enjoying less privacy than those who did not offer themselves or their work for public approval. The distinction was not always predictable. In 1940, the United States Circuit Court of Appeals in New York dismissed a suit brought by William James Sidis. In 1910, he had been an eleven-year-old prodigy in mathematics who lectured to famous mathematicians. But in the 1930s, Sidis lived in a hall bedroom in one of Boston's shabbiest neighborhoods and worked as a clerk. When *The New Yorker* described his adult life—the humorist James Thurber had rewritten the article—Sidis sued for invasion of privacy. His attorney argued that he had been a private citizen, not a celebrity, for more than two decades. The court called the article a "ruthless exposure" but ruled that, because Sidis had been a public figure, in effect he still was.

In recent years, the courts have increasingly held that the public's interest in learning about fellow citizens should be elevated. In fact, the reasoning in privacy cases is like the reasoning in libel cases: a steadily evolving concept of serving the public interest by reporting private citizens' involvement in newsworthy events and more latitude for reporting the actions of public officials and public figures.

The most extreme case, *Time, Inc. v. Hill*, was decided by the Supreme Court in 1967. An article in *Life* reported that a new play, based on a novel about a family held hostage in its home by escaped convicts, had been "inspired" by the true-life ordeal of the James Hill family. Hill brought suit for invasion of privacy, arguing that the article gave the impression that the play "mirrored the Hill family's experience." He won the suit in a lower court, but the Supreme Court applied the rule that it had defined earlier in the *New York Times v. Sullivan* libel case. In matters of public interest, the Court held, a plaintiff must prove that the "defendant published the report with knowledge of its falsity or in reckless disregard of the truth."

EXERCISES

1. Keeping in mind the college editor's problems discussed in this chapter, interview the editor of your college newspaper. Ask him or her whether the newspaper has problems like those Tim Grieve confronted. Be certain to cite at least some of Grieve's problems. Then write a report of about 250 words on your interview.

2. Consider the definition of "defamation" in this chapter as you read the front page and continuations of the front-page stories in your city's newspaper. How many stories do you consider defamatory or so nearly defamatory that you would not print them?

3. Think first of a public official (governor, mayor, member of the city council, and so forth), then of a famous entertainer (actor, singer, writer, and so forth). Read again the short section on invasion of privacy and then write whether you believe the public official and the famous entertainer merit the same or different rights to privacy.

AP/UPI
Style

The Associated Press and the United Press International, two large news-selling organizations, have developed a uniform writing style to be used in all their stories. The agencies publish two different stylebooks with almost identical entries explaining how to write articles in AP/UPI style, and many newspapers use these books to establish a uniform style in all the stories they print.

This chapter contains about 10 percent of the entries in an AP or UPI stylebook, chosen because of their usefulness. As they are in the stylebooks, the entries in this chapter are presented alphabetically. We have italicized our examples to set them off. In everyday usage these words, abbreviations, and expressions are not italicized.

abbreviations and acronyms A few universally recognized abbreviations are sometimes required. Others are acceptable, but, in general, avoid alphabet soup.

Apply the same guidelines to acronyms—pronounceable words formed from the letters in a series of words: *ALCOA, NATO, radar, scuba,* etc.

Guidelines:

1. Use *Dr., Gov., Lt. Gov., Mr., Mrs., Rep., the Rev., Sen.,* and abbreviate certain military titles before a name outside direct quotations. Spell out all except *Mr., Mrs.,* and *Dr.* before a name in direct quotations. See **titles.**

2. Abbreviate junior or senior after a person's name. Abbreviate company, corporation, incorporated, and limited after a company name.

3. Use *A.D., B.C., a.m., p.m., No.,* and abbreviate certain months with the day of the month. See **months.**

   Right: In 450 *B.C.;* at 9:30 *a.m.;* in room *No.* 6; on *Sept.* 16.

   Wrong: Early this *a.m.* he asked for the *No.* of your room. The abbreviations are correct only with the figures.

Right: Early this *morning* he asked for the *number* of your room.

4. Abbreviate avenue, boulevard and street in numbered addresses: He lives on Pennsylvania *Avenue*. He lives at 1600 Pennsylvania *Ave*. See **addresses.**

5. Certain states, the United States and the Union of Soviet Socialist Republics (but no other nations) are sometimes abbreviated. See **state(s).**

6. Some organizations are widely recognized by their initials: *CIA, FBI, GOP, TVA,* which are acceptable. Even then, an abbreviation is not always necessary. If it fits the occasion, use *Federal Bureau of Investigation,* for example, rather than *FBI.*

Do not use an abbreviation or acronym in parentheses after a full name. If the abbreviation would not be clear without this arrangement, do not use it. Do not reduce names to unfamiliar acronyms solely to save a few words.

addresses Use *Ave., Blvd.* and *St.* with a numbered address: 1600 Pennsylvania *Ave*. Spell out without a number: Pennsylvania *Avenue*.

Lowercase standing alone or in plural uses: the *avenue,* Massachusetts and Pennsylvania *avenues*.

Do not abbreviate similar words, such as alley, drive, road, and terrace. Capitalize as part of a formal name: Printers *Alley*. Lowercase standing alone or in plural uses: the *alley,* Broadway and Tin Pan *alleys*.

Use figures for an address number: 9 Morningside Circle.

Spell out and capitalize First through Ninth as street names; use figures with two letters for 10th and above: 7 *Fifth* Ave., 100 *21st* St.

ages Always use figures. When the context does not require *years* or *years old,* the figure is presumed to be years.

Hyphenate an age used as a compound modifier before a noun or as a noun substitute. Ages in apposition are set off by commas.

A 5-year-old boy. The boy is 5 years old. The boy, 7, has a sister, 10. The woman, 26, has a daughter 2 months old. The law is 8 years old. The race is for 3-year-olds. The woman is in her 30s (no apostrophe).

capitalization Avoid unnecessary capitals. Use a capital letter only if you can justify it by one of these guidelines:

1. Capitalize proper names of a specific person, place or thing: *John, Mary, America, Boston, England.*

2. Capitalize common nouns such as *party, river, street* and *west* as an integral part of a proper name: Democratic *Party,* Mississippi *River,* Fleet *Street, West* Virginia. Lowercase common nouns that stand alone: *the party, the river, the street.* Lowercase common noun elements in all plural uses: the Democratic and Republican *parties,* the Hudson and Mississippi *rivers;* Main and State *streets.*

Capitalize popular, unofficial names that serve as a proper name: *the Combat Zone* (a section of Boston), *the Badlands* (of South Dakota).

3. Capitalize words derived from a proper noun and still dependent on it for their meaning: *American, Christianity, English, French, Marxism, Shakespearean.*

4. Capitalize the first word in every sentence.

In poetry, capital letters are used for the first words of some phrases that would not be capitalized in prose.

5. Capitalize the principal words in the names of books, movies, plays, poems, etc. See **composition titles.**

6. Capitalize formal titles before a name. Lowercase mere job descriptions and formal titles standing alone or set off by commas.

composition titles In titles of books, movies, plays, poems, programs, songs, works of art, etc., capitalize the first word and all succeeding words except articles and short (four letters or less) conjunctions or prepositions. Use quotation marks for most:

"The Star-Spangled Banner," "The Rise and Fall of the Third Reich," "Gone with the Wind," "Of Mice and Men," "For Whom the Bell Tolls," "Time After Time," the NBC-TV "Today" show, the "CBS Evening News."

dates Use figures without letters: *April 1.* Not: *April 1st.*

When a month is used with a specific date, use the abbreviations *Jan., Feb., Aug., Sept., Oct., Nov.* and *Dec.* Spell out other months.

When a phrase lists only a month and a year, do not separate with commas. When a phrase refers to a month, day and year, set off the year with commas.

January 1972 was a cold month. Jan. 2 was the coldest day of the month. Feb. 14, 1976, was the target date. His birthday is May 15.

days Capitalize them: *Monday, Tuesday,* etc. Other guidelines:

Spell out days of the week in stories for morning newspapers. Use *today, tonight,* etc., but not *yesterday* or *tomorrow,* for afternoon editions. Avoid an awkward placement: *The police jailed Tuesday,* etc.

doctor Spell out if not a title: An apple a day keeps the *doctor* away.

Use *Dr.* (or *Drs.* in plural) as a title before the name of a physician, including direct quotations: *Dr. Jonas Salk.* Drop the title after first reference.

Dr. may also be used with *the Rev.* in first reference to Protestant clergy who have doctor of divinity degrees: *the Rev. Dr. Norman Vincent Peale.*

Do not use *Dr.* for those who hold only honorary doctorates. With other doctorate degrees, use *Dr.* with care; the public often identifies *Dr.* only with physicians.

dollars Always lowercase. Use figures and the $ sign in all except casual references or amounts without a figure. The book cost $4. Dad, please give me a *dollar. Dollars* are flowing overseas.

For specified amounts, it takes a singular verb: He said *$500,000 is* what they want.

For amounts of more than $1 million, use the $ and figures up to two decimal places. Do not use hyphens: *He is worth $4.35 million. He is worth exactly $4,351,242. He proposed a $300 billion budget.*

The form for amounts less than $1 million: *$4, $6.35, $25, $500, $1,000, $650,000.*

geographic names   The authority for spelling place names in the U.S. states and territories is the U.S. Postal Service Directory of Post Offices. But do not use the postal abbreviations for **state** names (see separate entries), and abbreviate saint as St. and sainte as Ste. in U.S. names.

The first source for the spelling of all foreign place names is Webster's *New World Dictionary*. Use the first-listed spelling if an entry gives more than one. If the dictionary provides different spellings in separate entries, use the spelling that is followed by a full description of the location. Also:

1. Use *West Germany, East Germany,* etc. for divided nations.

2. Use *Cameroon,* not *Cameroons* or *Cameroun.*

3. Use *Maldives,* not *Maldive Islands.*

4. Use *Sri Lanka,* not *Ceylon.*

The last three exceptions conform with the practices of the United Nations and the U.S. Board of Geographic Names.

If the dictionary does not have an entry, use the first-listed spelling in the Columbia Lippincott Gazetteer of the World.

Follow the styles adopted by the United Nations and the U.S. Board of Geographic Names on new cities, new independent nations, and nations that change their names. If the two do not agree, the news services will announce a common policy.

Capitalize common nouns as an integral part of a proper name, but lowercase them standing alone: *Pennsylvania Avenue, the avenue; the Philippine Islands, the islands; the Mississippi River, the river; the Gulf of Mexico, the gulf.*

Lowercase all common nouns that are not part of a specific proper name: *the Pacific islands, the Swiss mountains, Chekiang province.*

girl   Applicable until 18th birthday is reached. Use *woman* afterward.

governmental bodies   Capitalize the full proper names of governmental agencies, departments, and offices: *the U.S. Department of State, the Georgia Department of Human Resources, the Boston City Council, the Chicago Fire Department.* Elsewhere:

1. Capitalize names flip-flopped to delete *of: the State Department, the Human Resources Department.*

2. Capitalize widely used popular names: *Walpole State Prison* (the proper name is *Massachusetts Correctional Institution—Walpole*).

3. Lowercase when the reference is not specific: *Nebraska has no state senate.*

4. Lowercase generic terms standing alone or in plural uses: *the Boston and Chicago city councils, the department.*

graduate (*v.*) A person may *graduate* from a school. It is correct, but unnecessary, to say he *was graduated*. But, do not drop *from* in: John Adams graduated *from* Harvard.

granddad, granddaughter, grandfather, grandmother, grandson, house of legislature Lowercase most nongovernmental uses: a fraternity *house*, a *house* of worship, the *house* of Tudor, bring down the *house*, like a *house* on fire.

Capitalize proper names of organizations and institutions: *the House of Delegates of the American Medical Association, the House of Bishops of the Episcopal Church.*

Capitalize a reference to a specific legislative body: *the U.S. House of Representatives, the Massachusetts House, the Virginia House of Delegates, the House of Commons, the House of Lords, the House of Burgesses.*

legislative titles Capitalize formal titles before names; lowercase elsewhere. Use *Rep., Reps., Sen.* and *Sens.* before names in regular text, but spell them out in direct quotations.

Spell out other legislative titles (*assemblyman, assemblywoman, city councilor, delegate,* etc.) in all uses.

magazine names Capitalize, without quotation marks. Lowercase magazine unless it is part of the publication's formal title: *Harper's Magazine, Newsweek magazine, Time magazine.* Check the masthead if in doubt.

months Capitalize the names of months in all uses. Use the abbreviations *Jan., Feb., Aug., Sept., Oct., Nov.* and *Dec.* with a specific date. Do not abbreviate any month standing alone or with a year alone.

nationalities Capitalize the proper names of nationalities, peoples, races, tribes, etc.: *Arab, Arabic, African, Afro-American, American, Caucasian, Cherokee, Chinese, Eskimo, French Canadian, Gypsy, Japanese, Jew, Jewish, Latin, Negro, Nordic, Oriental, Sioux, Swede.*

No. Use this abbreviation for number with a figure to indicate position or rank: *No. 1 man, No. 3 choice.*

Do not use in street addresses, with this exception: *No. 10 Downing St.,* the office and residence of Britain's prime minister.

Do not use *No.* in the names of schools: *Public School 19.*

numerals A numeral is a figure, letter, word or group of words expressing a number.

Roman numerals use the letters *I, V, X, L, C, D* and *M.* Use Roman numerals for wars and to show personal sequence for animals and people: *World War II, Native Dancer II, King George VI, Pope John XXIII.*

Arabic numerals use the figures *1, 2, 3, 4, 5, 6, 7, 8, 9* and *0.* Use Arabic forms unless Roman numerals are specifically required.

people, persons Use *people* when speaking of a large or uncounted number of individuals: Thousands of *people* attended the fair. Some rich *people* pay no taxes. What will *people* say? Do not use *persons* in this sense.

Persons is usually used for a relatively small number of people who can be counted, but *people* often can be substituted.

Right: There were 20 *persons* in the room.

Right: There were 20 *people* in the room.

People is also a collective noun that requires a plural verb and is used to refer to a single race or nation: The American *people* are united. In this sense, the plural form is *peoples:* The *peoples* of Africa speak many languages and dialects.

percent One word. It takes a singular verb when standing alone or when a singular word follows an "of" construction: The teachers said 60 percent was a failing grade. He said 50 percent of the membership *was* there.

It takes a plural verb when a plural word follows an "of" construction: He said 50 percent of the members *were* there.

percentages Use figures and decimals rather than fractions: *1 percent, 2.5 percent, 10 percent.* For amounts less than 1 percent, use a zero and decimals: *0.5 percent, 0.03 percent.*

president Capitalize as a formal title before names: *President Kennedy, Presidents Kennedy and Johnson, President John Smith of Acme Corp.*

Drop the title after the first reference.

Lowercase in all other uses: The *president* left today. He is running for *president.* Lincoln was *president* during the Civil War.

The first name of a present or former U.S. president usually is not needed, but may be used in feature or personality stories. Use a first name if needed to avoid confusing one with another: *President Andrew Jackson, President Lyndon Johnson.*

royal titles As with all other titles, capitalize royal titles before a name; lowercase standing alone or set off by commas. See **titles.**

Some examples:

Queen Elizabeth II of England; Queen Elizabeth; Elizabeth, queen of England; the queen of England; the queen.

Prince Rainier of Monaco; Prince Rainier; Rainier, prince of Monaco; the prince of Monaco; the prince; a prince rules Monaco.

the duke of Windsor; the duchess of Windsor.

Prince Charles; Charles, prince of Wales; the prince of Wales; the prince; Charles, heir apparent to the British throne.

Princess Caroline of Monaco; Princess Caroline; the princess.

slang Slang terms are not generally regarded as conventional. They are used, however, even by the best speakers, in highly informal contexts.

Examples: *short snort* for a drink of liquor or *bash* for a party.

Use slang terms with caution; they often pass into disuse in time. If slang is used, do not self-consciously enclose it in quotation marks unless it is a direct quotation. Provide a definition for any unfamiliar term.

state(s) Usually lowercase: *New York state, the state of Washington.* Also: *state Rep. William Smith, the state Transportation Department, state funds, state church, state bank, state of mind, state of the art.*

Capitalize as part of a proper name: *the U.S. Department of State, Washington State University.*

Always spell out the names of the 50 U.S. states standing alone.

Rule of thumb: Spell out *Alaska* and *Hawaii.* Abbreviate any of the 48 contiguous states with six or more letters; spell out those with five or fewer. The list:

Ala.	Conn.	Ill.	Md.	Mo.	N.M.	Ore.	Texas	Wis.
Alaska	Del.	Ind.	Maine	Mont.	N.Y.	Pa.	Utah	Wyo.
Ariz.	Fla.	Iowa	Mass.	Neb.	N.C.	R.I.	Va.	
Ark.	Ga.	Kan.	Mich.	Nev.	N.D.	S.C.	Vt.	
Calif.	Hawaii	Ky.	Minn.	N.H.	Ohio	S.D.	Wash.	
Colo.	Idaho	La.	Miss.	N.J.	Okla.	Tenn.	W.Va.	

time Specify the time in a story if it is pertinent: *a wreck at 3 a.m.* Tuesday gives a clearer picture than simply a wreck Tuesday.

Time zones usually are not needed: *a wreck at 3 a.m.* provides a clear picture without the time zone.

For planning purposes, provide times in a note above the body of the story: *Editors: The meeting begins at 10 a.m. PST.*

In the continental United States use the time in the dateline community.

Outside the continental United States provide a conversion to Eastern time, if pertinent: *The kidnappers set a 9 a.m. (3 a.m. EDT) deadline.*

The forms:

1. Use figures except for noon and midnight. Use a colon to separate hours from minutes: 11 a.m. *EST, 1 p.m.* today, 3:30 *p.m.* Monday. Avoid redundancies such as *10 a.m.* this morning. Also, if clear: *4 o'clock.*

2. For sequences, use figures, colons and periods: *2:30:21.6* (hours, minutes, seconds, tenths).

3. The time zones in the United States and Greenwich Mean Time may be abbreviated as *EST, PDT, GMT* etc., if linked with a clock reading: *noon EDT, 9 a.m. MST, 3 p.m. GMT.* Do not abbreviate if there is no clock reading. Do not abbreviate other time zones outside the United States.

4. Capitalize each word of the proper name: Chicago observes *Central Daylight Time* in the summer. But: Denver is in the *Mountain time zone.*

titles   Capitalize only formal titles when used before a name. Some specifics:

1. Lowercase and spell out all titles not used with a name: The *president* spoke. The *pope* gave his blessing. The *duchess* of Windsor smiled.

2. Lowercase and spell out all titles set off from a name by commas: the *vice president*, Nelson Rockefeller, declined to run again. Paul VI, the current *pope,* does not plan to retire.

3. Capitalize *Mr., Mrs., Miss, Ms.,* etc., when used.

4. Capitalize formal titles with names: *Pope Paul, President Washington, Vice Presidents John Jones and William Smith.*

5. Lowercase titles that are primarily job descriptions: *astronaut John Glenn, movie star John Wayne, peanut farmer Jimmy Carter.* If in doubt about whether a title is formal or merely a job description, set it off by commas and use lowercase.

6. Capitalize *duke, king, queen, shah,* etc., only when used directly before a name.

7. Set long titles off with a comma and use lowercase: *Charles Robinson, undersecretary for economic affairs.* Or: *the undersecretary for economic affairs, Charles Robinson.*

8. If a title applies to only one person in an organization, insert *the:* John Jones, *the* deputy vice president, spoke.

women   Women should receive the same treatment as men in all areas of coverage. Physical descriptions, sexist references, demeaning stereotypes and condescending phrases should not be used.

To cite some examples, this means that: Copy should not assume maleness when both sexes are involved, as in: *Jackson told newsmen . . .* or in *the taxpayer . . . he* when it can easily be said *taxpayers . . . they,* etc.

Copy should not express surprise that an attractive woman can also be professionally accomplished, as in: *Mary Smith doesn't look the part but she's an authority on . . .*

Copy should not gratuitously mention family relationships when there is no relevance to the subject, as in: *Golda Meir, a doughty grandmother, told the Egyptians today . . .*

Use the same standards for men as for women in deciding whether to include specific mention of personal appearance or marital and family situation.

INDEX